In the Names of
Ibis Headed Thoth & Starry Crowned Isis,
of Hard Visaged Athena & Brightly Winged Hermes,
of the Clever Legba & the Wise Erzulie Freda,
of the Melodious Sarasvati & the Elephant Headed Ganesha,
and of all other Divinities
of Wisdom, Knowledge, Art & Science:

a Geas

is hereby placed upon all who read these words!

If

you should steal this book
or borrow it and return it not
to its proper owner, who is:

or if

you should attempt to use the knowledge contained herein
for any act or spell
that would injure or enslave any innocent sentient being,

then shall

all your tools and weapons turn against you,
all beauty and joy depart from your life,
and all your cunning and your skills
bring you nothing save sorrow and despair,
till you have made full restitution for your crime.

Caveant Malefactores!

Philip Emmons Isaac Bonewits

REAL

MAGIC

AN INTRODUCTORY TREATISE ON

THE BASIC PRINCIPLES OF YELLOW MAGIC

(Revised Edition)

Philip Emmons Isaac Bonewits

ⓦ WEISERBOOKS

York Beach, Maine, USA

First published in 1989 by
Weiser Books
P. O. Box 612
York Beach, ME 03910-0612
www.weiserbooks.com

Library of Congress Cataloging-in-Publication Data

Real magic / by Phillip Emmons Isaac Bonewits.-rev. ed.
p. cm.
Bibliography: p.
Includes index
ISBN 0-87728-688-4
1. Magic. 2. Psychical Research. I. Title
BF1611.B58 1988   88-13099
133.4'3--dc19   CIP
CCP

Printed in the United States of America

08 07 06 05 04 03 02 01
 14 13 12 11 10 9 8 7

Contents

Preface

There are few experiences in the life of an author more embarrassing and sobering than the rereading of a work written by him or her several years previously. The process of dissatisfaction begins within a few days of the book's first publication, and gets worse as the years roll by. There you are as an author, growing (one hopes) in your knowledge of your field and maturing (one hopes even more) in your ability to phrase things precisely as you wish. And there is the blasted book, its "ancient" words frozen forever into unforgiving print, following you about like an overly enthusiastic puppy for the rest of your life (and beyond?). Soon you begin to hope that people will forget about the book and will start paying more attention to your later (and you think better) writings.

But so many people have told me in the last few years that they consider *Real Magic* to be some sort of classic or other, that I have been persuaded to allow it to be republished, more or less in its original form. A few major and several minor changes have been made in the text, but the majority of updating materials have been collected into a new appendix at the back of the book.

There are some matters, however, that should be touched upon here, because they deal with how the book as a whole was originally written and with how I would change things now, had I the opportunity to do the entire text over again from scratch.

I will start by apologizing to the 51% of my readers who are of the female persuasion. At the time *Real Magic* was being composed, this author, like most other male writers in 1970, had absolutely no awareness of just how sexist the standard English language writing style could be. Naturally male pronouns were used as general terms throughout, since I didn't know any better. But in order to set a point straight once and for all, I will state that it is my firm opinion as a professional occultist that *any form of magical or psychic activity that can be performed by a man can be performed equally well by a woman, and vice versa,* with only the minor exceptions of those spells and other techniques connected directly with the physiological processes of reproduction (if a spell requires the user to produce their own menstrual blood or sperm, for example, one gender or the other is probably going to have difficulty doing it). Social and/or personal programming may convince a person that, as a woman or man, they "cannot" perform a certain kind of magical or psychic act, or may prevent them from getting specialized training they need, but these are artificial sexist limitations and not eternal laws of Nature.

In point of fact, race, creed, color, gender, sexual preference, occupation, technological sophistication, virtue or place of planetary origin are really matters of very little importance when it comes to understanding and using the basic principles of magic; though of course psychological and cultural differences will affect points of training, temperament and style.

Secondly, let me note for the benefit of those critics who have complained that I do not support my claims "sufficiently," and who use this supposed lack of verification as an excuse to reject the entire book, that I would have needed to at least triple the size of the work in order to include the hundreds of research citations and footnotes that I purposely omitted from the first editions. Indeed, the multiple volume expansion and revision I hope to start soon will have all of this supporting evidence for those who do not have the time to look the subjects up themselves, nor the charity to assume that I am not a bald faced liar.

For now, let me merely assure the reader that just about all of the research results referred to in this book are quite well known to specialists in their various fields, and can be found by anyone willing to look the particular topics up in the para-psychological, anthropological, medical, historical, occult and other appropriate technical literatures. Just because it may be possible to draw unusual conclusions from the data is no reason to automatically doubt the validity of the evidence itself.

Thirdly, now that I am becoming older and wiser, I feel a need to apologize for the rampant egotism that permeates the book, as well as for my lack of charity towards both the parapsychologists (who have made magnificent strides in recent years) and towards some of the more conservative occult movements of the western and eastern mainstreams. They can't help it if their academic and cultural environments require them to be stodgy in order for them to survive with their careers and/or social standings intact. And apologies are probably also due to those many kind readers who sent me letters of support and criticism, and to whom I never had the time or secretarial help to reply. I'm afraid that I really am terrible at keeping up with correspondence, but each of your letters has been filed in an appropriate category and many of them will be consulted and their suggestions followed in my future writings and lectures.

The "occult fad" of the early 70's has faded out, having been replaced by new fads of meditation, "ancient astronauts," vampires, "pop psychology," flying saucers and jogging. But rest assured, by the mid-80's another groundswell of interest in parapsychology and the occult will erupt (or be created by the New York publishing industry) and by that time enough research will have been done in all of these "fringe" areas of knowledge and speculation that their overlaps will be obvious to every open-minded and imaginative thinker on the planet.

When thousands of kids are bending silverware with their bare minds, and thousands of parents are keeping tabs on their teenagers through telepathy, and thousands of pacifists are using psychokinesis to defuse nuclear weapons, it's going to be real hard to put the genie back into the bottle. We can accomplish all these things and more by the turn of the century, with a little help from the Gods and a lot of old fashioned elbow grease, assuming that the madmen who run this planet allow us all to survive that long. Everybody think strong thoughts!

Lughnasadh, 16 y.r.
August 7, 1978 c.e.

Introduction

This book will not be what you expect it to be; it isn't even what *I* expected it to be. It will have full meaning only when it is obsolete.

Almost everyone these days is interested in the occult, and the charlatans and hacks have been quick to capitalize. There are many intertwined reasons for this sudden increase in interest. In part, it is the age-old quest for knowledge (that is, power); in part, the stirring of ancient instincts in a time of crisis for the species; in part, pure terror of modern technology and a feeling of helplessness in the face of the monsters we have created. The total number of reasons for our modern obsession with magic and ESP runs into the infinite. I do not know them all, I never shall.

And here is Lesson One for the aspiring human (a goal far above that of becoming a mere magician or mystic): *Never be afraid to say "I don't know" or "insufficient data."* Saying this is never a sign of weakness but may in the end prove to be your greatest strength.

As you will have noticed if you have read even lightly in the fields of magic, mysticism, and ESP, books on these subjects have certain similarities. They are almost invariably composed of a mixture in varying proportions of two kinds of material. They may take the Documentary approach and be "scrapbooks" or "recipe collections," miscellaneous hodgepodges of superstitions, science, and "primitive horrors." Or they may be works of Salvation, telling the reader how he can gain various powers on his way to Enlightenment, at which point all these powers are discarded; this is called the theurgical, or religious approach, and derives from the Greek word *theurgy* which originally meant "divine work" and later came to mean "the use of magical means to attain religious salvation."

Further, almost all these books are highly moralistic, their authors constantly dragging religion and ethics into the study and interpretation of supposedly natural phenomena. The amount of cultural bias and bigotry in this field is astounding. Since we live in a predominantly Christian culture, the majority of the old manuscripts available to us reflect this Christian orientation. Hence all the balderdash about curses "coming home to roost," demons dragging off magicians or witches by the hair, magicians needing to pray to the Christian God in order for their spells to work, all sex magic being evil, and so on. It is essentially the same mentality that over the centuries has ascribed diseases to demonic possession and lightning bolts to whatever god happened to be in vogue. And Hindu, Chinese, and Arabic manuscripts on magic all reflect the religious attitudes of *their* authors. In fact, to a certain extent you could say that even the works of modern ethnographers and parapsychologists are biased by what Ashley Montagu and others have referred to as "the superstitions of the modern religion of Science."

As a rule these books are all written by self-appointed "experts" who either implicitly or explicitly claim their infallibility in spreading the Absolute Truth. Often they maintain that their writings are Eternal Truths held by an ancient Secret Society for centuries, or else Revealed to the author by Superhuman Beings. Now naturally the Society cannot reveal itself to the public for a scrutiny of its claims, or it wouldn't be a Secret Society anymore, would it? And the Superhuman Beings just happen to be on the next plane over right now, and are unfortunately impossible to contact, though they *did* show great wisdom in their choice of prophets, didn't they?

It is a strange mechanism, though an almost universal one, that a person who happens to have a genuine talent, either psychic or scholarly, in one small area of occultism, instantly becomes an "expert" on anything and everything even vaguely connected with the occult. After his (or her) death his reputation and the supposed accuracy of his pronouncements grow at a truly magical rate until a mini-religion has developed around him. Everything our prophet had to say is printed and reprinted, with errors conveniently "forgotten." An Edgar Cayce, for example—a man who was a superb psychic diagnostician and peerless healer. Then he began sounding off on everything from flying saucers to reincarnation to the reappearance of Atlantis (which he predicted would rise in 1959, 1963, 1968, 1970, and 1972, depending on which edition of his book you read). The upshot was that his followers made a fool of him and cast doubts on what were probably quite genuine gifts.

By this time you may be wondering where this beating of not-so-dead horses is going to lead. Is it to prepare for my demonstrating that I am somehow different from my predecessors? Right! It is because I believe this book to be unique, the first truly scientific and interdisciplinary examination of worldwide patterns in occultism. It is the result of training and education probably impossible until this decade, impinging on a particularly weird mind that had been shaped by some pretty unusual experiences.

For the past few years I have been lectured, bellowed at, and sworn at by some of the best minds at one of the world's finest universities. For surviving this harrowing experience with my sanity and individuality intact, I received in June of 1970 the world's first Bachelor of Arts degree in Magic and Thaumaturgy. Suddenly, at the ripe old age of twenty-one, I find myself an Authority. Now it is indeed true that I am technically the world's only *academically qualified expert in magic,* but that alone means little. After all, a brand-new LLD is not quite ready for the Supreme Court (though his appointment might be interesting), a new MD is not prepared to perform a heart transplant, and an AB in Art does not make you a Michelangelo. Today a Bachelor's degree is only the beginning; it shows that the student is prepared to *really* start studying.

Am I really an "expert" in anything then? And if not, why

am I writing another book to clog an already glutted market; that is, other than needing the money, being on an ego trip, or having considerable publicity value as a "first"? There are many natural and "supernatural" talents that I lack, but I am lucky enough to possess a knack for something fairly rare in today's technology—an ability to organize information and form patterns or "generalizations." In an age of specialists, there are very few GP's; the only other one I can name off-hand is Buckminster Fuller, who is far above my level. But you might say that, like the human species, I specialize in not specializing.

Like everything else in life, this has both advantages and disadvantages. I can never work alone of course, since I must have access to dozens of experts in many different fields in order to fill gaps in my data. This means, and I will say it right now and get it over with, that *there are thousands of people who know more about specific small areas and aspects of my field than I do.* In compensation though, my grasp of the interdisciplinary approach (the use of data and methods from many different arts and sciences), gives me a freedom that specialists never dream of, a loosening of boundaries and limitations of thought that generates endless streams of new ideas to examine. Many, indeed most, of these new possibilities and theories never pan out, but the few that do would never have been discovered otherwise. I can stand back, you might say, and see tapestries of thought where specialists can see only ravelings of random threads (though granted they can see those individual threads more clearly than I can).

The thing that makes me unique then and entitles me to be called an "expert" is that *I am the first to put occultism under the interdisciplinary microscope, dissecting and examining it in a scientific but flexible way, and reporting my results in plain language.* This last aspect, more than any other, is the one most likely to upset Establishment scientists and Establishment occultists.

But enough of this self-flagellation/adoration. A few words about my methods, aims, and outlook are now in order, though they will not necessarily appear in that order.

First, I wish to make the point that *this is not a book of theurgy;* if you are looking for salvation, enlightenment, or instant nirvana, you came to the wrong place. This is instead a book of *thaumaturgy,* from another Greek word meaning "the art and science of wonderworking." Within these pages I will present some of the most basic *Laws of Magic* and illustrate them with examples. Not too many examples though, for there are plenty of scrapbooks of occultism on the market from which you can select your own favorite cases to compare with my findings. Indeed, one of my major purposes is to provide a theoretical framework in which the general reader can place his information so that it will make the most sense and be the most useful. Only when *you* have tested something for yourself should you really believe in it.

Second, in this book you will find few, if any, Absolute Truths, and no statement herein is to be taken as one: "All things are relative including this statement." This is a book of theories, probabilities, possibilities, conjectures, hypotheses, speculations, and occasional wild guesses. I will usually label everything for what it is. Statements with no quibbling or qualifying adverbs or adjectives are items with such a high probability rating, say 95 percent plus, that to argue over them would waste more time than is worthwhile. If you disagree with such statements, or indeed anything in the book, *test it yourself!* If you find proof that I am wrong, by all means let me know about it. I am always ready to receive comments, corrections, and new data (though I *will* refuse to accept any packages that tick).

Third, I am betraying nothing and no one when I describe principles that used to be Sacred Secrets. As Aleister Crowley says in *Magick in Theory and Practice:*

> In such a work of practical Magick as the preaching of a new Law, these methods may be advantageously combined; on the

one hand, infinite frankness and readiness to communicate all secrets; and on the other, the sublime and terrifying knowledge that all real secrets are incommunicable.

Again, Dion Fortune says in *Psychic Self-Defense:*

As so much has already been made known concerning the esoteric teachings, and as the circle of students of the occult is becoming rapidly wider every day, it may well be that the time has come for plain speaking.

And both these quotes are over forty years old! Now I can no more make you a magician than a drama coach could make you Sir Laurence Olivier; you must combine real talents with many years of hard training. Perhaps I can help you learn how to memorize your lines, put on makeup, utilize props and scenery, recognize cues, or move your body on stage, but if you are to become a great performer, the source of that greatness must come from within. And drama critics (that is, occultists) must study too. As to whether or not everyone has the necessary talents and only needs to be trained, all I can say is: insufficient data.

And as for the traditional fears that "certain information" might get into the Wrong Hands, it is a problem that I have discussed with many philosophers, scientists, mystics, and magicians, and I have decided that these fears are no longer relevant, if indeed they ever were. I base my decision in part upon the following considerations: The question of exactly *who* the "wrong hands" are has never been satisfactorily answered in my opinion; it usually means anyone of a different religious, philosophical, economic, or political background. Also, every science has had this charge laid against it; to a certain extent the secret of the atomic bomb will always be in the wrong hands, and the same knowledge that enables a doctor to cure can also be used to kill. Moreover, I have always distrusted compulsive secrecy since, despite its claims, it is rarely altruistic and usually ends as an excuse for tyranny. Then, as we will see, those who use psychic powers for destructive and negative ends mess themselves up more than they do anyone else since, among other things, you must have a balanced outlook on life in order to be sucessful in magic. Finally, it is necessary for the data in books such as this to become available to the greatest number of people as quickly as possible since (a) several governments including our own have already instituted research on a massive level into methods of psychic control, and (b) this planet is in such trouble, politically and ecologically, that it is highly doubtful that the species will make it to the year 2000. We will *need* a few "miracles" to survive, and the tossing of all these extra variables into the situation can't make things much worse than they are and will probably improve matters. Here in the West our ethical technology lags about 500 years behind our physical technology, and a new emphasis upon humanistic and, if you will, "spiritual" values is absolutely vital. But the public is unlikely to accept a new emphasis unless it is something that can be tested and proved.

I refuse to place myself in a position that "entitles" me to decide what other people should or should not be allowed to know. And I intensely dislike organizations—religious, political, or other—that attempt in any way to keep knowledge from the public. Anyone willing to undergo the necessary self-disciplines for study in any field ought to be allowed to learn all he can. Therefore this book contains literally *all* that I feel I know securely enough to explain to others. Granted that it is an elementary text, its contents should be enough to enable any person to go as far as he wants in the field, merely by extending logically what he will learn here.

One of my major tools of writing as well as of research is a little-known rule known as Occam's Razor, formulated by a Bishop William William of (surprise!) Occam. It says, "Entities are not to be multiplied without necessity," which is another way of saying "Let's not make things any more complicated than they absolutely have to be." Where a simple explanation, interpretation, or hypothesis will work, don't bother with a fancy one full of big words. If one theory or guess explains several things and requires less stretching of the imagination than another, use it! Now I am perfectly aware of the devastating blow that universal use of this rule would deal modern scholarship, not to mention politics or religion, but I will use it anyway. Just don't tell anybody.

Occam's Razor is used to slice away at many complicated subjects, and as you have no doubt found out by this time, occultism (ancient, medieval, and modern) is probably the most complicated and hairy subject in human history. The beliefs and patterns of occultism around the world form a tangle almost impossible to slice, however sharp the razor.

One of the major purposes of this book is to examine these old beliefs and patterns to see if they form a coherent whole— to see if some of them correspond to other patterns within areas of present human knowledge that are at least *fairly* clear, and to see how and if these patterns can be "translated" into terms suitable for testing in a modern laboratory.

Another purpose is to expose the errors and outright frauds that have been cloaking and choking the occult for centuries. "Occult" means "secret and hidden." Well, the occult shall be hidden no longer, the Veil of the Temple shall be rent, a task that only the Fool dare perform because the angels are afraid.

This is a book meant for the general public first and the scientific and occult communities second. This will make even more scientists and occultists angry with me since there is nothing they hate so much as a "popularizer." Nonetheless I intend to keep the technical jargon to a minimum (I can't avoid all of it), and not hide my occasional ignorance in a cloud of verbiage. Any technical term or phrase that I'm forced to use will be defined once or twice in the text and again in the Glossary; it will also be printed in *italics*, though *italics* are also used for emphasis or other purposes. Long phrases will be abbreviated wherever possible. If in avoiding seventeen-syllable words I should accidentally simplify matters to the point of outright error, I rest assured that *someone* will gently bring it to my attention. I also reserve the right to make horrible puns, mangle my metaphors, exaggerate or understate things for irony, and even to ignore the great god Proper Grammar, if in doing so I manage to get my point across.

There may be some who think that my errors are due to other causes or even (horror of horrors!) that the book is "unscholarly" because of its sometimes breezy style. So in order to slip in thanks to my many benefactors, confound the unbelievers, and show how sneakily we interdisciplinarians can "stack the decks," I will note here that *before publication* the manuscript was examined and dissected by a score of expert scholars and authorities, as well as some lesser lights, from many different arts and sciences. Each was asked "Are there any major errors of fact or logic concerning your field?" Each replied with either a "No" or a "Yes, and here they are." All of them were generous, kindly, brave, cruel, and absolutely merciless—for which I am eternally thankful.

Not all of them were "believers" either. Several objected to the entire book's premise. However, about 90 percent of all corrections and additions suggested were incorporated into the text before it was sent to the publisher. Those points that were not accepted were of two kinds: (a) requests for footnotes and research citations that—if I had included all of them—would have given the reader five or ten footnotes per page or else an Appendix twice the size of the text, and (b) points where reviewers contradicted each other—and there were quite a few of these—or where the abstract opinion of a reviewer differed from the concrete personal experience of the author.

Of course there are still going to be errors left even after all this effort, and naturally nobody is to blame for them except myself. After all, I *wrote* the book. However, if an error was something which even *these* distinguished scholars couldn't find, or which they considered unimportant to the general public, *I* am certainly not going to feel guilty. I will simply do my best to correct matters in the next edition. As I will say many times throughout the book, I not only expect but I *want* mistakes to be found.

At this point, therefore, I wish to extend warm thanks to the following for their gracious assistance and helpful advice (since many are not known outside their fields, I will note for the reader the studies and skills of each). It is due solely to these people that the reader can be assured that the book he holds in his hands is as accurate and scientific as modern knowledge can make it.

Allen Angoff: Administrative Secretary, and the staff of the Parapsychology Foundation, Inc.

Dr. Mark Elton Bartel, M.Crim., DJs: Criminology, law, archaeology, Hebrew-Judeo studies, Kabbalah.

Dr. Lowell John Bean, PhD: Anthropologist—specializing in the California Indians and shamanism.

Dr. Owen Chamberlain, PhD: Physics, winner of the Nobel Prize.

Licenciado José Feola, PhD: Biophysics, parapsychology, President of the Minnesota Society for Parapsychological Research.

Dr. Joseph Fontenrose, PhD: Professor Emeritus of Classics, mythology, comparative religions; a scholar and a gentleman.

Dr. Vonnie Gurgin, D.Crim.: Criminology, statistics, philosophy of science, sociology of knowledge; symbolic interactionist.

Dr. Lewis R. Lancaster, MTh, PhD: Oriental languages and religions, Tantra.

Reverend Sigurd T. Lokken, BD, MTh: Lutheran minister and theologian.

Donald McQuilling: Physics, philosophy; president of the California Society for Psychical Study, Inc.

Dr. Thelma Moss, PhD: Neuropsychiatry, parapsychology.

John Raymond: Journalist, hypnotist, occultist; friend.

Dr. Francis Israel Regardie, DC: Probably the foremost Western occultist of our time.

Mrs. Ellie Reynolds: Psychic, book reviewer, and critic; friend.

William G. Roll, B.Litt.: Parapsychologist, *the* authority on "poltergeist" phenomena.

Dr. Michael Scriven, D.Phil.: Philosophy of science, parapsychology.

Donald Simpson: Inventor, artist, electronic technician.

Allen Spraggett: Author, journalist, parapsychologist.

William Tobin: Chemistry, geology, teaching.

Chelsea Quinn Yarbro: Author, dramatist, mime, critic.

Dr. Hans J. Zwang, MD: Neurology, medicine.

Thanks are also due to Victor Anderson, Howard Harrelson, and Ralph Oyer, students of the occult; Charles Hixson, computer programmer and statistician; Pamela Stockwell, and Susan Pierson, who typed the manuscript; James Robeson, longtime friend and ne'er-do-well; Carole Tobin, who provided much needed support; Julia Vinograd, poet; and especially to my students of *Magic 1-A*, the members and staff of the California Society for Psychical Study, Inc., and the members of the Order of Wizard Lore of the Associated Guilds of the Society for Creative Anachronism, all of whom patiently listened to and gleefully attacked every basic theory that eventually became a part of this book.

And finally, of course, thanks are due to my parents, without whose assistance my production would have been impossible.

Rethe 1, 1971   P. E. I. B.
Berkeley, California

The Laws of Magic

Unity

Identification

Association

Evocation   Invocation

Words
of   Names
Power

Personification

Contagion

Unity

Cause & Effect

Similarity

Infinite Data

Knowledge

Infinite   Universes

Synchronicity

Self-
Knowledge   Finite   Senses

Unity

Personal Universes

Perversity

True Falsehoods

Unity

Pragmatism

Polarity

Synthesis

Unity

Dynamic Balance

PEIB

A qualitative diagram showing
their primary interrelationships

CHAPTER ONE

The Laws of Magic

"Law: a statement of an order or relation of phenomena that so far as is known is invariable under the given conditions . . . the observed regularity of nature."
—*Webster's Third New International*

Over the centuries a collection of basic magical and mystical axioms has surfaced in culture after culture throughout the world, even in cultures that were totally isolated. These we can, and will, call the *Laws of Magic*. Like the law of gravity or the law of diminishing returns, these magical laws are not legislative acts (as some theologians have tried to make them) but rather they are descriptions of the ways that phenomena in a field—in this case magic—seem to interact and behave. They are the results of observation, testing, and theorizing until a coherent whole is produced.

Not all these laws are consciously known or understood by those using them, and not all will automatically appear in every single culture with a tradition of magic. To understand them, it is not necessary that you become a magician yourself. In fact, it is often easier for an outsider to discover and organize these laws.

For example, suppose a physiologist is watching Arnold Palmer play golf. Now the scientist may understand everything that's going on inside Palmer's body when he swings his club; that is, he will know what neurons are discharging, what hormones are being released into Palmer's bloodstream, what muscles are contracting and releasing. The fact that he knows all this, however, won't make him a pro like Palmer. As for Palmer himself, he probably doesn't understand everything going on in his metabolism; all he knows is that he moves his body in such and such a way and sinks a putt. Knowing how to play golf does not make him a physiologist. The scientist has a slight advantage here because he can study athletes from many different sports.

The situation described here is similar to the relation between a professional occultist and a professional magician, where the former would be the physiologist and the latter, the athlete. An even better comparison would be the occultist as scientist and the magician as engineer. A person can be a superb occultist and a lousy magician and vice versa; the basic talents involved are not the same and only rarely do they show up in the same individual. I, for example, am a much better occultist than I am a magician; and most of my colleagues are better magicians than they are occultists.

Now all magicians believe in the *Law of Cause and Effect,* that *exactly* the same actions done under *exactly* the same conditions will always be associated with *exactly* the same results. Actually the whole theory of causation gets shaky as soon as you look at it twice, and those "exactly's" are hard to get, but it works quite nicely for day-to-day planning. This is not a law limited to magic, but I'll toss it in here to keep things neat.

We will examine in this chapter some of the most basic and important Laws of Magic, give a brief description of their meaning, relate them to the workings of the mind, show some of their interrelationships, and throw in a few examples for good measure. But before we do, consider the words of J. W. N. Sullivan's *The Limitations of Science:*

> But these laws are purely descriptive laws. They are just statements of fact, like saying gold is yellow. Kepler gives no reason why his laws should be as they are. The observation and recording of laws is the first step in scientific procedure. Science

begins by hunting for uniformities amongst natural phenomena. The scientific man finds, for instance, that light is propagated in straight lines, that unsupported stones fall to the ground, that heat passes from a hotter body to a cooler one. In this way he introduces a sort of order into whole groups of happenings. And this sort of knowledge is often quite sufficient for practical purposes. Indeed, in many cases of great practical importance science has not yet advanced beyond this knowledge.

The *Law of Knowledge* is the most basic of all the laws. It states that "understanding brings control," that the more you learn the stronger you are. If you know all there is to know about something, then you have absolute and total control over it. Now this is the basis of all modern science and technology, and obviously matches the way the human organism—or any other that we know of, for that matter—actually works. The more data input the organism has about phenomena either inside or outside its body the greater a possibility it has of solving problems and thus surviving. The key phrase for this law would be: "Knowledge is power."

Its major sublaw is the *Law of Self-Knowledge* which says that the most important kind of knowledge is knowledge of oneself. This also has a very logical basis. Constant review and reorganizing of the contents of your mind and body lead to more effective survival. You might say that only when the machine is cleaned and greased are you thoroughly tuned for living. Its key phrase would be: "Know thyself."

All the other laws depend upon these two; it is wise to keep them in mind at all times. I don't really think that these need any more explanation or defense, and since this is not *officially* a book of philosophy or phenomenology, we can go on to the others.

The *Law of Names* is related to both the Law of Knowledge and the *Law of Association*. It states that knowing the complete and total true name of a phenomenon or entity gives you complete control over it (almost all phenomena in magic are personified and can be considered to be "entities," or beings). This law is based on two premises. First: in simpler languages than our own a name is a definition of that which is named. This is true also in complex languages, though you often have to search long and hard for the name-meaning of a word, especially one with foreign roots. Knowing the name, you know that which is named. As you get more information about the thing named, the name changes and evolves to fit the new data, often getting longer in the process.* If you can only learn the full name of a strange phenomenon, you will fully understand it and therefore control it. This is the connection with the Law of Knowledge.

Second: names are associational devices (memory gimmicks, used to remind you of something) both as aspects or descriptions of a phenomenon and as root, or "germ," sounds. We will go into those a bit more deeply when we hit the Law of Association. The key phrase for the Law of Names could be: "What's in a name?—everything!"

A sublaw of the Law of Names is the *Law of Words of Power*. This says that there are certain words that are able to change and influence the inner and outer reality of those saying them. Now every word can be considered to be the name of something, but this is not the major emphasis here, even though the most powerful words of power are usually corruptions of the names of the old gods.

Words like "abracadabra" or "osorronnophris" or "she-hamphorash" may have little or no meaning to those saying them, but their meaninglessness is irrelevant. The power is thought to lie in the *very sounds* of the words themselves,** thus linking this to the subject of Mantra, which we'll get into later. (I'm sorry that I am forced to keep saying "later," but everything in magic is incredibly interwoven, and I am required by the printed page to present things one at a time.) The key phrase here is: "A word to the wise is sufficient."

---

* For example, it is helpful to know that the Pope is often an archantidis-establishmentarian.

** Though the speaker must be in a special frame of mind, of course.

The next major law is the *Law of Association*. If two things, "A" and "B," have something in common (anything!), that thing can be used to control both, and "A" and "B" have a mutual influence on each other, depending upon the size of the thing shared. The more they have in common, the more they influence each other.

When the hunter runs down and kills a lion, he may eat the lion's liver thinking that this will give him strength; or a warrior may eat the brains of his slain enemy in order to assimilate his opponent's courage or cleverness. A communicant in church eats a piece of bread which is believed to be the body of Christ so as to gain some of Christ's attributes. All these are examples of "ritual cannibalism," and are essentially the same. The lion has strength and a lion's liver. If I have the lion's liver, then I will also have the lion's strength. The same mechanism of association is operating in each example.

Now the Law of Association is rarely used in its pure form, except for selecting the window dressing and props for casting a spell. Instead, two major sublaws hog the limelight. In fact, these two were the first to be "discovered" by modern anthropology * and were thought to underly the whole of "primitive" magic. Actually, use of the term "primitive" should be avoided since many many so-called savage cultures are just as complex as our own.

These two sublaws are the *Law of Similarity* and the *Law of Contagion*. The first is the basis of "sympathetic magic" and basically says that effects resemble causes. If you want to make a broom fly, you have to put bird feathers on it, wave it around, chirp over it, and so forth. Remember, any object, idea, or person which reminds you of, or is connected (that's *associated*) with a particular phenomenon or entity, partakes of that entity's power and can be used as if it were the entity itself. Thus the feathers, chirping, and other props are con-

---

* Or so the anthropologists say. Actually it was Sir James Frazer in 1890 who was the first to isolate these laws; but anthropologists refuse to allow him into their company.

nected with the idea of flying and can be used to produce the power of the phenomenon "flight." So the key phrase for the Law of Similarity would be: "Lookalikes *are* alike!"

The Law of Contagion has an undeservedly bad reputation because of publicity given to "voodoo" and "curses" in non-literate societies. Sure, it can be used to kill, but it can also be used to cure. The law states that "things once in contact continue to interact after separation." The emphasis here is on objects or persons that have been in *physical contact* with each other. Thus you might use hair or fingernail clippings to help cast a curse because the clippings are associated with (they remind you of) the victim. Or you might touch a sick child with "holy water" in order to cure her of illness. So our key phrase here is: "Power is contagious."

These two sublaws often work together. One example might be the ritual cannibalism discussed earlier. Another would be the area of "fertility" magic, which usually consists of letting the kids do their thing out in the fields before plowing. Or you might take a bottle of your best wine and pour it over the growing vines to insure the crop's high quality. Almost all religious rituals invoke these two sublaws, as when a priest makes the sign of the cross with holy oil or water on the body of a believer, or when the rice of fertility is tossed at a wedding.

Association is used in a reverse manner in "ridicule rituals," in which an enemy's associations are twisted and distorted in order to render them powerless. For example, in the famous so-called Black Masses the rituals and prayers would all be done backward, and ugly or obscene things associated with the normally sacred and powerful. It is also common to use the enemy's gestures, symbols, words, and names in contradictory, muddled, or ridiculous combinations in order to destroy his power.

The Law of Association, with its various sublaws and interactions with other laws, is probably used more than any other law. Now, since magic is predominantly a function of the mind and its thinking patterns, you might expect that this most frequently used law might have an intimate connection with the way the human mind works. Well, you won't be disappointed, since the major function of the brain seems to be association.

As far as most psychologists can tell, thinking, feeling, and memory are the result of data correlations (associations) between information that has already been organized and the new data constantly being received. When data are associated, patterns are produced. The total mind, or personality or "world view," consists of millions of patterns all summing up as a *metapattern* (the word we'll use in this book). Anything can be data ("data" is now used as a collective noun, though technically 1 datum + 1 datum = 2 data—well, 3 actually, since their relation is also a datum) whether it's perceptions, memories, fantasy images, beliefs, values, techniques, rules, or any pattern these may form in combination. Your memory is a collection of many of these previously organized patterns. New information is compared with data already organized, in the memory or elsewhere, so that various correlations and associations can be tried on for size. New associations form new patterns and modify old ones; one new piece of data may drastically alter an entire large pattern. The larger patterns are highly conservative, though, and a man may go insane rather than admit he must change his metapattern. It is well known that those who do succeed in making major alterations in their metapatterns are usually the most fanatic converts: St. Paul and Lenin come immediately to mind.

So where's the connection? The Law of Association can be considered to be a restatement of these principles of the human mind: "Any datum correlating with previously organized data adds to the total content of that data pattern, increasing understanding and thus control of the phenomenon under consideration."

Please remember that this data organizing doesn't have to take place on a conscious level; in fact, in normal life, very little of it ever does. Having a lock of someone's hair, or knowing his secret name, or his ancestry, or having a wax image of him can all be considered methods for gaining more data about him. Some of this may be received and organized on a subconscious or even psychic level. Every new corner of a pattern gives you a new handle you can use to yank out the pattern when you need it. Or, if you are going to do a spell of a more abstract sort, you would surround yourself with colors, lights, smells, sounds, pictures, textures, and anything else you could think of—touching every sense of the body—to remind you of the matter at hand. Thus you would keep certain patterns associated with these items on the surface of your mind and increase the intensity of your concentration. The key phrase we will use for the Law of Association is: "Commonality controls."

The *Law of Identification* combines those of Knowledge, Association, and Personification and states that by maximum association between your metapattern and that of another entity, you can actually *become* that entity and wield its power. Now by maximum association and organization of all data about an entity or phenomenon, you increase your knowledge. The instrumental act of role-playing the part of the entity gives you still *more* data, as you begin to get an idea of how the entity feels from the inside out. You then examine your personal metapattern from the point of view of the entity's metapattern. This is, of course, more intense association, but it is conceived of as "becoming" the entity. All thoughts of separation vanish, and you can do anything the entity can, because you *are* the entity.

Unfortunately most people become so thoroughly lost inside their target entity that they are unable to get out. They even lose all thought of themselves as being anything *but* the entity. The two beings are neither separate nor equal, and the stronger submerges the weaker. Depending on your society and culture, this is known either as sainthood or insanity. This law is primarily theurgic, since once you succeed you're in no condition to do any more experimenting, nor do you really want to. When the identification is temporary we have something called "divine" or "demonic" possession. Our key phrase here might be: "You can become another."

The *Law of Synthesis,* or the Union of Opposites, states that the synthesis of two opposing ideas or data will produce a third idea that will be truer than either of the first two. This third idea will not be a compromise but will be something brand new.

This law comes in very handy, though it is used in the West more for mystical purposes than for magic. Basically, it allows for the simultaneous holding of two conflicting data without anxiety or cognitive strain. It is a method-pattern in the mind that advocates various types of adaptive conduct. It allows you to change belief more smoothly and alter value patterns when necessary. It allows the redeployment of attention from unpleasant contradictions, thus relieving the strain that would otherwise exist.

Since the strain has been tranquilized, old and new data can be considered in peace. The final result will be something *new* which will be in essence a synthesis of the original beliefs.

There are reams of material on this law, showing up everywhere from the Jewish Kabbalah to Tibetan Tantra to Karl Marx—who had the principle down right, but whose followers botched up the results due to insufficient data. The key phrase for this law would be: "Synthesis reconciles."

Closely related is the *Law of Polarity* which says first that anything can be split into two completely opposite characteristics and second, that each of these polarities contains the essence of the other in its own essence.*

This law shows up often in mysticism in comments about the "blackness of white and the whiteness of black," etc. In fact, the very essence of black is contained in the essence of white and vice versa. This alone should be enough to take

---

* Dr. Regardie prefers to say that each polarity contains the "potentiality" of the other within its essence.

care of those still amateurish enough to believe in pure "Black Magic" or "White Witchcraft" or similar nonsense. However, knowing how stubborn religious fanatics are, it's unlikely that anything will get through to them. They will have burned this book by now, anyway, and be vainly tossing hexes in my direction or trying to light a burning pentacle on my front lawn.

The most famous phrasing of this law in Western occultism is "as above, so below," or "the macrocosm is in the microcosm." The last phrase is very interesting, since believers set up one-to-one relationships among all parts of the mind, body, and spirit and the structure of the universe. This has led to some interesting fun and games with palmistry, astrology, phrenology, divining by entrails and so on, all based on alleged correspondences. While it is true that everything in the universe *can* be made to relate or correspond to everything else, the *usefulness* of such correspondences must always be tested. No matter how pretty a pattern may be, if it doesn't work when applied to other patterns, its only value is aesthetic. (Though I will admit that in some fields, such as mathematics, a pattern may sit doing nothing but looking pretty for years before someone finds an application for it.) The key phrase we will use here is: "Everything contains its opposite."

The *Law of Balance* states quite simply that if you wish to survive, let alone become powerful, you must keep all aspects of your universe balanced. You need a certain amount of energy or power in order to survive. If you have too little or too much power you will kill yourself. This is one reason why the followers of *both* "White Magic" and "Black Magic" are headed down dead-end streets. Fanaticism is to be avoided, for the further you go toward an extreme, the less flexible and adaptable to change you become. Since naturally you can also be *too* flexible as well as not flexible enough, it follows that what is needed is to strike a *dynamic* rather than a static balance. As you can see, this law fits in with the larger group of "paradox laws," that is, those of Synthesis, Polarity, and True Falsehoods. The key phrase we shall use here is: "Strike a balance."

The *Law of Infinite Data* states that we will never run out of things to learn (this is also referred to less seriously as the *Law of Infinite Elbow Room*). It is a basic working assumption and, as such, serves the purposes of preventing stagnation and despair and encouraging constant research for new data and, thus, survival. It is also a stimulus to ordinary garden-variety caution, since you can never tell when something new and/or threatening is going to pop up. Our key phrase with this one is: "There's always something new."

The *Law of Finite Senses* throws some additional light on the subject. You cannot hear, taste, smell, or touch things with your eyes unless you are a small child with natural *synesthesia,** or else a grown-up, tripping out on acid or mescaline. Your eyes are limited to only one form of sensory scanning: of a very small portion of the electromagnetic spectrum, visible light. All our senses are similarly limited, both as to type and range of scanning for data. We haven't come to the end of the available data: We haven't seen everything in the universe there is to see, and there is no indication of any end to come. Nor have we any proof that the data available to our normal senses is all the data there is. Therefore, by the *Law of Pragmatism,* the working principle that the total amount of data is infinite is a "true" principle. The key phrase for this law would be: "We can't see everything."

The *Law of Infinite Universes* says that there are an infinite number of ways to view the universe and therefore, again by the Law of Pragmatism, there are an infinite number of universes. This law is a necessary result of the infinite amount of data. If data is infinite, then the patterns and metapatterns possible from manipulating that data are also infinite in number—in fact, it is probably a higher order of infinity, but we will let the mathematicians worry about that.

* Senses that have not yet been separated from each other.

It is interesting to note that both the Hindu and Buddhist theologians have believed in this law for thousands of years before our modern astronomers even got around to stating the possibility of an infinite number of stars and planets. There are more than 100 billion stars in our galaxy, more than 100 billion galaxies in our physical universe, and many astronomers quite seriously believe that there are other clusters of galaxies running around in different physical universes.

There is another point to consider in this law. Every being that perceives is unique. You are made up of billions and billions of different atoms and molecules in a unique energy pattern. If even one of these atoms changed, so would you. In fact, while reading this sentence, you just did. Several millions of atoms were inhaled and exhaled: several billions of atoms and molecules in your cells did their thing, some breaking down and others building up. You are not the same person you were ten seconds ago, and though your metapattern is strong enough to keep you from noticing it, your mind has changed as well. Brain cells have died, others have stored the sensations coming from different parts of your body—these very words are now changing you. Only the saving conservatism of your metapattern allows you to retain an identity.

You have a sensory system that absolutely no one else has; most people come with standard equipment that's fairly similar, but *no two beings sense the world in the same way*. In that sense (sorry), we all live in different universes and there are at least 3½ billion universes hanging around this planet at any one time. This is just counting human beings on the planet Earth, remember, and there are more than 100,000,000 Earthlike planets in our galaxy alone. All these uncountable numbers of universes are changing constantly.

Remember your universe depends upon your sensations and how you classify them. The former is a matter of your physical equipment; the latter, of your cognitive organization. *Change either one and you move to a different universe.*

People who are blind or deaf live in universes where there are no such things as light and sound. If you change your metapattern, then you also move to a different universe.* The *least* efficient way is to change both your sensations and your mind at the same time by the use of drugs. The key phrase to remember for the Law of Infinite Universes is simply: "Infinite universes exist."

However, it is now time for my Two Minute Sermon on Drugs in Magic: As far as beginners are concerned, drugs have a very limited use in magic. Primarily they can be used to convince oneself that there is indeed more than one way to see the universe(s). On other occasions, mild stimulants or tranquilizers are of use in altering your metabolism for reasons we will get into later. Although all magic requires one to be in an altered state of consciousness, not all altered states allow you to do magic while in them. Hard drugs such as heroin ("smack"), methamphetamines ("speed"), or soporifics ("downers") are not only utterly useless from the ritualistic point of view, but are enormously destructive to the physical, mental and emotional health of the user. A magician cannot afford to be addicted to *anything* except possibly fresh air, healthy food and good loving.

Soft drugs, such as various hallucinogenic herbs and fungi, are often used in shamanistic systems of magic. *But* these require many years of expert training (a kind of training unavailable in this culture), especially since many of the herbs and fungi are extremely poisonous in the wrong amounts. Until you have managed (a)to track down a genuine tribal shaman who will agree to train you, and/or (b)to have had at least ten to fifteen years of experience as a magician, I seriously and sincerely suggest that you avoid taking any drug assisted short-cuts. Such efforts are most likely to cause you a lot more trouble than they are really worth and will produce nothing of lasting value. End of Sermon!

The *Law of Pragmatism* is very simple: "If it works, it's

* *The Incomplete Enchanter* series by L. Sprague deCamp and F. Pratt is based on this premise: The hero uses symbolic logic to switch universes by changing his metapattern to one of a world where magic works and science doesn't. *See* Bibliography.

true." Another way to say it is Crowley's "maximum convenience." This means anything: concept, method, dream, myth, hunch, data, or input organization, including all the different patterns these can form. It is after all just a statement of how organisms work. If a datum, pattern, or metapattern helps the organism survive, then as far as the organism is concerned, it has acted upon the "truth." If something doesn't help but instead hinders survival, then the organism will reject that thing as "false." Or die. The key phrase is as simple as the law: "If it works—it's true!"

Put this together with the Law of Infinite Universes and we come to an interesting result: *Truth can be defined as a function of belief!* This flies in the face of modern scientific attitudes that "truth" is "that which can be tested in a lab." Then there is the fact that the whole of modern science is *based upon belief in Scientific Methodology,* a practical belief, and therefore "true," but hardly an Absolute Truth.

Those who really examine their own biases (noticing their unverified assumptions about an "objective" reality) and specialize in Scientific Methodology are far more flexible than those who have been trained to receive their beliefs from on high. Sullivan, commenting on the fact that the first "law of motion" is based on a theoretical situation that can never exist in the physical universe (and is therefore impossible to verify by observation or experimentation) said: "They chose the law because it was the most convenient possible law to choose. It introduced an unrivaled simplicity and economy into the complicated phenomena of motion. For it must be remembered that what scientific men mean by truth is in the last resort convenience. Scientific men are pragmatists in practice, whatever they may think they are in theory."

So if my belief in a "real" Thor helps me to start a thunderstorm, then it is "true" that Thor exists. Which may or may not help the theologians reading this.

This brings us to a very important sublaw—the *Law of True Falsehoods.* This refers to data which contradict one's usual metapattern but which nonetheless work. Now your metapattern is considered to be "true" or "real" since you have survived, and therefore it has worked. So we can then have two contradictory truths. In any other system this might lead to great anxiety or even insanity. In magic, however, we have the Law of Synthesis, so that two truths may be held without strain until a final decision can be made. You might decide that there is no real contradiction or you might have to synthesize a new truth. Until you do, though, we have what we can call True Falsehoods. In magic, more than anything else, "it's the thought that counts." So the key phrase here should probably be: "If it's a paradox, it's probably true."

One unexpected benefit of this last law, as well as a slight explanation for those who violate these laws we've been discussing and still manage to get good results, is that someone who sincerely believes that he can break or ignore all or some of the laws of magic, probably can! This is because his universe doesn't contain the possibility that his spells might backfire or refuse to work if he doesn't follow the laws. Therefore they won't. I should warn you, though, that such depth of belief is nearly impossible to instill artificially. If you were such a person, you aren't now, because I have just entered a bit of doubt into your universe. I apologize, and hope that this volume will make up for your loss by increasing your efficiency.

The final (I promise) major law that we shall look at is the *Law of Personification* with its two sublaws of *Invocation* and *Evocation*. The main law states that any phenomenon may be considered to be alive and to have a personality; in short, to be an entity, and that this is often useful and therefore true.

It is a well-known fact of human nature that we tend to personify inanimate objects. If you crack your head on the side of a door, you will curse it just as if it were alive and could be hurt by your abuse. This alone is useful because it harmlessly relieves your angry tension. Although the theory of Universal Animism is no longer as popular as it used to be among anthropologists and students of so-called primitive religion, it remains true that we still personify things, especially in times of shock or crisis.

I herewith offer my pet theory: Human beings have the longest childhood of any animal. The growing child finds that he receives the overwhelming majority of his data input from his parents or other people. When he starts complicated thinking and associating, the one pattern he knows best is *people* so he associates information in terms of the *people-pattern*. Everything is thought of in terms of relationships to this single pattern that has the earliest and strongest grip on him. Later, as he grows, he learns other patterns to use for associations, but none ever takes the place of his first important pattern, particularly in a time of crisis when the *people-pattern* screams "run to the people for help" and an image of mommy and daddy flashes across his mind.

Hence the ease with which men personify objects and even abstract ideas. And thus, the universal tendency to make our gods and demons in our own image; not to mention the theological point that manlike gods justify childish behavior on the part of people. So our key phrase for this law will be: "Anything can be a person."

The *Laws of Invocation* and *Evocation* say that you can conjure up from, respectively, the inside of and outside of your metapattern, real entities. These entities are only personifications of patterns, of course, but so is every entity, including your friends. Often, as Crowley says, "It is *more convenient* to assume the objective existence of an 'Angel' who gives us new knowledge than to allege that our invocation has awakened a supernormal power in ourselves." (The emphasis is Crowley's.) It is also usually more *comfortable* to personify, since the paranormal in ourselves is often terrifying.

These two laws may be considered the same depending upon whether or not you believe in an objective universe outside your own mind. The key phrase we will use for these two laws is: "Beings within, beings without."

This completes for now the listing of the major Laws of Magic. That there are others I have no doubt. Also there are many methods and procedures that some people would like to raise to the ranks of laws. What we have done here is to examine certain principles that you will find in almost every book that you will read on Western, Eastern or Tribal systems of magic.

Now there will also no doubt be some who would like to throw some sort of "moral law" into this list. I have yet to meet a descriptive moral law (unless self-imposed) that was a universal in magic, and I refuse to clutter up a book of science with legislative laws that belong more in the realm of religion and ethics. Though I personally believe no science should ever be used to destroy human life, I can force my view neither upon the laws of ballistics, if a gun is pointed in my direction, nor upon my readers—who would probably point guns at me if I tried.

Those who wish may include morals under the Law of Cause and Effect, of course, which holds in magic as it does in other sciences. Like the clumsy boy with the needle and thread, as they sew, so shall they weep.

As you read and do research in occultism, you will find that you come across various Laws, Principles, Rules, Methods, Ways, Paths, Techniques, Commandments, Revelations *ad nauseam*. Most of them should easily translate into general or specific cases of the basic laws; if you find a brand-new one, let me know. With the exception of authors like Crowley and Fortune, though, you will find that any principles in your readings have been buried under tons of abstractions, moralisms, prejudices, and pure garbage by people who are themselves without principles, except in their fat bank accounts. These days, occultism is spelled o¢¢ulti$m.

CHAPTER TWO

Fun and Games with Definitions

> *"When I use a word," Humpty Dumpty said, in rather a scornful tone, "it means just what I choose it to mean—neither more nor less."*
>
> *"The question is," said Alice, "whether you can make words mean so many different things."*
>
> *"The question is," said Humpty Dumpty, "which is to be the master—that's all."*
>
> —*Through the Looking-Glass*

Lewis Carroll has just presented us with one of the toughest problems in linguistics, the question of whether a word means what we want it to mean or whether we should consider words to possess innate meanings, whether we like them or not. This is something we used to plague our English teachers with: Are grammar books and dictionaries collections of the way we *do* use words or *should* use words?

Be that as it may, though Establishment scientists and occultists get away with complicated technical jargon, we mere mortals need words with clear, specific, and comprehensible meanings. But language is a tricky thing indeed. No sooner do we have a word, than up pop synonyms, homonyms, antonyms, unclenyms and cousinnyms; and we are instantly trapped in a quagmire of symboling rivalry.

Now ideally a language is a set of symbols, together with rules for their use, that is held in common by a group. A language can be something used by hundreds of millions of people like Russian, English, or Chinese; or it can be used by smaller groups like the languages of musical notation, computer programs, mathematics, or other obscure codes.

Though words *have* to have common meanings so that people can use them to talk together, nonetheless people often use the same words for many different things or several words for the same one. It may give you a notion of how hairy this is, to learn that most of this chapter will be devoted to defining three little words that everyone "knows"—"occultism," "science," and "magic."

A word like "dog" is a *sign* that may be written or spoken. When you read or hear this sign and associate it with a concept in your head, you have just turned that sign into a *symbol.* The description of the concept, "a furry, four-footed mammal that makes a certain kind of noise and has a certain smell, etc." is a *definition* of "dog." As you can see, definitions are almost always much longer than the words they define. Problems arise, as we said, when people have different definitions for the same word or use different words for the same concept.

If you tell a few friends that you have just seen a gritz, they will probably ask you what a "gritz" is. You would begin to describe it, saying maybe, "Oh, it was about forty feet high, had four limbs, was very noisy, very ugly, and hadn't used a deodorant in weeks." If you stop there, one friend might think you'd seen an elephant, another a giant aardvark, yet another Godzilla, and so forth. As your description-definition gets longer, your friends will begin to agree as to what you saw and how sober you were at the time. But if a lot of people should see a gritz, not to mention the closely related grotz and gratz, over a period of many years, and they should all try to describe them, you will have millions of people most of whom might recognize a gritz if they saw one but each with his own private definition of exactly what a gritz is (*I* know, but I'm not talking).

Now with all this out of the way we can attempt to tackle the business at hand, defining a few major terms that we will be using throughout this book. "They've a temper, some of them . . . however, *I* can manage the whole lot of them! Impenetrability! That's what I say!" *

Occultism: The word "occult" means "hidden" or "secret." That's all. But the word conjures up images of robed and cowled scholars poring over dusty tomes in quest of strange and miraculous powers, of naked lamas floating across the snows in far-off Tibet, of old crones tossing bits of powdered toad and other unsavory items into boiling caldrons, of strangely dressed men with swords and chalices intoning hair-raising incantations in forgotten tongues, while within the circles and triangles chalked upon the floor unspeakable *things* begin to take form from the swirling mists, and of the gods know what else.

Why such confusion and nonsense? Because, just as with the gritz, many people for many years gave different descriptions of the concepts involved. All these definitions, the good and the bad, formed patterns and were used and handed down for generations. Occultism is naturally the study of that which is occult.

Science: The word means "organized knowledge," period. How organized it has to be is unspecified, though the general idea of internal testing for consistency is usually a part of the mythos. For some strange reason, though, the words "occultism" and "science" have been turned into antonyms as if they were by nature opposite in every way. It is necessary to examine a few of the arguments of those who wish to separate the two realms of "science" and "occultism."

Originally all technical and scientific knowledge was occult. There is not an Establishment Science today that cannot trace itself back to a time when its subject matter was part of "occultism." Physics and chemistry were once the property of the Physical Alchemists, in fact the word "chemistry" comes from the same Arabic root as "alchemy." The contents of medicine, astronomy, animal husbandry, botany, meteorology, and a

* Professor H. Dumpty again.

host of other -ologies were the duties and skills of priests, witch doctors, sorcerers, medicine men, and shamans.

All these disciplines became what they are today only when they became literally disciplined,* that is systematized to a greater degree than ever before and subjected to rigorous testing. Only when they became the property of the many rather than the few did they leave the realm of the occult.

Very well then, "science" is systematized knowledge; but how organized does it have to be before we can call it a science? Most areas of "occultism" have some sort of organization, though it is often pretty haphazard. Where do we draw the line?

One of the major ways that one decides whether or not something deserves to be called scientific is the presence or absence of people performing a mysterious ritual known to anthropologists as the "Scientific Method." Unfortunately there are actually *two* "Scientific Methods," distinct but interlocking; one is passive and called "observation," the other is active and called "experimentation." Until a few centuries ago observation was all the rage, but then we began inventing fancy equipment and techniques. Soon experimentation began getting all the publicity, became popular and efficient, and was used more and more until most people began to think that science *was* experimentation. Nobody noticed that there were still a lot of scientists who were observing, not because they didn't *want* to experiment, but because they couldn't.

Put it this way: paleontologists, economists, anthropologists, historians, meteorologists, archaeologists, astronomers, and many other scientists have little or no control over the things they study. No matter how showy atom-smashers and spacecraft are, there are still some subjects that just can't be manipulated or meddled with in a laboratory. It'll be a long time before a geologist can start an earthquake or volcano for the purpose of experiment! In fact, about all these sciences

* In the West the Greek philosophers were the first to try.

can do is investigate new ways to refine their observation and equipment.

Normally, however, the two methods work best together. You look at something and get all the info you can that way and organize it as best you can. But if your subject is amenable to manipulation, you can make a hypothesis or two ("hypothesis" is the scientific word for "wild guess"), set up an experiment to test your hunch, and then compare the results with your previous data. Then you make another hypothesis, another experiment, integrate your results again, and just keep going. When you have a whole bunch of interlocking hypotheses, you have a "theory" for which you must devise a bigger and fancier experiment. Several theories may combine into something called "a law of nature," which is just a bigger theory.* When you get right down to it, all the "laws" of modern science are whopping big guesses. *But* they are *educated* guesses! This whole arrangement of hypotheses-theories-laws is like a pyramid: Every layer depends upon those below. If one brick should prove faulty, the entire structure may topple. Depending upon whether the researcher involved is honest or not, his response to the discovery of a false brick will be either to tear down the whole structure and begin again or else to find some smooth-looking plaster to hide the cracks. Every known "law of nature" we have today is built upon the ruins of previous laws and theories, and a thousand years from now, twentieth-century science will be derided as sheer superstition and stupidity. Even that crowning achievement of modern physics, Einstein's Theory of Relativity, will have been modified drastically before the end of the 1990's (this non-psychic prediction is based on rumblings I've been hearing among the local physicists).

So far then, not all sciences are able to use experimentation. Given time though, for good or evil, probably all of them

* Other methodologists rearrange this order. One starts with laws and arranges them into theories, upon the basis of experimental results. From these theories new laws can be deduced. Actually both methods interweave in a chicken-or-egg way.

will be. Under the prodding of power-hungry governments and advertising agencies, psychology and sociology have made great strides toward complete control of their subjects. Unfortunately their subjects just happen to be us!

Now occultism is full of observation, in fact it consists of almost 99 percent observation. (This is because there has been much more writing on mysticism than on magic, the former being the passive side and the latter, the active side of the same coin of the realm of occultism.) But physics and biology were totally observational just a few centuries ago.* They found methods of experimentation, why can't occultism? You say that it's been too long. Had occultism been amenable to experimentation wouldn't it have been investigated a long time ago?

A valid question. But notice something here: We started out with the things furthest away from human minds, and as we gradually got closer to home, different sciences popped up as organized. Man went through astronomy, geology, physics, chemistry, paleontology, mathematics, biology, and medicine till we finally got to anthropology, sociology, and psychology (I know I left out a lot and I know that different parts of the world got these in slightly different order, but the basic pattern is there). The last three named are among the youngest of the sciences, and not one hundred years ago there were people who claimed these studies were "unscientific." To date, we've gotten closest to the human mind with the infant science of parapsychology, only recently let in through the back doors of the halls of Establishment Science, when the Parapsychological Association was finally admitted into membership in 1969 in the American Association for the Advancement of Science (which is sort of a super-AMA for Establishment scientists, designed to keep out the riffraff).

So we can quite accurately say that every modern science has grown out of occultism (usually via technology). In fact, occultism is dwindling rapidly and today includes mostly

* Despite some abortive attempts by the ancient Greeks.

such things as magic and mysticism, both of which deal with
powers of the mind that psychology and parapsychology can
only glimpse. Remember that occultism, that which is known
only to a few, is the child of the Unknown or that which is
known to nobody. As knowledge is ferreted out of the Unknown, it must always pass through a stage in which it is a
part of "occultism," before the few who first find it are able
to transmit it to others, so that it can become a part of "science." This is precisely what has happened to physics, chemistry, and most of the "hard" sciences.

For the purposes of this book though, this definition of
"occultism" is just a bit too broad. Einstein's Theory of Relativity is said to be understood completely by less than twenty
people in the world, but most people would not consider it
a part of occultism. Bits and pieces from a hundred disciplines and areas of study float around within the realm of
occultism. Occasionally some of them interlock into patterns
that we call magic, mysticism, philosophy, religion, metaphysics, mythology, phenomenology, and a dozen other things
(including superstition, fraud, and ignorance). Though the
larger meanings should be kept in the back of your mind,
when I say "occultism," I will usually be referring to those
sections of it dealing with the powers of the mind, *as yet*
unknown to more than a few.

Mysticism: We won't spend too much time on this term.
The word comes from a Greek root meaning someone or
something connected with the ancient Greek "Mysteries."
These were religious rites run by various orders, schools, and
fraternal organizations. From the very beginning the emphasis had been upon the religious and spiritual, and gradually the term absorbed the concept of "secret religious doctrines." That figures, since the initiation rites were secret
indeed. Any person who went through the rites of a Greek
Mystery became a "mystic" and was called "blessed" or occasionally "christos." (This is the origin of "Christ," which
contrary to popular opinion was *not* Jesus' last name—

"christos" means "anointed," which was one of the hon-
orific titles for the messiah, so Paul just translated "messiah"
into "christos.") The initiates kept their secrets well, and we
know next to nothing about what really went on during the
rites or what was taught. For that matter most of these Greek
"mystics" would not fit our modern concepts of what a mystic
is, and of those Greeks who *would* fit our concepts, few were
graduates of the Mysteries.

In any event, the important point to recognize is that
mysticism is theurgic and designed to bring spiritual salvation. By nature it is passive and contemplative, though it
deals with much of the same data that the more aggressive
magic does. Throughout history, men and women have easily
and often moved from magic to mysticism and back again.
We will find as we study that something that is valid in one
field usually works in the other as well. There can be no clear
dividing line, and indeed to attempt to draw one would violate the laws of both. Anyone trying to make a neat dividing
line would probably be making a very great mystic.

Magic: Now we are ready to define "magic," right? Wrong!
First we are going on a tour of Asia and Europe, to pick up
still more data to support our previous arguments. We start
our tour with a visit to Persia to consider the "Magi." Most
people associate this word with the "Three Wisemen" who
supposedly showed up to worship the infant Jesus at his birth.
The visitation of newborn saviors and avatars by kings and
wisemen is a common theme in nativity myths, but in the case
of Joshua bar Joseph is at least a possibility; first because
some astronomers now believe that there may have been a
supernova or comet of great brightness around 6–4 B.C.
(when he was actually born) and second, the Magi would
have noticed it, figured something unusual was up, and gone
looking. Besides, any Magus worth his salt would certainly
recognize a messiah when he saw one.

The Magi were Zoroastrian priests, devotees of a religion
which, by the way, shaped much of Christianity. But they were

far more. The 1768 edition of the *Encyclopaedia Britannica* has a lovely little paragraph on the Magi that is even better than the one in their 1968 edition: "The priests of the magi were the most skillful mathematicians and philosophers of the ages in which they lived, insomuch that a learned man and a magian became equivalent in terms. The vulgar looked upon their knowledge as more than natural, and imagined them inspired by some supernatural power: and hence, those who practiced wicked and mischievous arts, taking upon themselves the name of magians, drew on it that ill signification which the word magician now bears among us."

"Magus" is the singular of "Magi" (one Magus plus one Magus equals two Magi—bet they never taught you that in grade school). Though both the words "Magus" and "magician" are essentially the same, during the Middle Ages the title "Magus" was reserved for the superior magicians.

Both words come to us through Latin via the ancient Greek word *magos* which in turn came from the Old Persian term for a particular tribe in Media (modern-day Iran-Persia). The word was later used to refer to the priests of this tribe, which apparently had nothing else to recommend it, and was later extended to the Zoroastrian priests who inherited the territory (the Magi had some cousins in Eastern India known as the "Magas" who were the priests of the mountain and forest peoples). I was hoping that the root *mag-* could have been traced back to a fancy definition in the Indo-Aryan language, but there we seem to have hit a stone wall. If the root is a tribe's name, it probably means "the people" or "humans," and though this can lead to some interesting metaphysical gymnastics, it doesn't help us much linguistically. Those interested in learning more about the Zoroastrian Magi can check out *Herodotus,* Book One, Chapter 101.

There are also some interesting entwinings with *magister,* a master or teacher in ancient Rome or at a medieval university, from the Latin for "great" or "master" which was *mag-*

nus. Later most magicians, philosophers, mystics, and alchemists were also called *magistri.* And if you ever run across *mage,* it's another variation on "Magus." Did you notice that we've managed to get every single vowel to follow *mag-?* We've had "Mag*a*s," "Mag*e*," "Mag*i*," "Mag*o*s," and "Mag*u*s." One extra little goodie here is that there was a city called Magnesia on the Mediterranean coast of Asia Minor, and that this city was famous for its lodestones, and that this is where the name "magnet" comes from. Later when we see how important the electromagnetic field is to our work, we may begin to wonder. . . .

However, having toured through Persia, India, Asia Minor, Greece, and Rome we can now start on "magic." Hold onto your sanity, we have a long way to go. One of the first things you will notice, if you do any reading in this field at all, is that there are more definitions of "magic" than there are magicians, mystics, philosophers, occultists, theologians, and anthropologists put together (you wouldn't actually want to put them together, they would be at each other's throats in seconds . . . Hmmm, come to think of it, it might not be such a bad idea . . .).

I would like to give you some idea of the range of opinions involved if you haven't already found out. Those of you who have done your homework can skip the next few pages if you wish.

Now there is a technique used by many authors when they find themselves (a) with nothing to say, (b) painted into a corner, and/or (c) getting paid by the word. This is known as Presenting Evidence, or "padding." Padding with quotes is usually done when the author is afraid to present his own opinion, or else is anxious to show that he is widely read and has access to a xerox machine.

So, lest by some strange mischance some knave should accuse me of padding or of having base motives in my frequent use of quotes, I shall plead my case here and now. First, other writers are often much wittier and/or clearer than I could ever hope to be. Second, I wish to show in many cases that I am not alone in my opinions or grabbing them out of midair, that there are accepted authorities who agree with me and can thus shed some of their "respectability" on my work. Third, in occultism things often *become* whatever they are repeatedly called, whether they were so in the first place or not. Fourth, I often wish to show that proponents of very different schools of thought are unwittingly in agreement with one another and the juxtaposition of quotes from their work may clearly show the similarities. Finally, I fully expect to present my own synthesis and opinions about the meaning of the word "magic" at the end of the chapter.

With all this out of the way we can now take a look at what several different people in different times and places had to say about "magic."

MAGIC originally signified only the knowledge of the more sublime parts of philosophy; but as the magi likewise possessed astrology, divination and sorcery, the term magi became odious, being used to signify an unlawful diabolical kind of science, acquired by the alliance of the devil and departed souls.
—*Encyclopaedia Britannica* (1768 again)

Magic is the Highest, most Absolute, and most Divine Knowledge of Natural Philosophy, advanced in its works and wonderful operations by a right understanding of the inward and occult virtues of things; so that true Agents being applied to proper Patients, strange and admirable effects will thereby be produced. Whence magicians are profound and diligent searchers into Nature; they, because of their skill, know how to anticipate an effect, the which to the vulgar shall seem a miracle.
—"Goetia of the Lemegeton of King Solomon"

Magic is the art of effecting changes in consciousness at will.
—William Butler

A magical device constructed according to the
directions found in an ancient Disc of Shadows.

Magic is a comprehensive knowledge of all nature.

—Francis Barrett

Magick is the Art and Science of causing changes to occur in conformity with Will.

—Aleister Crowley

Yet when the sociologist approaches the study of magic, there where it still reigns supreme, where even now it can be found fully developed—that is, among the Stone Age savages of today— he finds to his disappointment an entirely sober, prosaic, even clumsy art, enacted for purely practical reasons, governed by crude and shallow beliefs, carried out in a simple and monotonous technique. This was already indicated in the definition of magic given above when in order to distinguish it from religion we described it as a body of purely practical acts, performed as a means to an end. Such also we have found it when we tried to disentangle it from knowledge and from practical arts, in which it is so strongly enmeshed, superficially so alike that it requires some effort to distinguish the essentially different mental attitude and the specifically ritual nature of its acts. Primitive magic—every field anthropologist knows it to his cost—is extremely monotonous and unexciting, strictly limited in its means of actions, circumscribed in its beliefs, stunted in its fundamental assumptions. Follow one rite, study one spell, grasp the principles of magical belief, art and sociology in one case, and you will know not only all the acts of the tribe, but, adding a variant here and there, you will be able to settle as a magical practitioner in any part of the world yet fortunate enough to have faith in that desirable art.

—Bronislaw Malinowski
Magic, Science & Religion

Wherever sympathetic magic occurs in its pure unadulterated form, it is assumed that in nature one event follows another necessarily and invariably without the intervention of any spiritual or personal agency.

Thus its fundamental assumption is identical with that of modern science; underlying the whole system is a faith, implicit but real and firm, in the order and uniformity of nature. The

magician does not doubt that the same causes will always produce the same effects, that the performance of the proper ceremony accompanied by the appropriate spell, will inevitably be
attended by the desired results, unless, indeed, his incantations
should chance to be thwarted and foiled by the more potent
charms of another sorcerer. He supplicates no higher power;
he sues the favor of no fickle and wayward being; he abases
himself before no awful deity. Yet his power, great as he believes it to be, is by no means arbitrary and unlimited. He can
wield it only so long as he strictly conforms to the rules of his
art, or to what may be called the laws of nature as conceived
by him. To neglect these rules, to break these laws in the
smallest particular is to incur failure, and may even expose the
unskillful practitioner himself to the utmost peril. If he claims
a sovereignty over nature, it is a constitutional sovereignty
rigorously limited in its scope and exercised in exact conformity with ancient usage.

Thus the analogy between the magical and the scientific
conceptions of the world is close. In both of them the succession
of events is perfectly regular and certain, being determined by
immutable laws, the operation of which can be foreseen and
calculated precisely; the elements of caprice, of chance, and of
accident are banished from the course of nature. Both of them
open up a seemingly boundless vista of possibilities to him who
knows the causes of things and can touch the secret springs that
set in motion the vast and intricate mechanism of the world.
Hence the strong attraction which magic and science alike
have exercised on the human mind; hence the powerful
stimulus that both have given to the pursuit of knowledge.

—J. G. Frazer
The Golden Bough

We must see magical behavior as the response to a situation
which is revealed to the mind through emotional manifestations, but whose essence is intellectual. For only the history of
the symbolic function can allow us to understand the intellectual condition of man, in which the universe is never charged
with sufficient meaning and in which the mind always has more
meanings available than there are objects to which to relate

them. Torn between these two systems of reference—the sig-
nifying and the signified—man asks magical thinking to provide
him with a new system of reference, within which the thus-far
contradictory elements can be integrated. But we know that
this system is built at the expense of the progress of knowledge,
which would have required us to retain only one of the two
previous systems and to refine it to the point where it absorbed
the other.

—Claude Lévi-Strauss
The Sorcerer & His Magic

So what have we got? Most of the writers are agreed that
"magic" is a type of organized knowledge, that the magician
follows what he considers to be natural laws, and that this
knowledge is the possession of a small minority. Does this
sound familiar?

Malinowski, following Frazer's example, quite piously tries
to separate religion from magic from science. Lévi-Strauss, in
Structural Anthropology, swiftly demolishes these attempts.
But Malinowski's reasoning is sloppy even to the non-an-
thropologist, to wit: "religion" is supposed to be the use of
nonphysical means to nonpractical ends; "science" the use of
physical means to practical ends; and "magic" the use of nonphysical means to practical ends. Now riddle me this, Bronislaw: Is a Catholic priest saying a mass for rain during a
drought performing magic or religion? How about a sorcerer
performing a spell to damn an enemy to eternal unrest, thus
using nonphysical means for a nonpractical end, isn't that
religion? Oh yes, and what do you call someone using physical
means for nonpractical ends, an "artist," possibly? Though
separations *can* be made, and sometimes *must* be made,
Malinowski's separations are so poorly constructed that a hip-
pogriff could fly through them.

The quote from Lévi-Strauss deals exclusively with *Placebo
Spells,* as indeed does his entire article. He ignores the many
cases of curses and cures that happen *without* the knowledge
of the subject. Additionally, noting his last comments, one

wonders why a system of magical reference could not be re-
fined to a point where it absorbed all others? This has in fact
been done in some of the more complicated and sophisticated
systems of occult philosophy, especially in Eastern Tantra and
in the pages of the Mystical Kabbalah.

So far we have the following: "Magic" is an art and a science for dealing with particular types of knowledge, the
manipulation of which will produce results that will astound
and amaze the uninformed. This sounds a great deal like
quantum mechanics, cybernetics, and astrophysics, as well as
other even more "occult" sciences. Where is the difference
then between "magic" and "science"?

Only this: *The science and art of magic deals with a body
of knowledge that, for one reason or another, has not yet been
fully investigated or confirmed by the other arts and sciences.*

If the contents of magic and other parts of occultism are
not now fully recognized sciences, they will be someday. Occultists need not fear that their realm will ever totally disappear, for by the Law of Infinite Data there will always be a
few facts left to discover. Magic and mysticism are but small
parts of occultism; even when they are fully understood and
controlled, there will be plenty of work left to do. Only the
coward and the fraud need fear the "invasion" of occultism
by modern science.

CHAPTER THREE

Parapsychology, the Apologetic Science

Parapsychology is the youngest, yet, at the same time, the oldest known science. So far, the relationship between magic and parapsychology could be considered similar to that between an observational science and an experimental one (except, of course, that magic has as much art as science in it).

Para- is a Greek prefix used for "above," "beyond," "other" (though originally it meant "beside"). Placed in front of "psychology," it gives us a term that means both "the study of the unusual in psychology" and "the psychology of the unusual." In point of fact, the word "parapsychology" is usually defined as "the study of paranormal phenomena." Now "paranormal" means literally "above the normal," or "beyond the common," or "other than the usual." So, since "super" means "above," and the "natural" is that which is "common," "usual," and "normal," it would seem that all this is really a sneaky way to get around saying "supernatural." It is.

Parapsychology had enough problems getting accepted by Establishment science as things were, without any extra difficulties. So the early researchers decided that it was safer to say that they studied "paranormal" rather than "supernatural" phenomena. (Does this mean that the science of parapsychology will soon be encroaching on the territory of official religions? Right, the first time!)

Now since "paranormal" is a long word, and I am basically lazy, we can now introduce the word *"psi."* This is short for "psychic," which means "of the mind-soul" and "of the supernatural." So we can talk about *"psi* phenomena" or *"psi* powers," instead of writing "paranormal" over and over again.

Do you get the feeling that we are going to get bogged down in definitions again? I'm sorry to have to keep doing this, but as we said before, in magic things often *become* what we call them. It is therefore of the utmost importance that we all agree upon our use of terms, if we are to get anywhere at all. Linguistics and psycholinguistics are vital parts of the study of magic. One of the reasons this book is being written is to give you a set of terms at once clear and precise. In this chapter we are going to examine the subject matter of parapsychology; this will necessitate the defining of special words and terms (plus some special conventions of our own).

The people who studied *psi* phenomena ("happenings") and powers quickly divided everything into two parts: *Extrasensory Perception* and *Paraphysics* (that's "mind over matter"). Since like Caesar, I have a great deal of gall, I have divided *psi* into three parts, adding *Hypercognition* ("superfast thinking"), plus a new area of *Anti-psi* for the barbarians. We are now going to examine these divisions and their contents, and *psi* what we can *psi.*

First I must mention that parapsychology is as plagued as occultism is by a lack of universal terminology; so the list of terms following are my own, those I have found most useful. Other researchers may use different words for the same thing, or the same word for different things. Other conventions we will use include: "-er" at the end of a term like "ESPer" means the *person using* the *talent,* who is also the person we will call the *agent;* "-ing" at the end will mean the *process* of using the *talent* (as in "ESPing"); the word "talent" when in italics will refer to a special *psi* ability. Finally, since this is a mix of traditional with coined terms, we will feel free to mingle Greek, Latin, and French roots in a way most scientists would find horrifying.

The first category of *psi* is that of *Extrasensory Perception*, or "ESP." This is (and there will be no arguments about the objective existence of the *talents* discussed) the reception of data without using the normal sense channels. It is sometimes called the "sixth sense," somewhat stupidly, since even normally we have more than five. This is because the so-called sense of touch is actually several senses and includes the "sense" of heat, cold, pressure, pain, and pleasure. We also have a "sense" of time, space, balance, weight, muscle tone, and so on, most of which (including hearing!) are modifications of "touch." We can in fact normally receive data in only three different ways—by pressure, as in "touch" and "hearing," by chemical interaction as in "taste" and "smell," and by receiving electromagnetic waves as in "sight." Since all incoming data is translated into electrochemical signals to the brain anyway, all our "senses" are ways of manipulating and interacting with portions of the electromagnetic spectrum of energy, either directly as in "sight" or indirectly as in the other "senses" (matter is only sticky energy, remember).

ESP should probably be called Extrasensory Sensation instead of Extrasensory Perception, because "perception" technically refers to the *classification of sensations*, but we will use the traditional term for two reasons. First, because ESP is so firmly entrenched that we could never get rid of it; and second, because it is precisely the *classification* of data received through ESP that makes things so complicated. There is a vast difference between the way data is *received* and the way it is classified, or *input*—a difference that we will constantly have to watch, because it is the source of most confusion and error in both occultism and parapsychology.

Telepathy comes from the Greek for "far-sensing" and refers to the direct communication of data between minds. This communication may be one-way or two-way, and the data may be pictures, ideas, sensations, or emotions. The simpler the message, the more likely it is to get through and the greater distance it will go (see the notes on Dr. Kogan later in this chapter). As a rule, emotions and associations or attributes travel best.

Clairvoyance, from the French, means "clear seeing." It is the reception of data that *seems* visual, without the medium of another mind (if another mind were involved we would have telepathy and not clairvoyance going on). If, for example, I wake up in bed with an image in my head of something happening thousands of miles away—a not uncommon occurrence really, considering the number of cases of this sort reported *—it is obviously impossible that photons of light could have traveled all that way and into my darkened room from the place where they are actually bouncing around. I have no idea of *how* I am receiving the data, I only know that it is being input as if it were visual.

A common type of clairvoyance is when you seem to see an image of a person or thing in your room, often this image is connected with a sudden death. This is called by some a "veridical hallucination," to separate it from other kinds of hallucination, the difference being that in a "veridical hallucination" the content is fact, not fancy. Many, if not most, spontaneous cases of ESP involve a death or catastrophe. We will find this of great importance later on.

Clairaudience, again from the French, means "clear hearing," and is data input as normal sound even though the actual hearing of sound is impossible. Again this is without the medium of another mind. Most spontaneous clairaudience takes the form of hearing "voices" or "sounds" connected with a recent death or tragedy.

If the data should be received by ESP but input as if you were "tasting," "smelling," or "touching" then we could say that what was going on was *Clairgustance, Clairolfaction,* and

---

* A quick glance through old parapsychological and psychic research journals will give you plenty of "spontaneous cases" to examine and compare.

Clairtangency. As you may have guessed, these are terms coined by me.

Suppose, for another example, that my brother is drowning in Lake Erie (provided the pollution were thin enough to allow him to sink), and I am sleeping in my room 3,000 miles away. Suddenly I have a dream in which I "feel" cold water surrounding me, "smell" a horrid stench, "taste" raw sewage in my mouth, "hear" my brother's cries, and "watch" him sink beneath the scum. Provided that there was no telepathy involved, we would then have a case of all five *clair- senses* operating at once. So as you can see, I did not invent the last three terms just for the sake of neatness. There are many spontaneous cases on record, such as "smelling" smoke and "feeling" heat when a loved one's home is on fire, that simply do not fit under clairvoyance or clairaudience. To date these have all been lumped under clairvoyance or called *General Extrasensory Perception* (GESP), a term used when two or more types of ESP are operating at the same time.

Though I am sure that the same basic mechanism is responsible for all the different types of *clair sensing*, there is *something* determining the way in which the data is input. I feel that it will help to avoid confusion and sloppy thinking if we use these extra terms.

There is one more *clair sense* to be discussed and that is *Clairsentience*, more properly referred to as *Clairempathy*. We will use the second term because "sentience" as a root means "feeling" and includes both the concepts of "touching" and "emotion." Since we already have clairtangency for the first concept, and because "empathy" is more precisely limited to "emotion-perception," we will use clairempathy as a more exact term. It is the reception of data, usually emotional, from objects or surroundings—again, without normal channels or the medium of another mind.

Most people just say that a place or object has good or bad "vibrations" and leave it at that. A haunted house, for example, usually has some pretty heavy "vibes." When clairempathy is limited to objects, it is often called "psychometry," a term we will not use if we can possibly help it because it is also the name for a very technical science of psychological measurement and statistics, and the use of it here can only cause confusion.

We will pause here for a moment to discuss the person who is a *Total Empath*. He is someone who simply "absorbs" the local "atmosphere" wherever he may be. Sometimes called "sensitives," these people are as a rule totally defenseless against psychic attack or even undirected strong emotion in their vicinity. Unless he or she is taught methods of psychic "shielding," the *total empath* will find himself helplessly absorbing and reproducing strong emotions in situation after situation. All in all, this can lead to a pretty miserable life, and *total empaths* tend to die young—from emotional exhaustion—or wind up in mental institutions.

Some *empaths,* however, can control this absorption and can literally "drain" others of their psychic energy. Sometimes known when habitually irresponsible as "psychic vampires," they can suck up energy from others whenever needed. They are not *total empaths,* who definitely belong to the realm of ESP and ESP only; rather they are on the borderline between ESP and *Anti-Psi,* because they can walk into a room and absorb all the energy there, thus canceling out all *psi* for everyone else.

ESP has two other major types: *Astral Projection* and *Mental Projection.* Tentatively, these will both be defined as being GESP combined with concepts of "traveling" either through normal three-dimensional space or through various "astral planes."

The difference between astral projection and mental projection is that in astral projecting you hallucinate the image of a slightly translucent body, called the "astral body," which rises from your physical body and carries your center of consciousness with it. The reason I say that this astral body is only a hallucination (though granted it is a veridical one) is that the image is usually an exact visual duplicate of the way the *agent* looked before he began projecting, including as often as not, an "astral" nightgown or pajamas. I have yet to meet a single occultist who would admit that pajamas have astral bodies. Then again, in those rare instances where the *agent* has a maimed or crippled body, his astral body is usually perfect and unblemished.

Another indication is the famous "silver cord" that shows up so often (but not always) in astral projection. The cord is basically an umbilical one connecting the navel of the astral body to the navel of the physical body. This cord can grow to just about infinite length, stretching out behind you as you travel. Some experienced *agents* actually loop it around trees and telephone poles in order to anchor themselves. There is great concern in the literature about this cord breaking or being cut, as this severing is believed to cut you off forever from your physical body which will quickly perish. I just wonder if this anxiety is related in some way to the trauma involved in the *first* cutting of the cord at birth. The Eastern scriptures on rebirth talk constantly about "cutting the silver cord."

The evidence would indicate that the astral body found in astral projection is actually an illusion created by the *agent* to comfort him in his fear that he might be separated permanently from his physical body. It provides him with a set of "coordinates" to enable him to find his way back. I note the fact that mental projection is rarer than astral, and requires more training and self-confidence. Also mental projection is universally said to be less tiring than astral. Apparently the effort of keeping a translucent body together (cord, nightgown, and all) distracts and exhausts the *agent*. One experienced astral projector with whom I have discussed this, mentions that he can often move his astral body instantly from one place to another, simply by changing the coordinates of his consciousness.

One objection made to this "veridical hallucination" theory of astral projection is that there have supposedly been cases where actual photographs of astral bodies were taken while their owners were at home. I can answer this by suggesting the more likely possibility that the astral projector may have used one or more methods of "mind over matter" to control either the photons in front of the camera or else the film directly (as a gentleman named Ted Serios seems able to do).

The only other theory of astral projection, the traditional one, is that the astral body represents a "finer form of matter" that is similar to the "ectoplasm" produced by mediums. Since energy is matter and since the energy-pattern generated by even a thought may have physical analogs, it is impossible to rule this theory out entirely. It might even be possible that the astral projector uses some form of *Atomic Psychokinesis* to manipulate photons or some other type of subatomic matter, in order to produce the astral body. It's just that this is much less likely—mainly because manipulation of matter by the mind is much harder than hallucinating—than that the body image is only just that: imaginary.

However, this is a veridical hallucination, and we still have the problems of the "astral planes" to be considered. Though most occultists today consider these "planes" simply to be various parts of the mind, to the *agent* these planes are completely real and solid to his astral body. If our astral projector should meet another astral projector or some entity upon these planes, both are capable of doing damage to each other's astral body—damage which is firmly believed to be reflected in the physical body left behind. Thus, you can meet injury or death while traveling through the astral planes if your "astral double" is damaged.

Probably the Law of True Falsehoods is involved, since the *agent's* belief is the critical variable. Throughout these astral planes you will meet many entities, usually personifications of the patterns within your own metapattern, and we all have some pretty nasty "demons" locked up in our subconscious minds. Fortunately we also have a few "angels," and a battle between the two groups can be very interesting to watch (though also rather dangerous—the Good Guys don't always win, remember!). If you meet another astral projector, then you are probably using the astral planes as an input mechanism for telepathy. But as one occultist put it, "It cannot be denied that it is somewhat encouraging to be knocked down by a demon whose existence you were unaware or unsure of before."

Two areas of *psi* that sit near each other, about halfway between ESP and *Paraphysics* are *Animal-Psi* and *Plant-Psi.*

Animal-Psi involves many different phenomena of unusual natures either occurring between humans and animals or between animals and animals or animals alone. Some of these are familiar to all of us—the dog or cat that travels thousands of miles to find his home after being lost; the dog who howls at his master's death or at the approach of danger; the cat who shows awareness of the impending arrival of his master at an unusual hour, and so forth. A few experiments—far too few in recent years—have been done in the lab (mostly the experimenter's thinking about food or danger and watching the animal for any reaction) that demonstrate the occasional use of telepathy between humans and animals.

The existence of *Animal-Psi* in such matters as migration patterns and animal-to-animal communication is strongly to be suspected. Here is a place where cross-fertilization between zoologists, animal psychologists, and parapsychologists could be most fruitful. Having worked for a veterinarian, I can recall many cases in which the attitudes of the animals or their owners were the critical factor in cures and recoveries.

Plant-Psi got its greatest publicity when an enterprising researcher decided to hook an electroencephalograph to some plants and record their reaction when he injured tissue by burning or slicing leaves. He found that he didn't even have to touch the plants to cause a reaction, *the mere thought of* *hurting the plant* was sufficient to cause the needle to swing wildly! Later experiments were done * involving the cursing and blessing of plants, with definite results ascribable only to the blessings and curses. For those of you who are vegetarians because you cannot stand the thought of causing pain to dumb animals, I have unhappy news. When you slice a tomato, *it screams!* As you sit there munching your soybeans, imagine the psychic atmosphere over the fields at harvest time. . . .

Now we can move on to *Paraphysics,* different types of *psi* involving apparently mental control of matter. Of the various forms of paraphysics the one with the most laboratory evidence accumulated in its favor is *Psychokinesis,* or PK. The word means "mind-moving," and that is precisely what PK is. (*Telekinesis* is a common synonym for PK, but we will not use it in this book.) From the earliest experiments forty years ago, to the most recent, evidence has shown that people *can* move matter and control what should be the random movement of small objects such as dice.

When an object or person floats across the room, this form of "floating PK" is called *Levitation.* This might have some connection with the traditional skills of Eastern adepts in making objects heavier or lighter, something we could call *Mass Control.*

Teleportation and *Aportation* are the instant movement of beings and things (respectively) from one point to another apparently without going through space as we know it. Teleportation has been done only in fiction, myth, and scripture, though sufficiently often to raise suspicion. Aportation, however, has been done in the laboratory. These experiments were rare and were done in the earlier days of parapsychology when the researchers were concentrating on mediums and spiritualists. Most of those tested failed, but a few were able to perform under the most stringent lab conditions, using aportation to move small objects such as shells, rings,

* At McGill University in Canada and elsewhere.

junk jewelry, and so on, into sealed rooms. Something to note here is that the few animals that were aported in experiments always arrived dead. Perhaps a being has to transport himself (that is teleport) in order to survive the trip. Both aportation and teleportation seem totally farfetched. Can we grab some further evidence for them from other disciplines? Yes, we can: I am told by my physicist friends that moving matter faster than the speed of light (something theoretically possible with APK—see later in this chapter) will take that matter out of our three dimensions. I have an unverified report that physicists recently managed to Aport a quantity of Argon gas a distance of twenty feet in a lab. Unfortunately when it arrived it was "wrong," that is, reconstructed improperly. Is it possible that "instructions" upon proper reassembly could be *sent* along with the matter transmitted? Let us check some other subjects for an answer to this question as well as for additional data.

Take mythology and symbology, for example. Mircea Eliade in his writings on *The Symbolism of the Centre* and *Binding and Loosening Gods* has given us, purely by accident (I think!), what amounts to "instructions" on how to think in order to Teleport, as well as "explanations" of the physical and mental mechanisms involved.

Every culture, says Eliade, has the concept of a special place which is the Centre of the World-Universe. This is a place where all planes of existence intersect; for example, Heaven-Earth-Hell, Past-Present-Future, and so forth. Any spot so consecrated may become the Centre, and all these Centres coexist, that is, they are all the same Centre.

Remember our discussion in Chapter One about constant change? A person walking across the room is not the same person in any two instants of his trip. Thus we can consider, strictly from mysticism, folklore, and the Laws of Magic, that motion is as relative a concept as time, an attitude currently accepted by modern physics. Add to this the Buddhist concept of perpetual Creation-Destruction-Re-creation. By merely continuing to exist, I have "destroyed" my previous selves and "re-created" new ones. If I were to let myself be "destroyed" at one spot and "re-created" at another, the spatial transition would be instantaneous, just as that described in the literature of Teleportation. We find from studying religion, magic, and folklore that all such concepts as time, space, motion, matter, and energy are totally relative, and can be transcended by the skilled. Einstein, anyone?

Let us return to Eliade. The "eternal present," where, when "time" is nonexistent, is called "stasis" or "nonduration." Various symbols of this in three dimensions include "immobility," "motionlessness," "stability," etc. If you live in this state, you are called "he whose thought is stable"; you are in the *nunc stans* (Latin—"stable-now"). The Buddhist term for "instant" is the *ksana,* which also means "the favorable moment." Any instant may become the *ksana;* illumination is instantaneous (*eka-ksana*) and usually symbolized as a lightning flash. Thus the difference between "moment" and *ksana* is *qualitative.* The *ksana* is coexistent with every instant of time —past-present-future. By jumping into *ksana* from the present, you should be able to jump off again into any point of past or future. This, however, is perilous, as *all* time and *all* space surround you at the *ksana-Centre;* probably deep hypnosis as to destination and return (as well as retention of sanity) would be necessary. A point to remember about *ksana* is that it may be equally described as "no motion" or as "motion too fast to be measured."

Myth is full of references to "breaking through" planes of existence, usually with the "difficult passage" motif. Some illustration of the Law of Synthesis is almost always involved, as well as an emphasis that the passage or breakthrough must be instantaneous. Any hesitation brings death.

Binding and Loosening Deities are also common throughout the world. They use knots and snares, physical or magical, for both attacking and defending. The Magic of Knots is twofold, binding and safekeeping, snaring and healing, keeping powers in or out: All depends on the intent, whether for attack or defense. Compare the symbology of binding with that of Greek phrases referring to the Fates as "weaving the *web* of Life" (or cutting it), various widespread concepts of the universe as a *web* of forces, of the air as woven or webbing, the silver cord of astral projection, the "thread of life," the climbing of a rope in the Centre, the fact that words like "fascination" are derived from words for binding, and the fact that "the human situation" is almost always expressed in terms of bondage, limitation, and so on.

After discussing the above, Eliade brings us to two major conclusions; first that everything in the universe is connected in a *Web* with everything else, and second that it is traditional for certain deities (usually sky or ocean gods) to be in charge or command of this universal webbing or bondage. Then he examines another motif, the myth of the "Escape from the Labyrinth." This is really an escape from life's bondage, or more accurately, "enlightenment" and escape from the tyranny of profane reality. One may never escape the *Web* entirely, except by entering Nirvana or oblivion, but one can free himself from one section of the *Web* in order to travel about it.

The magician, or "mayin," can bind or loose because he controls "maya" ("maya" in Sanskrit equals "illusion" equals "bondage"), and thus can control the illusion we call "reality." The magician therefore should be able to escape from one part of the *Web* and go to another. He does this by consecrating one spot as the Centre of the *Web*, and then another spot. By concentrating on both spots as being the same Centre, and by overcoming the apparent contradiction involved, he can create a *ksana* and leap instantly from one Centre to the other along the *Web*. He can thus be in two places at once, a traditional magical ability known as "bilocation."

What we have from all this is, therefore, a complete psychological orientation for the act of teleportation. Note that the variables involved in the folklore, mysticism, and religion sources are the same as those noted by modern physics as necessary for such a thing as teleportation or aportation to occur—the transcending of the highly relative concepts of time, space, and motion. Note that "movement too fast to be measured" will take you, during a "moment too short to be measured," from one place to another without going through the "space" between. Does this sound anything like "moving faster than the speed of light will take matter instantaneously from one spot to another, leaving the time-space concepts entirely"?

See how simple it is? Now do it!

However, this is supposed to be a chapter on parapsychology, so let us return to that arena. I hope this last digression has provided some insight into how the interdisciplinary approach can generate fascinating (but not binding) possibilities and shed new light on old concepts. Speaking of old concepts, most books on parapsychology would end right here in their discussion of Paraphysics, claiming that they had covered all available information, just as the head of the U.S. Patent Office tried to get Congress to close it in 1830, on the grounds that everything important had already been invented.

So now we will come to a new kind of Paraphysics, with terms invented by me. After all, as everyone knows, giving something a definite name that will allow for testing is usually the first step in dragging it out of the Unknown. This new section is *Atomic Psychokinesis* (APK)—the use of PK upon matter at molecular, atomic, and subatomic levels. As we shall see later, the smaller the object, the easier it is to use PK on it. Thus there is no reason not to extend PK on down to these levels.

Most of this section on APK was suggested by studies of spontaneous cases of strange phenomena, as well as traditions of belief and folklore in many societies. For example, one kind of APK would be *Transmutation*, the alteration of the basic structure of matter by rearranging electrons, protons, neutrons, and so on. Changing water into wine, or lead into gold would then become examples of transmutation rather than of "miracle" or "alchemy."

We also can have *Psychopyresis,* the igniting and control of fires, done by speeding up atoms with PK (this is because temperature is a function of how fast an object's atoms are moving). Mysterious fires play a large role in the tradition of the supernatural, and many spontaneous cases have been reported of children who could start fires just by "wishing."

Then there is *Psycholuminescence,* the control of photons and thus of light.* This could account for tales of halos, auras, mysterious lights, and a host of similar phenomena. In fact, from the occult literature, it would seem that psycholuminescence is about the easiest form of APK to do. Does this have anything to do with the fact that the photon is one of the smallest known subatomic particles? (Or should I say "least energetic"?)

Suppose you wanted to move a large amount of air molecules around to evoke winds, rain, and so forth. Then you would have *Weather Control.* When you read about rainmaking and other weather rituals, you will often notice that they are designed to facilitate the use of APK. Note here that those of my friends who have tried weather control all agree that it is easier to do in the Midwest than here in the San Francisco area, also that meteorological conditions in the Midwest are much less stable than on the coast. Thus practical results of weather control fit well with official theories of weather.

As we have seen, almost any phenomenon in magic can be given a name that can be fitted into the field of parapsychology, regardless of whether the parapsychologists or magicians appreciate the fact. But how about something like cursing or faith-healing? Both of these would seem too broad and vague to have anything to do with parapsychology, and you

---

* Also quite logically of radiant heat, ultraviolet light, radio-waves and. . . .

certainly wouldn't expect them to be the same thing. But they are!

If we are going to allow the use of APK on atoms, photons, and air molecules, why *not* upon living cells? We can call this *Cellular Psychokinesis* (CPK). Despite great efforts by professional skeptics, the facts remain that (a) people can be killed by curses without knowing that they have been cursed, and (b) people have been cured of genuine physical diseases at places like Fatima and Lourdes, as well as by local witch doctors. Add to this the fact that at places like Canada's McGill University experiments have been done in which curses and blessings were the only possible cause of damage and accelerated growth of plants and animals. Finally, hypnosis has been used to speed up the rate of cell growth in damaged tissue, healing burned skin, for example, in two or three days —without leaving scars. In fact, it is entirely possible that if the human body is capable of speeding up the multiplication of new cells in cases of severe body damage, we may eventually find that cancer and similar diseases are only cases where this type of CPK has happened without control. Spontaneous cures (medical terminology for "we don't know what happened") in cancer are almost always associated with a change in attitude on the part of the patient, who simply *refuses* to die.

For those who regularly perform faith-healing or curing rituals, there is an interesting phenomenon you should be aware of. It is an overlap between CPK and telepathy, in which the disease is absorbed accidentally or deliberately by the healer, who exhibits the same symptoms for a short time, after which the disease vanishes from patient and healer alike. This is literally a form of CPK *Assimilation* and can be very dangerous to the practitioner.* I know, I've had it happen to me when I was careless.

* Since, if rules are broken, the healer may not be able to get rid of the disease assimilated. Pomo shamaness Essie Parrish contracted diabetes and arthritis this way.

We have one last form of paraphysics to look at, also a brand-new term for an old "supernatural" phenomenon, but this time someone else is responsible for the coinage— William Roll, of the Psychical Research Foudation near Duke University. The new term is *Recurrent Spontaneous Psychokinesis,* or RSPK. The *old* term was a very famous one, "poltergeist," or "noisy ghost."

Mr. Roll spent many years traveling around the world investigating "poltergeist" activities, and he came up with some results that are shaking up parapsychologists and physicists alike. First, he noticed that there was always one person, called the *agent,* who was the center of the activity. Since there was no sense in postulating some other entity such as a ghost or spirit, he used Occam's Razor and wound up with the term RSPK.

Second, he found out that RSPK was not, as had been previously believed, always associated with a frustrated teeny-bopper. Though adolescents were indeed the most common *agents,* there were many much older.

Third, Mr. Roll found out that the *agent* did not have to be frustrated sexually—almost any kind of frustration would do. One *agent* in Florida had never gotten along with his father. When he got a job in a new city, he transferred his dislike of authority to his foreman and started throwing things around the warehouse by RSPK.

Fourth, the *agents* themselves were almost never bothered by the flying objects; they simply accepted it all very calmly. Mr. Roll apparently had not yet connected this with the phenomena known in psychology as *belle indifference* in which the hysteric patient is unconcerned about such things as a paralyzed arm or a loss of voice. They seem to react with an air of inner satisfaction and outward calm, probably because their symptoms *do* give them a form of satisfaction by relieving anxiety, resolving conflicts, and bringing sympathy and attention.

Fifth, he found out—and found out the hard way—that

RSPK *will* attack people after all. Just after his reassuring an anxious mother of an *agent,* "Don't worry, poltergeists never attack people," a bottle flew across the room and hit him on the head! Never tempt a poltergeist.

Almost all RSPK activity involves the movement of objects through space; the rest are matters of APK in which objects explode or implode (I don't know if RSPK activity has ever included other forms of paraphysics such as CPK or Aportation; Mr. Roll didn't say). The last and most interesting discovery that he made was that these movements of physical objects (anything from knick-knacks to couches to walls) soon began to follow a predictable pattern! The distance an object was moved depended on two factors: its weight (mass?) and its distance from the *agent.* Light objects close to the *agent* were tossed the greatest distance. On the other hand, a heavy piece of furniture could not be moved unless the *agent* was very close and even then it wouldn't move much.

Mr. Roll charted these movements on a graph (see page 52) and showed it around back at the lab.

One day a visiting physicist saw it and said the equivalent of, "You dolts! Don't you recognize it?" It turned out that the graph was an almost perfect picture of a "Vortex Field" (going clockwise in the Northern Hemisphere), and when expressed mathematically was none other than a standard "Exponential Decay Function." This is a formula for describing the conversion of energy from one form to another form. So what the graph seems to be is a picture of the conversion process of "psychic" energy to kinetic energy in a standard energy conversion function. But everybody knows that "mind over matter" is impossible. Don't they?

Remember my comment about having the gall to divide *psi* into three parts, when everyone else is using only two? Well, I won't cease here. I will tell you how I stumbled on the principle of *Hypercognition.*

While strolling through my parapsychological dictionary or research reports, I kept tripping over a little beastie called

RSPK Chart:

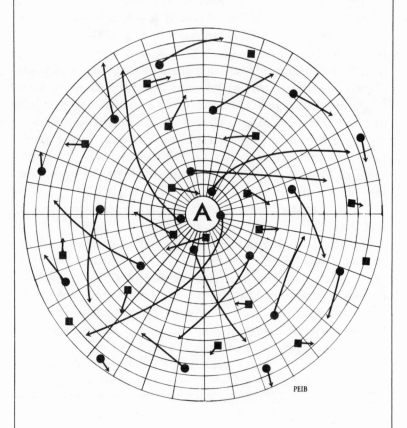

PEIB

A highly stylized depiction of the major data discovered by William Roll. The letter A in the center represents the Agent or "poltergeist," circles are light objects and squares are heavy ones. Arrows suggest the direction and distance of psychokinetically induced movements.

Precognition. Now precognition is an unruly creature, constantly getting mixed up with the various *clair senses.* You see, precognition used to be the term for looking into the future in general, just as his twin brother *Retrocognition* was the term for looking into the past in general.

What caused all the confusion was the fact that none of the *clair senses* is limited by space *or time.* With clairvoyance, for example, you can look into next week as easily as next door. Not only that, but there seemed to be two distinctly different ways of looking into the future! For example, while waking up in the morning I might get a clear vision or hear a voice telling me something about the future. Or I might suddenly have a flash of "intuition" that something was going to happen, *without a pseudo-sensory experience!* The first type of experience was usually more reliable than the second. The question was: Was the same thing happening in both cases?

Nor was I alone in noting these two different ways of prediction. Allen Spraggett in his book *The Unexplained* quoted a conversation he had with Jean Dixon, one of America's most famous prophets (the terminology is hers): "There is a distinction between my ESP, or psychic gift, and my visions. A vision comes directly from God. It's divinely inspired. You can't talk about a vision and psychic power in the same breath. Whereas something foreseen by ESP may be averted, a vision is inflexible. What I see in a vision is fated to be."

Other examples in the literature can be easily found, but it is obvious here that Jean Dixon's "visions" (usually in Roman Catholic window dressing) are basic clairvoyance. But what about her "ESP" or "intuitions"?

I decided that though it was possible that the same mechanism was involved in both types of prediction, it was equally possible that there were two distinct mechanisms or *talents* involved. Given the *clair senses* as one way of figuring out the future, how else could you do it? Obviously you could sit down, evaluate the data on hand, get some new data (normally or via ESP) about the present, and finally come up with a prediction based on the known probabilities. In other words: think!

But for this to be something special (*i.e.*, "paranormal"), you would have to do it *very* fast. Fortunately we already have a precedent of sorts in the form of the "human computers" who, though they are often very stupid in other areas, can solve incredibly difficult mathematical problems in mere seconds. Also remember that these days probability calculations are completely mathematical.

So we have hypercognition: Superfast reasoning, often using data received via ESP, usually at a subconscious level, resulting in an accurate statement and presented to the conscious mind as a "flash" of "inspiration" or as a "hunch." If you do this and arrive at a prediction about future events, this is precognition. If you arrive at a statement about the past, then it's retrocognition. In effect your mind has temporarily kicked into high gear, turning into a super analog computer and churning out results in a fraction of a second.

Retrocognition, by the way, is just one possible explanation for some of the "evidence of reincarnation." If you personify and identify with a pattern of information received by retrocognition, you would probably input the data as "memories of a past life." Another possible explanation will be considered when we discuss the *Switchboard*.

There are other advantages besides neatness in separating hypercognition from the *clair senses*. For one thing, it helps to explain why people such as Jean Dixon, Edgar Cayce, Gerard Croiset, Peter Hurkos, and others who are usually quite good at prediction can make occasionally such huge blunders. Invariably their good predictions were usually the result of "visions" and their bad ones the result of "hunches." No matter how good you are at precognition, your results are only going to be as good as the data you have to work with. If you have incorrect or incomplete data, then the result of your probability calculation will be poor.

The *clair senses* vs. hypercognition dichotomy also helps explain why the results of "hunches" can be changed (though it doesn't explain why "visions" are "inflexible"). Obviously, if at the time you are precognizing, you can't or don't check out the future actions of every entity involved, or else don't bother to specify that all possible future changes are to be included in the calculations; then it is quite likely that someone can change the course of events after your prediction is made.

Spraggett said in his book that the problems for the "skeptics" was to explain the seers' hits, and the problem for the "believers" was to explain the misses. This dichotomy of *clair senses* vs. hypercognition does that nicely, without resorting to pseudo-religious discussions of the inflexibility or plasticity of "fate." For that matter, I'm not all that convinced that the results of ESPing into the future are all that absolutely impossible to change. It may be that the *clair senses* are really types of hypercognition, in which the results are accurate to a 99.9999 percent rating (that is, higher than regular hypercognition). The whole area needs far more research, especially when you consider our recent discussion of the relativity of time.

Insufficient data!

Now for the barbarians, we will examine another area that is brand new to the parapsychologists and old hat to the occultist; that is the area of *Anti-psi*. This is the realm of those *talents* that frustrate, avoid, destroy, or generally mess up regular *psi*.

We can start with *Catapsi,* the generation of "static" that cancels out regular *psi* powers within its range. Now I'm not just talking about skeptical researchers, though it is true that the rabidly skeptical type of person is usually pretty good at generating Catapsi static. I'm sure that everyone knows one or two people in whose presence it is difficult or impossible to think or concentrate, people who through no fault of their own are just plain *annoying.* Catapsi is very much like this, operating on psychic levels instead of (or in addition to) the psychological ones. Catapsi can frequently be considered to be the psychic equivalent of "white noise," in that so much power is being broadcast in an absolutely random pattern that coherent signals simply can't get through. It can be very hard to shield against, especially if you don't have a clear idea of exactly what's going on. On the other hand, if a person has a strong ability to generate Catapsi in a controlled fashion, they can be a very useful addition to any magical working group, since when directed this talent is effective for both psychic attack and defense. Certainly if you feel that you may be *talented* in this way, you should start practicing control.

There are many well-known psychics around the world who have repeatedly shown their genuine *talents,* only to have them fail in the presence of particularly hostile examiners. The concept of Catapsi offers us a possible explanation for this, though it should not be used as an all-purpose excuse!

From my personal experience and research I have become familiar with the fact that particular people inhibit the action of *psi* powers when these powers are tried in their vicinity. On several occasions very nice people have had to be removed from the room in order that an experiment or housecall succeed, simply because they were unwittingly generating static.

Catapsi should not be confused with *Splodging,* a widespread general broadcasting of emotion so strong that it drowns out all other competing *psi,* and so strong that even normally *untalented* people can pick it up. It usually occurs in anxiety states, and the *Splodger* is rarely aware that he is doing it. It has been called the equivalent of a "psychic yell" and often makes its recipients very uncomfortable. If we consider Catapsi to be the production of pure "static," we can consider Splodging to be the broadcasting of a specific signal at such a loud volume that it drowns out all other signals in the vicinity.

There is also the area of *Apopsi* (from roots meaning "avoidance"); this is the *talent* for being completely immune to any *psi* activity directed toward one. These people are the exact opposite of the *total empaths* mentioned previously. If you try to cure them, curse them, or do telepathy with them, absolutely nothing gets through. It is as if they had an impenetrable shield around them which nothing of a psychic nature can pierce. Just as the Catapsi-er mentioned above usually has a very hostile personality, so the Apopsi-er usually has a very withdrawn, unemotional nature. In fact, they usually have the greatest difficulty in expressing even the simplest and most normal emotions toward others.

Another *talent* is that of *Negapsi*, the "reversal" or "inverting" of *psi* activity in the vicinity. If you sent a blessing to a Negapsi-er he turns it into a curse, and vice versa. If he tries to do some precognition he winds up doing retrocognition. If he attempts to score high in an ESP test, he winds up scoring *below* chance.

The last known kind of *Anti-psi* is that of *Reddopsi* (from the roots "to give back," "return"). This is the ability to instantly return any *psi* aimed at you back to the point of its origin. If someone tries to curse a Reddopsi-er the curse will simply be sent right back to the curser, often without the Reddopsi-er consciously knowing about it. It's as if he were surrounded by a mirror, sending back everything aimed at him.

All of these *Anti-psi talents* can either benefit or harm the possessor, depending on how much control he or she has over them. Obviously if I am trying to use CPK to cure someone, there are going to be problems if the patient is using one of these *talents* uncontrollably. He might generate so much static that my CPK could not get through, or have such strong shielding that I can't get through, or turn my cure into a curse and kill himself, or send the cure right back to me—which wouldn't hurt me much but certainly wouldn't help him at all!

And since these powers, like all *psi* powers, can work in combination, it is entirely possible that the patient might use both Negapsi and Reddopsi and send me back my own cure as a full-scale curse! Needless to say, a vital part of any diagnosis is to make sure that the patient is not the victim of uncontrollable *Anti-psi* powers.

Speaking of the combination of *psi* powers, we might also note the interesting results when professional skeptics (generating Catapsi) try to do experiments themselves. Often they find themselves, much to their embarrassment, very good at such things as "water-witching" or *clair sensing*. Or they may, as mentioned before, score significantly below chance, thus exhibiting Negapsi. So it would seem that it is perfectly possible to switch from one form of *Anti-psi* to another, or to regular *psi*.

The various *Anti-psi talents* can be very useful if you have them under control, for both attack and defense purposes. Anyone who has ever been psychically attacked will know what a miserable condition it can be. If you have never been attacked, count your blessings—they're probably responsible. There are indeed such things as psychic attacks, though conditions of real disease or hypochondria and paranoia are often responsible for illusions of psychic persecution. Attacks usually take the form of a general feeling of unease, nausea, pain in the pit of the belly, and a definite lack of self-confidence. You literally want to crawl into a hole and die. In nine cases out of ten, the attacker will be in your immediate vicinity, and he may not be aware that he is attacking.

How can you defend yourself? Well, the literature on occultism is full of comments about "psychic shielding." They talk about imagining a spherical or egg-shaped shield completely surrounding you and protecting you. This of course is merely referring to the deliberate use of Apopsi. If you can master the other types of *Anti-psi*, you could use them as well. Just imagine that shield as reversing all harmful energies into helpful energies as they pass through it (Negapsi). Or visualize the outside of the shield as a perfect mirror, reflecting harmful energies back to point of origin (Reddopsi). Or imagine the shield as an energy field generating psychic static (Catapsi), thus disrupting all transmissions in your vicinity. Remember though, that if you are going to bother with shielding at all, it is best to specify that it is designed to defend only against attacks, that blessings and offers of help will be able to get through. One way is to have an automatic "burglar-alarm" system of shielding—one that is inactive most of the time but instantly goes into effect at the first reception of an attack. Contrary to science fiction, a psychic attack takes time to wear you down. If you notice the very beginning of the attack, it will be easy for you to defend yourself.

Then again, there is the school that maintains, "The best defense is a good attack." On several occasions when I have been attacked (and these often happen during the course of a superficially polite conversation), I have foiled the attempt by merely repeating Lewis Carroll's "Jabberwocky" while concentrating on generating as much Catapsi static as possible. To an attacker who is unfamiliar with Catapsi, it can be very painful, especially when aimed directly at him! On one occasion though, I just took a couple of tablespoons of antacid for my stomach while concentrating on pure contempt for my attacker. It's really a beautiful fact that an attitude of ridicule or humor, the reciting of nonsense poems or even Mother Goose will do more to freak out an opponent than anything else. This is of course because most humor involves the attitude of "I thought you were dangerous but you really aren't at all." This kind of self-confidence is perennially your most potent defense.

I might note here before going on that the overwhelming majority of people who have attacked or tried to attack me— usually for my own good, of course—have been highly moralistic members of the so-called Right-Hand Path (the official "Good Guys" in magic).

However, let us now leave these latest flights into what I'm sure some of my readers consider sheer fanta-psi, and return to the standard parapsychological research laboratory.

I'm sure that just about everyone these days is familiar with the standard research designs of present-day *psi* research. To date almost all experiments have been limited (at least in the United States) to testing for telepathy, clairvoyance, and PK. The telepathy and clairvoyance experiments usually deal with someone trying to guess cards in the past, present, and future. (They never yet have come up with a satisfactory experimental design for separating telepathy from clairvoyance, let alone clairvoyance from precognition—I have one, but *that* I'm not revealing until I can use it for my PhD thesis.) The PK experiments are usually done with people who try to move small objects such as dice in midair so as to affect their fall. I refer you to the writings of J. B. Rhine, *et al.*, the *Journal of Parapsychology*, and several hundred books now on the market.

The whole idea of these experiments is to see if the people being tested (the subjects) can do something that neither the laws of probability nor sloppy experimenting can account for. Obviously, in some areas of study, such as RSPK, direct experimentation is impossible.

Howsoever, these experiments, limited as they have been, *have proved the existence of GESP and PK*, usually at a very low level of 1 percent to 2 percent for ordinary people, but much higher when the subjects are especially *talented*. Hundreds of wiser statisticians and methodologists than I have examined the evidence, and they have not found it wanting. If we spent one-thousandth of the money on *psi* research that we spend on finding bigger and better ways to kill ourselves, we could get results in ten years that would knock established theories of science for a loop. Hmmm . . . could this be the reason for some of the opposition to *psi* research? Naahh. . . .

From all of the work done so far, however, we can draw

certain conclusions. For some strange (unusual? paranormal? magical?) reason, the same variables and patterns keep showing up in experiment after experiment.

Take emotion, for example. One of the earliest findings in *psi* research was that there had to be a strong emotion or motivation for high scoring. Once J. B. Rhine bet his prize scorer Hubert Pearce $10 for every correct guess. Pearce sat down and promptly got twenty-five out of twenty-five cards correct. The odds against that, by the way, are several trillion to one.

I do hope you know what ESP, or Zener, cards look like, since they've been using them for four decades. They consist of five cards each of five different geometrical designs; this makes it easy on the statisticians since there is a simple one-in-five, or "5.00" per "run," chance of guessing right by pure luck. The way statistics work, a person who regularly scores at 5.25 per run is considered a high scorer if he does it over several hundred runs (one run equals twenty-five trials or cards).

Too much emotion, however, would blow the whole experiment as badly as too little. Finally, the researchers came to the conclusion that strong emotion, combined with calm self-confidence, was associated with success (they are far too cautious, not to say paranoid, to use the phrase "causes success").

I have long been dissatisfied with the traditional ESP card designs because they were deliberately designed to be emotion-free. Who can get excited by stars, wavy lines, and plus signs? I would like to try some experiments with cards that were deliberately "loaded" with emotions, positive and negative. Say cards with dollar signs, swastikas, sex symbols, hammer & sickles, skull & crossbones, and so on.

Other variables they discovered would affect the results of *psi* tests were the health and alertness of the subject, when he last ate, drugs in his system, attitudes toward the experimenters, colors of the cards or room, the presence or lack of

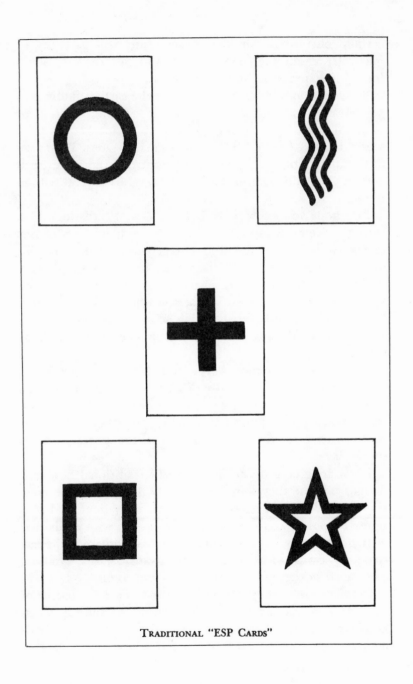

TRADITIONAL "ESP CARDS"

distractions (several sexy lab assistants had to be removed), his belief or disbelief in *psi*, and the experimenter's belief or disbelief in *psi*.

At this point I would like to report on some research done by Professor I. M. Kogan, Chairman of the Bioinformation Section of the Moscow Board of the A. S. Popov Society, USSR. For those like Dr. Rhine who refuse to accept any research results done in Russia, I can only say that the Russians, like everyone else outside North America, are about ten or twenty years ahead of us in *psi* research. Don't get mad at me, just write your Congressman and ask him why the United States is so far behind in the ESP race. Besides, Kogan's work has been supported by researchers outside the Communist world, including some classified U.S. government work.

Kogan's paper is entitled "The Information Theory Aspect of Telepathy." It was submitted by Dr. Kogan for presentation at the symposium entitled "A New Look at ESP," held June 7–8, 1969, at the University of California in Los Angeles. It is based largely upon articles published by him in *Radiotekhnika*, a Russian technical journal. It was translated and checked by Dr. F. J. Krieger and Dr. Thelma Moss, both of UCLA and both red-blooded American scholars, who presented it at the symposium.

It is a highly technical paper, half equations, but it makes many interesting points. I would prefer to let Kogan speak for himself, so I will quote him for most of the discussion:

The Information Theory Aspect of Telepathy

The fundamental consistency of phenomena related to telepathy and the existing representations of the laws of information transmission is shown. A brief description and analysis are given of the information content of some experiments conducted by the Bioinformation Section in the years 1966–1967. Formal algorithms are proposed which can be applied for use of telepathy as a channel for information transmission.

In the present section the question of the possibility of telepathy is posed in principle: Does it or does it not contradict our well-known laws of nature, including the laws of information transmission? And, in particular, do the existing observations agree with the widespread hypothesis of the electromagnetic nature of the field—the carrier of telepathic information?

At this point, Dr. Kogan takes off into a series of equations concerning the Laws of Information Transfer, the Laws of Radio Waves, and such. Then he describes samples of the experiments he is analyzing and dives into more equations, with the final result that:

> It can be seen from relations (11c) and (11d) that the transmission of telepathic information by the electromagnetic field of biocurrents is possible in principle over any distance. The smaller the information rate the larger the distance.

Then Kogan goes through four different methods of estimating the lowest possible wavelengths for telepathic information transfer, assuming that telepathy operates upon the electromagnetic spectrum. He comes up with these estimates of telepathic wavelength (λ), by (a) the power put out by the living organism—giving: $\lambda > 1$ to 100 meters; (b) the fact that telepathy goes around the curve of the Earth—giving: $\lambda \gtrsim 10$ meters; (c) observed frequencies of brain biocurrents—giving: $\lambda \gtrsim 300$ hundred kilometers; and finally (d) by the laws of information transfer—giving: $\lambda \gtrsim 10$ kilometers.

Then Kogan works out the highest possible wavelength, by known estimates of the maximum amount of power that the human organism can put out. This gives us a maximum of $\lambda = 1000$ kilometers. Thus we have the result that telepathic wavelengths are somewhat between 300 km and 1000 km from crest to crest. This puts them in the parts of the e-m spectrum known as Radio Waves (only a tiny part of which is used commercially in radio and television).

> This indicates that the facts of telepathic information transmission over small distances are attributable to the field of biocurrents with wavelengths of the order of hundreds of kilometers. . . .

In other words, we already put out lots more power than would be necessary for telepathy. He then goes on to explain why experiments done with attempting to shield e-m waves in "Faraday Cages" failed.

The conclusion about the range of superlong waves can also explain the failure of experiments with shielding, when, judging by existing publications, the arrangement of shielding did not affect the outcome of telepathic experiments, since in this range of frequencies shielding by elementary means (and only such means were used in the experiments) is completely ineffective.

Then he mentions that for long-range telepathy it would be perfectly possible for the waves to bounce between the Earth and the ionosphere, while still staying within known power bounds of the body.

Kogan came to two sets of conclusions:

It is clear that in obtaining these estimates, in our view, a series of sufficiently valid assumptions was accepted:

1. The antennas of the inductor and the percipient are the human body; this seems natural and generally encounters no objections.

2. The biocurrents that generate the electromagnetic field have a linear component.

3. For superlong waves, matching of the percipient's antenna is provided at the expense of the small velocity of propagation of currents along the nerve fibers, because of which the system behaves like a decelerating structure; it has been reliably established that this velocity amounts to several tens of meters per second.

4. The actual magnitude of the biocurrents is of the order of 1 micro-ampere and more; this has been established by biophysical experiments.

5. The propagation of superlong waves takes place in the spherical earth-ionosphere waveguide; this corresponds to modern ideas.

and:

An analysis of the experimental results permits us to formulate some quantitative and qualitative general features apparent in experiments of various types. These are:

1. In the experiments, the actual transmission rate of telepathic information was between 0.005 and 0.1 bit/sec.

2. The actually realized information-transmission rate decreased with increasing distance and, thus, in spite of what has often been presumed, the transmission of telepathic information in our experiments was a function of distance.

3. In the transmission of telepathic information, the percipient does not apprehend logical concepts such as the names of objects and in most cases they are not formulated; as a rule, the characteristics perceived are qualitative attributes associated with sensations (shape, color, hardness), indications as to types of actions (direction or search), and emotions. These are the most plausible code elements of transmitted telepathic information; apparently they also include digits.

4. The clearest perception of telepathic information occurs during comparatively short (up to 1 min) time intervals.

5. The results of the experiments carried out are not incompatible with the electromagnetic hypothesis of telepathy. This deserves further attention in connection with the recognized features of extra-long favoring their distant propagation.

Finally, let us look at Kogan's conclusion:

> The purpose of the present paper is to show the consistency of the results of telepathic experiments—both those described in the literature and those conducted in our Bioinformation Section—and our well-known ideas about nature. The possibility of obtaining definite results by intentionally conducted experiments speaks in favor of the existence of the telepathic type of phenomena. Formalized algorithms permit in perspective the use of telepathy for constructing information transmission channels.

Now, what is the significance to us of all this electrical stuff? It means that not only have we proved the possibility of telepathy as a method of communication, but we have also begun to figure out some of the ground rules.

Basically every human body is a walking radio station, broadcasting and receiving on ultra-long wavelengths of the standard electromagnetic energy spectrum. Anything that will affect the human neural system will modulate the radio waves broadcast and the efficiency of reception for those waves broadcast by others. *And 99 percent of all instructions for casting spells are ways of changing your neural system!* Also it would seem that the early Rhine hypothesis that everyone can and does use telepathy constantly has received support from Kogan's work.

The Chart of Telepathic fall-off is reproduced below, followed by an adaptation of it by a physicist friend to show probable static values:

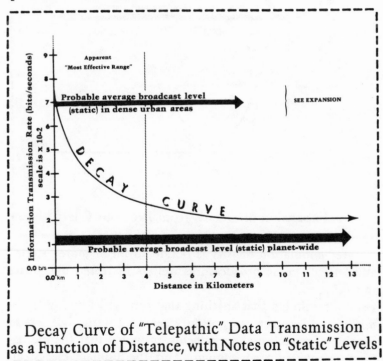

Decay Curve of "Telepathic" Data Transmission as a Function of Distance, with Notes on "Static" Levels

Adapted from I.M. Kogan by M. Brader & P.E.I. Bonewits

We also begin to understand why telepathy is more common in small isolated cultures than in large urban ones.

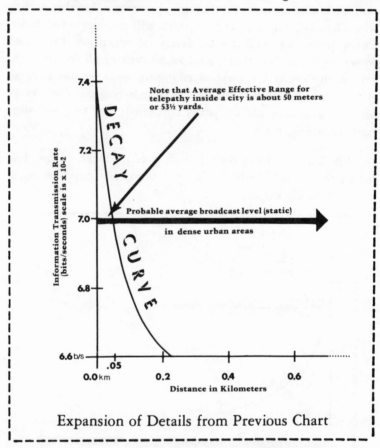

Note that Average Effective Range for telepathy inside a city is about 50 meters or 53½ yards.

DECAY CURVE

Probable average broadcast level (static) in dense urban areas

Information Transmission Rate (bits/seconds) scale is x 10-2

7.4

7.2

7.0

6.8

6.6 b/s

.05

0.0 km   0.2   0.4   0.6

Distance in Kilometers

Expansion of Details from Previous Chart

Greater population density is bound to mean more "static" and "noise" being broadcast, as well as increased difficulties in tuning in.

I am reminded that anything that can act as both a transmitter and receiver can not only generate static, but is also capable of setting up energy fields, provided that the mechanism is sophisticated enough. And the human biosystem, especially the brain and the rest of the nervous system, is just about the most sophisticated mechanism on the planet. Thus we can see that much of *Anti-psi* may have a physiological basis.

It also means that once we can get over the minor details of (a) building an artificial antenna-transmitter 10 kilometers across and (b) figuring out a translation method, *we will be able to build a machine that will be able to read minds and send out thoughts of its own!* Once we get to that point, I'm heading for a neutral country or else the UN. Such a machine could be the greatest thing to happen to man since the wheel, but knowing present political policies, the inventors of the machine would be tortured into using it as a weapon for some government. Fortunately there are defenses, only a few of which have been noted above.

So now we can get to the point of *why* I included a chapter, and a very long one at that, on parapsychology in a book about magic. Once standard magical methods are codified and translated there is no reason why they can't be used in the *psi* lab to increase scores. Also, parapsychology started out as very interdisciplinary; we occultists and magicians could learn quite a bit from *psi* researchers and vice versa.

Yesterday's science fiction is today's science is tomorrow's cliché. A hundred years from now you'll be able to float an ashtray across the room to you as easily as you now flick a switch and turn on the lights (though hopefully by that time nobody will be crazy enough to smoke cigarettes). It may surprise you to know that we *still* haven't any idea just exactly what electricity *is*, but that hasn't stopped us from using it for the past hundred years.

Finally, many of the magical and mystical phenomena that we will encounter will prove to be easily explainable in terms of *psi*. These new terms may not be as romantic as the old ones, but only the frauds and bigots have anything to fear. Following this logic, why is it that so many of the Establishment occultists (supposedly strong enough to protect themselves from Catapsi) are afraid to have their powers tested by "nonbelievers"? And why are so many Establishment scientists afraid to test those volunteers that *do* step forward?

After all, the least we can do is try and be *psi*-entific.

CHAPTER FOUR

Mantra, Mandala, and Mudra

In this chapter we are going to examine parts of a highly developed magical-mystical tradition of the East that is known as *Tantra*. Although the words "mantra," "mandala," and "mudra" correspond quite nicely to our words "incantation," "pentacle," and "gesture," an examination of their Eastern counterparts will be more useful to us than if we were to mainly check out our traditional Western terms. This is because the Sanskrit origin of the Eastern words will tell us a great deal about their specialized meanings; also, we will be able to look at various items of occultism from what to us is a new and different viewpoint. By concentrating on the Eastern systems and occasionally jumping back to the Western versions (rather than the other way around, which is the usual method in books available to the public) and by tossing in bits of data from a half dozen different arts and sciences, we will find that the supposedly huge differences between Western and Eastern occultism are not really all that great.

Now the origin of the word "Tantra" will itself tell us a great deal about this predominantly theurgic system of occultism; it comes from the Sanskrit *tan* meaning "to weave," "continue," "propagate," and "endure." The full word "Tantra" is often translated as "in the loom," in the middle of the *Web*'s woof and warp. So in the system's name alone we have more than a hint that its emphasis is going to be on association and patterning.

Tantra has quite a lurid reputation, and in order to understand why, we are going to have to make a slight detour into the history of Buddhism. To date scholars have presented two major views of Tantra. The first considers it a "corruption" of originally "pure" teachings, definitely inferior and sometimes unspeakably evil. The second sees Tantra as an inevitable result of Mahayana ("Protestant") Buddhism's constant attempts to absorb local beliefs and be all things to all people. The second view has now prevailed, at least among scholars of comparative religion, although the first is still popular among scrapbook collectors, missionaries, and theosophists.

Mahayana's cardinal principle was universal salvation. The *Bodhisattva* who refused to take his well-earned chance to enter Nirvana so that he might help others to become enlightened, was considered far superior to the *Arhat* ("saint") who went "selfishly" into Nirvana as soon as he could. We have an amazingly close similarity in some versions of spiritualism, in which "helpers" stick around the planet in order to aid the living and the dead. In Mahayana, no matter what the cost, all beings must be "saved."

The majority of the people in the geographical areas that Mahayana penetrated were, by Buddhist standards, "superstitious" and "ignorant." So Mahayana felt it necessary to meet them halfway and soon complied with their desires for ritual and magic. Mahayana moved into northwest India about 200 years B.C.E. right smack into the middle of the world's major trade routes.* Greeks, Egyptians, Romans, Persians, Siberians, Chinese, and miscellaneous Asians met and intermingled, and the ultimate result was an incredible mishmash of religious and magical beliefs. Parts of this became known as Tantric or Esoteric Buddhism ("esoteric" just means "occult").

* *See* Ch'en in Bibliography.

For our purposes here we can consider the basic system of beliefs as Tantra, and the religious-social-cultural additions to this we will call Tantrism, for reasons soon to become obvious. For there is actually more than one Tantrism, though they all have the same basis of Tantra. For example, those who did not convert to Buddhism became for the most part members of various sects labeled "Hindu Tantrism." (Hinduism is loose enough that any belief in India which is not easily fitted into a separate pigeonhole is lumped under "Hinduism.")

By the seventh century C.E. Mahayana had expanded in both northwestern and northeastern India, and it was heading into Tibet and Nepal. The local religion in Tibet was one of nature spirits and mountain demons, involving highly ritualistic methods of worship, and usually called *Bon*. Throughout Tibet all these magical beliefs and local gods were fitted into a careful system and safely "Buddha-ized," or so the missionaries of Mahayana thought. Actually Tantrism had become a religion in itself; it only dressed up as Buddhism, Hinduism, or Bon when necessary. As a rule, a man was a Tantrist first, a member of the other religions second.

Now Mahayana Buddhism did things in exactly the same way that early Roman Christianity did; they absorbed all local spirits worshiped and turned them into angels, demons, saints, and gods that could be easily fitted into the conquering religion (the major difference was that Buddhism spread by conversion and persuasion, rather than by sword and torch). Mahayana's tendency to absorb even Hindu deities into its pantheon resulted in Buddhism's being considered just another Hindu sect, and converts moved easily from one faith to another. The invasions of Islam in the eleventh century relentlessly destroyed Buddhism in India, but they did not destroy Tantrism. In northwest India, Tantrism absorbed a little bit of Islam and continued on its merry way. In the rest of India, Tantrism survived by masquerading as a sect of "Hinduism." In Tibet it had already absorbed the native Bon religion, though Buddhist terminology prevailed. (This is the majority view by now, but in Tibet there are those who claim that many of the beliefs of Tantrism and Mahayana originated there.)

So although Mahayana Buddhism continued elsewhere, notably in China and Japan, in its attempts to absorb native beliefs it wound up creating Tantrism which grew and eventually absorbed the Mahayana itself over a wide area. We will return to the history and beliefs of Buddhism later, but for now we can see how vital the advent of Mahayana was to the creation of the system later known as Tantra. It was the catalyst of *universality* that turned a pile of apparently unrelated and opposed concepts from dozens of different cultures and nations into a unified system of occultism. Thus, we have here yet another reason for studying Tantra, for it is the most intercultural and international collection of occult beliefs known to man. If you are looking for universals in occultism, Tantra is a place that must be investigated; because if something isn't found in Tantra, it's unlikely to be very much of a universal.

As some of you might have expected, Tantra holds to all the Laws of Magic. It does, however, place special emphasis upon the Laws of Association, Synthesis, Balance, and Polarity, phrased mainly in Buddhist terminology. The official goal of Tantra is theurgic, the attainment of salvation and enlightenment. But as you will soon notice, methods devised for theurgy can usually be used for thaumaturgy as well.

In Tantric Buddhism "enlightenment" soon became defined as the union of positive and negative, active and passive, masculine and feminine. (Buddhism's stance was apparently male-chauvinistic, since "masculine" was associated with "positive" and "active," and "feminine" with "negative" and "passive"—in Hindu Tantrism things were the other way around.) The aim of the syntheses of the dozens of polarities devised was supposed to be the realization of the nondual nature of reality (or was it the nondual reality of nature? Oh, well).

Another interrelationship with Buddhism soon developed in Tantra. In the *Śrī-kāla-chakra-tantra,* an early text of Tantric Buddhism now in the Cambridge University Library, the Buddha quite clearly says, "the macrocosm is in the microcosm." Those who can still remember this from the early discussion of the Law of Polarity will take one giant step forward. Truth was considered to reside within the physical body, and the body became the best medium by which the truth could be realized. The emphasis on universal salvation then fitted in neatly, since any merits a person gained automatically helped everybody in existence. The Tantric stress on the physical body as a means to enlightenment led inevitably to concentration upon ever-more-complicated rituals and ritualism.

If I were to give a free-association test to any dabbler in occultism, the instant response to saying Tantra would be a reply of "mantra." "Mantra" comes from a Sanskrit root meaning to "think" or "reason," usually out loud, since the concept of "sound" is also in the root. The use of sounds in Tantra has received more study and attention than any other aspect; partly because any sound or combination of sounds could become a mantra, whether that of a letter, syllable, name, creed, or truth.*

The Law of Names is a vital part of mantra, so we will now make the promised digression on this law.

Names have always been big things in mythology and folklore. Isis of Egypt refused to cure the god Ra of snakebite until he revealed his secret name; once she had the name, she was able to work the spell, but she had also gained total control over him. Ra and other gods are often referred to by their believers as "he whose name is unknown." Once the real name of Ra was known, evil sorcerers could command

---

* As with any other mundane word, the same mantric sound can have various meanings in different circumstances.

him to do their will. A similar prohibition against revealing or saying the secret name of a god shows up throughout the world. The Bible and Talmud are full of rules concerning the name of YHVH, sometimes called the Tetragrammaton, or "four-letter-word." This name was never to be spoken out loud, instead corruptions of "Yahveh" and later in Europe "Jehovah" were used. (Actually, since the early Hebrew manuscripts rarely used vowel markings at all, and never in the name YHVH, there is no way at all unless you speak Hebrew to tell the proper pronunciation—no matter what various "Kabbalistic-Mystery-Schools" tell you.) Almost every mythology in the world has at least one story of a god or goddess who gets into trouble because of the revelation of his or her real name, or because they swore by it and therefore could not evade their oath.

The Sumerian god Enki (who was the local water-and-fertility god just as YHVH was, and thus topdog of *his* religion) got more than slightly drunk one day with his daughter, the goddess Inanna—"the Queen of Heaven." He exclaimed "by the name of power, by the name of my power, to holy Inanna, my daughter, I shall present the divine decrees." These decrees were the one hundred basic principles of civilization and exactly what Inanna was after, so she could give them to her pet city. Though Enki tries, he is unable to go back on his oath.

I am sure that just about everyone is familiar with the story of Rumpelstiltskin. Our heroine has had impossible tasks set her, which a strange little man agrees to perform, on one condition. She must give him her first-born child—unless she can guess his name first. Fortunately our villain isn't too bright, because he is overheard by a bird while mumbling some rather bad poetry about his name. The bird tells the girl, she tells Rumpelstiltskin, and he freaks out.

The belief is common throughout the world that if you give a person a new name you give him a new soul. Sick people are often given new names, "so the demons won't recognize them." Then the medicine man may recommend a change of sex identity; boys will start to dress and act like girls, and vice versa (this again is to confuse the demons). The Hebrew-Roman mistake Saul had an epileptic fit after which he changed his name to Paul. The less said about *his* sex life the better.

In medieval Western occultism there is a great deal of emphasis on names of God as words of power. For example, the four letters YHVH are assigned all *sorts* of individual attributes, and whole philosophies are based on their combinations. The letters may be assigned sex values, values of "positive-neutral-negative," "active-passive," "finite-infinite," and YHVH knows what else. The Name of God is considered to be the highest concentration of divine power, some schools even maintaining that the entire Torah (the first five books of the Old Testament) is nothing but an elaboration of the name YHVH. Great and terrifying rituals were devised and dedicated to the soul purpose of transmitting one of the secret Names to properly prepared initiates. It was said that the carving of one of these names into the forehead of inanimate statues could give them life (see the "Golem" in Chapter Six). This was once supposedly done to a pagan bull idol who immediately said, "I am your god, you shall have no others," a somewhat confusing statement and open to interpretation, considering the circumstances. The Names of God were considered so real and tangible that you could actually "put on the Name of God" as if it were a garment.

I have found that medieval occultism was based predominantly on corruptions of one of the Hebrew Kabbalahs; "Kabbalah" just means "collection," and there were at least seven Kabbalahs, only *one* of which dealt with mysticism and magic, plus Kabbalahs of travels, folktales, medicine, and so on. Even the Torah and the Talmud were considered Kabbalahs. Thus it was from Semitic mysticism that we got most of our organized obsession with Names and Words of Power.

Every spirit, angel, and demon had a special name or two

plus a designated rank and duties. Conceivably many of these "angels" were originally members of the *Elohim,* the Ancient Hebrew term for a fusion of all the gods. They recognized *many* gods, despite what the Bible says; it's just that YHVH was in reality the national god of Israel. This fusion of gods eventually included such well-known "angels" and "archangels" as Raphael, Gabriel, and Michael. The suffix "-el" means "god," *not* "godlike" or "godly." (In the same way the Christian concept of the Trinity can be traced in many of its aspects to localized gods.)

Also many of the "demons" were in reality old gods and goddesses whose followers were conquered or absorbed by Judaism or Christianity; Baal and Astaroth are probably the best examples.

The medieval occultists figured out all sorts of ways to "discover" the names of various "angels" and "demons" hidden within the pages of the Bible. Francis Barrett in the classic *Book of the Magi* says:

> God himself, though he be only one essence, yet hath divers names, which expound not his divers essences or deities; but certain properties flowing from him; by which names he pours down upon us, and all his creatures, many benefits; . . . The Cabalists, from a certain text of Exodus, derive seventy-two names, both of the angels and of God, which they call the name of seventy-two letters and *Schemhampheres,* that is, the expository.

Barrett goes on to show how different names can be produced by taking initials from sacred phrases. For example, today the "angel Nasa" would be in charge of the National Aeronautics and Space Administration; he—obviously from the shape of rockets, the angel would be male—would be of the element of Air, and his rank would be that of a Count (down). You could also take the last letter of each word in a phrase, or other "divers" methods could be used. In fact, the very term "Schemhampheres" has become a Magic Word. Barrett was the first modern occultist to attempt to bring together all of Western occultism (around 1801), and it is interesting to note that he is almost unique in his belief that the power of these words and names is not in their sounds or forms but in the minds of those using them.

All the *Grimoires,* or "Black Books," of magic insist that you must know the true name of the demons and angels you are dealing with. Some of them, such as the "Lemegeton," or "Book of the Spirits," are largely telephone directories combined with a *Who's Who* of the spirit world. These books give the names, powers, ranks, appearances, and signatures of all major angels and demons, as well as collections of recipes for spells and charms. Except to the literary analyst and the thaumaturgical theorist, they are totally useless.

When one is drawing a pentacle it is important to have at least a half dozen sacred names, preferably in Hebrew, around the perimeters of the circles. In fact, a spell just couldn't be done without a few corruptions, mispronunciations, and misspellings of various names of various gods. Why, for that matter, did you think we called them "spells"? Fully half the words in any pseudo-Kabbalistic ritual will be names of God. Since Western occultism was monotheistic, all names were of YHVH, his friends or enemies. Even to this day most Western occultists, including many who claim to be Pagans, insist on cluttering up their rituals with the same monotonous mystic mispronunciations of mangled monotheistic mantras.

In Tantra things are a lot more flexible. You can use the names of the major gods in rituals, but you've got a lot more room. Among other things, this is because of the principle of *varna* which says that sound is eternal and every letter of the alphabet is a god! Words are collections of gods, and their meanings are not man-made, but are a function of the letters. Hebrew occultism approaches this concept, and the pagan Celts and Teutons came even closer with their concepts of "Casting Runes," but none made it quite this far. In Tantra, therefore, every word could be a "Word of Power." Even "garbage" is a sacred word, since it is a collection of the gods *g, a, r, b, a, g,* and *e.* You can see how this could lead to lots of fun and games in religion and meditation, especially when you consider how many people worship the great god just mentioned.

Closely related is the "germ" theory of sound in Tantra. Every entity has a "germ" sound, in the sense of germination, not infection—although the latter sense leads to some not un-Tantric ideas. By repeating the germ sound we can create the entity out of the void—he did not necessarily exist until we created him. Very few other groups in history have ever claimed this power to create gods; about the only ones I can think of are the Egyptian priests and the ancient Greek *Theurges.*

For example, the famous mantra "OM" is actually the diphthong "AUM." Some sects say that the *A* stands for Vishnu, the *U* for Shiva, and the *M* for Brahma. Others say that the *A* stands for Agni, or fire; the *U* is for Varuna, or water; and the *M* is for Marut, or air. In any event we have the combination of germ sounds "AUM" invoking a totality or sum of deities in the form of a trinity.

The solemn uttering of a great Truth is called *satya-vacana* and is supposed to be a very powerful act. *Dhāranīs* are one-phrase credos and very common as mantras; they are often abbreviations or summations of long *sutras* (books). Both *satya-vacanas* and *dhāranīs* show up frequently in West and East alike. The idea of "calling upon the name of the Lord" pops up all over our sacred books (*sutras*); no matter whether they are Oriental or Occidental. Saying "Jesus the Christ died for your sins" was a common method of casting out demons during the Middle Ages; today we say "your id doesn't like your ego" to get the same result. "In the Name of the Father and of the Son and of the Holy Spirit" tells you a lot about the Catholic religion; in one phrase we have a credo of the Trinity, a solemn Truth, and the invoking of the god(s?). But of course, as we all know, Catholicism has nothing whatever to do with a "superstition" like Tantrism. Ask any Catholic theologian.

One Eastern religion making rapid inroads in the West uses the mantra *Nam-myo-ho-renge-kyo* ("give voice to your devotion to the wondrous law of life: cause and effect"). The group, called Nichiren Shoshu, is basically standard Mahayana Buddhism, mixed with very strong Japanese chauvinism and militarism. The laymen's association, called the Soka Gakkai, actually controls the religion with an iron hand. Funds and donations, constantly requested, are funneled directly into the coffers of the Komeito Party which is now Japan's third largest political party. To say that the Komeito's neo-Fascist attitudes are causing worldwide concern would be putting it mildly. In fact, the entire Soka Gakkai is officially listed by the U.S. Government as "a subversive and fascist organization."

The group was founded in the late thirteenth century C.E. by a rather irritable Buddhist monk named Nichiren, who was thoroughly convinced that all other religions (especially competing Buddhist groups) were composed of traitors and devils. He thought himself a reincarnation of Gautama Buddha and died at age sixty of chronic diarrhea (Daruma's Revenge). The cult he founded became one of the few Buddhist sects in history to emulate Western methods of conversion—blood, pain, and death. Today his followers use a highly aggressive evangelistic method of making converts known as doing "Shakabuku" ("break and subdue"). I was swept into this group several years ago and kicked out three months later for heresy—asking awkward questions. The group has made over 11,000,000 converts, including 200,000 in America, by using these methods of hounding, threatening, and brainwashing in what the Japanese government has described as "a semi-gangster manner, using a military organization." Naturally most American members join honestly, never realizing what they are getting into. And the group does proclaim noble goals—an end to war, racism, and poverty, and so on. This is one of the best examples of how we should learn to separate the value of a mantra from the aims of those using it—for the mantra *is* very useful.

Another mantra becoming famous in America is the one of the Krishna Consciousness Movement. It is very easy to learn, it goes: *Hare Krishna, Hare Krishna, Krishna Krishna, Hare Hare; Hare Rama, Hare Rama, Rama Rama, Hare, Hare*. Now *"Hare"* (pronounced "hăr-āā") means "hail" and Krishna and Rama are a half dozen intertwined heroes and gods in the Hindu pantheon, so the mantra is fairly easy to figure out. The group now in America claims to go back to 1486 in India when Krishna supposedly reincarnated himself in order to present this mantra to the world. Though there are several flavors of Krishna and even more of Rama in Hinduism,* this group says that they are all the same god. Since we are of course living in the worst of all possible worlds and times (the *Kali Yuga*), we are incapable of making any but the most simplistic efforts toward attaining enlightenment, hence the use of the mantras.

We have a fairly large contingent of this movement in the Bay Area, and observation shows that, contrary to claims, its practitioners are far from instant saints. So far the movement has consisted of street people and hippies with melted minds, looking for a new crutch; so they dress up in orange bedsheets and tennis shoes, shave their heads and beg on the streets while singing the mantra to the tune of "This land is your land." During all this they sell poor-quality incense at inflated prices. All money collected is tax free and, in theory, goes to house and feed the members of the group and the poor. Actually most of it seems to have been used to make the local group leaders rich and comfortable.

Lest you think that such praying on the weak is something limited to "heathen" religions, I might also mention a group here in Berkeley called the Christian World Liberation Front.

* Such as chocolate ice krishna, vegetable Rama. . . .

It is literally a front group for the far-rightest "Campu$ Cru$ade for Chri$t," and does exactly the same things as the previous organizations mentioned. Here the mantra used is "Jesus Saves," and here too the switch is from one crutch to another, since none of the converts has enough brainpower left to understand any theology involved. Since the group has plenty of money, their emphasis is upon converting junkies and students and turning them into evangelists. They haven't had any success with the students, who resent the cooption of their revolutionary rhetoric, but the CWLF has converted many addicts and street people. Instead of shooting up smack or speed, they tear a page out of the Bible, melt it, and shoot *that* up. The junkie-evangelists horrify local ministers even more than the pseudo-Buddhist and pseudo-Hindu groups.

Yet another group using mantras in America are our local amateur revolutionaries. Their mantras include such gems as "Power to the People" and "Off the Pigs." Again they concentrate on recruiting drug-melted minds to be manipulated "for their own good" by the politicos. In all the time I was in Berkeley I met only two real Communists (both over sixty), but hundreds of self-proclaimed "Marxists," "Maoists," "Trotskyites," "Castroites," and so on. Yet very few if any had ever read *Das Kapital* or the lives and works of their heroes. Once again, we have a group that believes that the mere repetition of their slogans will change the world (as indeed they would if they knew how to use their mantras properly).

Few people realize that in America we have all been trained to have knee-jerk reactions to slogans, the American versions of mantras. Most sane people are able to make some resistance and learn to discriminate between sayings and slogans, but not those who have used alcohol or other drugs to destroy their minds. And here in Berkeley, we have a huge hard-drug culture under the iron hand of one of the strongest organized crime nests in the country. All soft and peace-inducing drugs have been ruthlessly banished, and the only things people can get now are drugs like heroin and methamphetamine (cut half the time with rat poison). The result is a large number of people living in a cramped ghetto who are so violent and paranoid that they will riot and rampage at the drop of a slogan. Such is the power of mantras over untrained or damaged minds that the entire University of California, Berkeley, has acquired a horrible reputation; all because of riots caused not so much by politics as by the Syndicate. But then, both the left-wing politicians and the right-wing politicians like things that way (and no, I am *not* implying that there are never *just* reasons for demonstrating). I just wonder if there could be any connection between this political state of affairs and the fact that organized crime in Berkeley is given a totally free hand by both local, state, and federal officials. I have yet to find a politician with the guts to open up this particular can of worms.

Fortunately the Buddhist, Hindu, "Jesus Freak," left- and right-wing groups seem to be embarking on a full-scale "Holy War," and with luck, they just might exterminate each other.

We have so far considered the uses and abuses of mantras as associational devices, but they have many other uses. The single-syllable ones, for example, are often used in breath control exercises. The popular mantras are also noted for their droning, hypnotic qualities. By the time you have repeated, *Om-mani-padme-hum* or *Nam-myo-ho-renge-kyo* or "Power to the People" or "Kill the Commies" or even "Eee-ee-kwals-emmm-seees-kwared" for the one-millionth time, you will not only begin to believe it, but you will also be well on your way to a magnificent hypnotic trance. Both the clinical hypnotists and Eastern masters would of course shudder at this thought (each for his own reasons, naturally). We will go more deeply into the uses of trances later.

Mantra, the use of sounds, leads to "mandala," the use of pictures and shapes. Both geometrical shapes and nongeometric pictures of animals and deities play a large part in mandala. A mandala is considered a type of "yantra," or diagram ("mandala" itself originally meant only "circle" * but has since expanded in meaning). Let us consider color elements first.

All schools in the occult arts have developed color scales, and Tantra was no exception. They relied mainly on the standard Indo-Aryan color scale that was also used by Western occultism. White was associated with good, life, enlightenment, and the "heavenly worlds." Blue was the color of the emotions, ESP, intuitions, and the astral planes. Green was for fertility, creativity, fields and flocks, and the "animal worlds." Yellow was associated with the mind and the "human worlds." Orange was the color of pride, materialism, and courage in battle. Red was for the body, blood, health, and the "ghostly worlds." Purple was associated with sexual and violent passions. Black was for evil, death, ignorance, and Hell.**

Much could (and will shortly) be written about the origins of this color scale, but the most important point lies in the phrase "is associated with." The colors were and are used as associational devices. Every god and goddess had a characteristic color or color combination that had to be used in their mandalas. Those with similar colors had similar aspects. If you wanted to invoke an entity, you were required to use his colors in the mandala.

Unfortunately very little is known about the effects of shape on personality. We have a thriving psychology of color, but little or no psychology of shape. Jung made some noble efforts in this direction, but his work has never been completed. Here is one area where magic can point out still more possibilities to psychology.

According to Tantra, the *Bodhi-mandala* (the circle

---

* Also in Arabic, *al Mandal* means "circle"; this gave rise to one of the most famous of medieval grimoires, the *Almadel*.

** The *Bardol Thodol* juggles these "worlds" around differently.

around the tree where the Buddha was enlightened) was what gave rise to belief in the efficacy of circle and other shapes. As in the West, the circle and the triangle were the favorite shapes for magical purposes. Just as he had his color, every deity had his or her own personal combinations of shapes and designs.

Pictures of from one to over a thousand deities, people, and animals were also an integral part of an entity's mandala. The entity's personal colors were of course required and in fact anything at all that was associated with the entity and which could be depicted in two dimensions could become a part of the mandala. As you have no doubt noticed by this time, Tantric mandalas were primarily Theurgic devices to help attain *identity* or union with a particular deity.

Perhaps the most well-known mandala (other than the national flags of the world) is the *Yin-Yang*, the symbol of the Law of Synthesis. Broken into its two pieces the shape became the popular paisley design in fabrics. I must admit, however, that there are other schools of belief about the origin of the paisley design; some say it comes from Arabian arabesques, some say from a funny-looking little mushroom that somebody accidentally ate one day.

Other well-known mandalas include: the fish and cross for Christ; the circle, swastika, and cross for the sun; the crescent and cup for the moon, and so on. Do you get the feeling that "symbols" can be mandalas? Right!

In France there are some very old mandalas painted on the walls and ceilings of certain caves by our Cro-Magnon ancestors. A painting of a bison with a spear in its heart was quite possibly expected to produce a bison with a spear in its heart. Among these paintings are some of a man wearing animal furs and horns dancing; here we are moving into the realm of *mudra.** These paintings are the earliest representations of magical beliefs and practices that we have available, and no student should overlook them.

* And possibly Shamanism. *See* Chapter Eight.

Among many nonliterate cultures mandalas are made by painting rocks or placing colored sand on the ground in various designs. Often the medicine man or his patient will sit in the middle of the mandala while the ritual is going on. Some tribes, such as the Yoruba, will use sticks to make a complex mandala in the dirt and then sprinkle food over it. They then come back the next morning and "read" the animal tracks made across the mandala in the night, as an alteration of the original patterns.

There is a great deal about mandala in Western occultism, where you will read about "magic circles," "pentacles," and so on. The magic circles and such were the designs drawn upon the floor or ground where the magician did his rituals. The pentacles were originally called "pentalphas," because you could take five letter A's and interweave them to form a five-pointed star. Since a picture of a man (head, two arms, two legs) fit so nicely inside a five-pointed star, this soon became the "good luck" symbol for man.* Pentacles ("five angles") soon became so popular that the term became synonymous for "talisman" (mandala). In the construction of a talisman, it was necessary to use all the designs, shapes, and colors, as well as names, associated with the operation or entity in question.**

After mandala and mantra the third member of the inevitable trinity is *mudra*—ritual and symbolic gestures, postures, dances, and movements in general. "Mudra" is from a Sanskrit root meaning to "seal" or "close off" a place, and many mundras are used for just that—to close and seal off, both physically and mentally, the place where a ritual is to be performed.

Mudras are associational and identification devices, and, as with mantra and mandala, every entity has characteristic mudras attached. Thus, you might shake your fist as a mudra

---

* Also the emblem for the Good Guys in Western occultism.
** If you would like to pursue this subject further, try reading *The Secret Lore of Magic* by Indries Sayed Shah. (*See* Bibliography.)

of "anger," bend back and open your arms as a mudra of "passion," go through a dance involving spear or hammer throwing as a mudra for a "storm god," and so on. Even *Kāma-kali*, or ritual sexual intercourse, is basically a mudra, though it has other aspects.

Very little has been written in the field of mudra,* as compared to what has been written about mantra and mandala. For the most part the psychology of dance and drama will give you the only ideas to be found about creating mudras. In Western occult literature, instructions in mudra are usually limited to how many times to walk around the circle, how to wave the sword in the air, how to assume postures of attack and defense, and so on. However, when the magician lifts his imaginary sword into the air to fend off an imaginary enemy, he is then using a mudra—one he had better have down pat, or he will be not-so-imaginarily dead!

Or if you can find a Catholic or High Anglican church that still uses the old mass, you can watch a beautiful series of interlocking mudras (and don't knock them—they used to be very powerful).

Before we continue to discuss Tantra, let us pause for a moment to sum up what we have found out about mantra-mandala-mudra. We have seen that Tantra like other occult systems had methods for organizing the entire environment to help the magical or mystical effort. We have seen that the "Three *M*'s" are predominantly association and identification devices.

To the believer in Tantra all things are relative. Myths offer a powerful fiction which can be used to control the fiction we call everyday life. Identification with an imaginary god gives us his imaginary powers which can of course be used in this imaginary world we live in. Thus, we can see the interweaving of the Laws of True Falsehoods, Infinite Universes, Association, and Identity. We also saw how other laws could be invoked by the use of the Three *M*'s, such as the

* Except by Gurdjieff and his followers.

Law of Names and the Law of Personification. We have also seen that these methods and beliefs of Tantra are applicable to other occult systems, that they often reflect cultural universals.

Note that in all these matters it is ritual and not intellect that is stressed. The mind, in fact, is often condemned as "getting in the way." * You will find that this anti-intellectualism is part and parcel of the theurgic approach, no matter what region of the world you are working in. Since we are more interested in thaumaturgical work, we can take this attitude with a grain of sodium-chloride.

As you could expect with a system stressing the use of the body as a vehicle to attain enlightenment, there is much in Tantra about body discipline and control. But not asceticism. For although asceticism and enduring ordeals can, to a certain extent, teach you the strengths and weaknesses of your body, they are primarily the tools of a body-hating philosophy. Tantra prefers to use exercises, carefully done to prevent damage, designed to improve both the condition and discipline of the body and the mind.

Changes in body and mind can be brought about by many different means, including ordinary physical exercise, mental exercise, drugs, hypnosis, concentration, or stimulation of the glands.

Physical exercises in Tantra can run all the way from push-ups and sit-ups to various types of Hatha Yoga to *Kāma-kali*. You must learn to be able to sit without moving for hours on end, you must learn how to control your breathing and slow down your metabolism; almost all of this is so that you will not be distracted when meditating or concentrating. Energy control is a very important part of the exercises; it is essential, for example, that during *Kāma-kali* the male be able to refrain from ejaculating under the most harrowing circumstances.

Then there are the mental exercises. These are usually

* Not only during the ritual itself, but even in its planning and evaluation.

devices to strengthen concentration and visualization. Once you have your body under control and not distracting you, you must then teach your mind not to wander off along interesting byways when you are concentrating. What exactly is "blue"? What does "square" mean? What is "stench"? What is the essence of "fish"? These and other questions are considered and answered by the aspiring Tantrist. As you can see, they are very useful for keeping him on his toes, sharpening both his sensations and his classifications.

As you sit reading this book, pause and close your eyes for a moment. Try to imagine a bright red circle in front of you. Change it into a square, a triangle, a bird, a sword, a man. When you can do this with your eyes open and see the figures even in broad daylight, * you are well on your way. Then start working on your other senses; imagine different sounds, smells, tastes, and touches. Current books now available on "sensitivity training," "games to play while stoned," and so forth may give you some help in this. Since we are a predominantly visual species, most of your efforts should be in the direction of manipulating visual images—so that when necessary, you can "conjure up" a mental shield or weapon, or so that you can get a clear and precise picture of your magical target.

In Tantra drugs have always played a minor but definite role. Hallucinogens and narcotics were often used and were of great value *to the trained user* (you just do not get the proper kind of training in our Western culture). They are, of course, association and identification devices *par excellence,* and they not only prove to the doubter the existence of other universes, but they can also give very detailed pictures of these alternate possible worlds. They also help the "dryness" and dullness that so often hits the student early in his training.

Hypnosis is very valuable and effective in causing changes in the body and mind. A few of the physiological changes that

* Without being drunk or stoned, that is.

hypnosis can cause include: catalepsy, increase in strength, paralysis, improved endurance, blistering, faster healing of injured tissue, improved sensation ability, pain killing, changes in the rates of normal metabolic processes, and the stimulation of various glands.*

The principle interest of Tantric trance, or *dhyana,* is its similarity to hypnotic trance. The practitioners of *dhyana* are quick, far too quick, to claim that there is little similarity involved. They have gotten away with this to date only because our definitions of hypnosis were so slack. Suppose, however, we define "hypnosis" as a state in which the following can occur at will: complete body and sensory control, increase in suggestibility, increase in concentration and elimination of distraction, and perhaps even increase in ESP abilities. Then we have a definition that is little different from that usually offered for *dhyana.*

Consider some more of the advantages of trance. When one is in a state of trance, various physiological changes already noted can be caused. Distracting incoming data can be eliminated and time perception stretched. This lack of distraction, brought about by body and sense control, holds the key to the major value of trance: improved concentration.

The interplay of concentration and trance is fascinating, all by itself. For trance is usually induced by concentration, and once the trance has been attained, the ability to concentrate increases a thousandfold. The entire mind can now thoughtfully and leisurely examine one piece of data or one pattern at a time. Also, for those with a "role-playing" theory of hypnosis, the mind can concentrate fully on the role of "a hypnotized person." What usually happens in Tantric role-playing, though, is that the person is now concentrating upon playing the role of a god or entity. Obviously, trance helps identification as nothing else can, and this kind of trance is often the result and aim of Tantric exercises.

Tantra and Yoga in unison developed a very complicated

* *See* Edmunds in Bibliography.

system of occult physiology. The most important part of all this, to the student of magic studying this "anatomy," is the concept of the "psychic centers," or *chakras*. The total number of *chakras* in the human body varies with different sects, but each of the major energy centers is "located" at or near a major organ or gland.

The Tantric ideal is to start energy in the *chakra* nearest the genitals and by controlling the muscles (the *sphincter urethrae* and *deep traversus perinei* for those snobs who insist on knowing) to prevent that energy from expending itself in orgasm. Instead, the energy is moved up through the body, successively stimulating each *chakra* until it arrives at the top of the head and produces exquisite bliss. One of the major ways this is done is *Kāma-kali.*

Kāma-kali is essentially a physical acting out (that is, a mudra) on several levels of the Law of Union of Opposites. A male has union with a female, energy beginning at the base of the spine rises to meet the waiting vacuity at the top of the head. (This is *not* a reflection on the mentality of Tantrists!) In Tantra this entire operation is carefully controlled to make sure that the sublimation of admittedly sexual energy is successful. As you can well imagine, *Kāma-kali* is responsible for the horror of the theosophists and others who assign Tantra to the Evil Left-Hand Path.

At this point, therefore, it is usual to print a pious cry about how far Tantra has departed from the unworldly and unsensual Buddha. Well, as we have seen, Tantra was never particularly Buddhist anyway. Other sects, Eastern and Western, have the equivalent of *chakras* and ritual sexual intercourse. I'm sure that the Buddha, with his usual tolerance, would have investigated the motives before condemning the actors. Believe me, it takes an incredible amount of courage and self-control to perform *Kama-kali*, far more than the average occultist has.

Other points of interest arise with the concepts of the various *chakras*. For example, there is the huge body of myth surrounding the pineal gland, the so-called third eye. This is supposed to give you visions when the *chakra* located there is stimulated. Ridiculous, of course. Except that scientists have recently found that the pineal gland when stimulated produces a natural hallucinogen. And the pineal gland is connected to the same area of the brain as the eyes.

Also we can note one last point about the *chakras*. Guess where the last *chakra* is, the one that gives bliss? Right smack in the middle of the brain's pleasure center.

Tantra is without a doubt one of the most highly organized systems of occultism on the planet. As we have seen in this brief examination, it is full of interesting and useful concepts for our work. The Three *M*'s, you will find, can be invaluable. Item after item of Tantra will be found to correspond to parts of our own occult tradition, with the advantage that Tantric ideas come from dozens of different cultures rather than just from Hebrew and Greek sources. Since Tantra does not really deserve its lurid reputation and is so very useful, why not use it?

Oh. You still think it's Evil Black Magic. Proceed.

Yin-Yang

PEIB

The oriental symbol of the Laws of Polarity and Synthesis

CHAPTER FIVE

Black Magic, White Magic, and Living Color

The Bad Guy wears a black hat, and the Good Guy is riding the white horse.

This is the general level of intellect employed when the subjects of "Black Magic" and "White Magic" come up. If you have read very closely between the lines, you might have gotten an idea that I don't care too much for either group. You're right.

My disgust with the entire concept stems both from study and personal experience. I have examined the "principles" and practices of both sides, without finding any moral superiority on either hand. Also I have belonged to and worked with groups calling themselves Black and those calling themselves White, and I was totally unable to find any real or important differences in their day-to-day activities.

The whole idea of White as Good and Black as Evil is purely the result of cultural bigotries. For example, if you were to walk into a room that was airtight and without a single source of light, you would find yourself blind and helpless. But what would happen if that same room were to have its walls and ceilings covered with thousands of 100 watt light bulbs, and you were to walk in? You would find yourself blind and helpless.

In this chapter we will examine the concept of "color" from the physical and cultural viewpoints. We will consider how associations are built up around colors and color combinations. We will then see how these associations became twisted and entwined in our Western culture. An examination of the myths of the "Right-Hand Path" and the "Left-Hand Path" will be made, followed by a slight detour into medieval and modern witchcraft and wizardry. Then we can sum up the "differences" between Black and White magic. We will also note a few points about psychological attitudes toward light and darkness and how they have contributed to the confusion. Finally, another system of color classification for magic, highly similar to that traditionally used in beliefs about "auras," will be explored. In short, something to offend everybody!

To begin, then, there are three different things involved in the determination and classification of a color: *hue, value,* and *chroma. Hue* refers to position in the spectrum of visible light, running from 7000 angstroms for red to 4000 angstroms for indigo-purple. (An angstrom unit is one hundred millionth of a centimeter and is used to measure wavelengths on the electromagnetic energy spectrum.) *Value* is a matter of how much light is reflected, how bright something is. If all light is reflected then the *value* is "white," if no light is reflected then the *value* is "black." The scale of color *value* runs from white through millions of grays to black; none of these are really colors at all in the sense that orange or green are; in fact, these *value* names are called the *achromatics.* We might also note here that a perfect 100 percent white or black has never been produced and, due to the structure of the eyes, probably couldn't be seen or comprehended anyway. Thus we have, in the words of a recent popular song, "only shades of gray." *Chroma* is a measure of the "purity," "saturation," or intensity of a color; its scale runs from 000 for the *achromatics* to 100 for the spectrum colors. Thus though white has more *value* than black, neither has any purity at all. Think about it.

Now using this system, a sunny sky might be scored like

this: *hue* is blue, *value* is light gray, *chroma* is 40. Not very romantic, is it? But this is the way modern physics handles the subject.

Throughout the years, scientists and artists have developed all sorts of systems for "scoring," or classifying colors. But remember the Law of Infinite Universes; not everyone is going to see colors in the same way. The method of having the three yardsticks of *hue, value,* and *chroma* is strictly a Western convention. Non-Western cultures may use totally different ways to determine their color concepts.

A non-Western system of color classification that will provide the most drastic example is that of the Hanunoo tribe of the Philippines. They also have three yardsticks, and one of them is the same as our *value:* lightness vs. darkness. The second is of *dryness-redness* vs. *wetness-greenness,* and what we call our colors can often cross from one side to the other; for example, a fresh vegetable might be considered *wet-green* only to become *dry-red* later on, without any change in what we would call "its color." The third dichotomy is of *strong-indelible* vs. *weak-fadable.* Without using our "natural" system at all, they manage to get thousands of color names out of this system. The Hanunoo's attitude to colors and color combinations is determined by elements of *their* culture, not by any value "inherent" in the colors themselves.

So then, "color" is an interpretation of the ways in which photons hit your retinas; *not* a matter of Good or Evil, positive or negative, and so on. So what happens to cause these other matters to be confused with colors?

All these photons hit your eyes in various patterns with assorted kinks and bendings, and an electrochemical message is sent to your brain. The pattern the message presents is compared with previous patterns, so that it can be identified. Your reaction will be based on the associated patterns that match the new data. Throughout your life you have built up associations with various color patterns, some the result of personal experiences and others given you by your culture.

Remember that nothing has any meaning at all except in relation to something else.

Suppose that when you were ten years old you gorged yourself on green apples and were thoroughly sick. Ever afterward the color apple-green might be very unpleasant to you and you might associate it with Evil, even though other people like the color. If in your society only members of royalty could wear purple, then your reaction to a man wearing a purple suit would be quite different from your reaction to the same man wearing red or green. The first case shows a personal, and the second a cultural association with colors.

Note, however, that in both situations the associations are purely arbitrary. The color apple-green does not cause sickness; many apples are quite safe to eat when green. Purple became the color of royalty only because the dye to make cloth purple was rare and the process tedious, therefore only kings could afford it (but see the notes on purple later in this chapter). Given different situations, cultures, or individuals, the reactions to the colors would change. Before you continue reading, it might be a good idea to think about your personal attitudes to various colors—the information will come in handy later.

Color combinations provoke cultural responses even more than single colors do. The combination of white-and-red produces a strongly negative reaction in Western culture, evoking images of the Red Cross, blood on skin, and gore-soaked bandages. Even in ESP tests there is a strong aversion to this combination; subjects will avoid guessing Zener cards printed in red on white backgrounds (funny thing, but white printing on red backgrounds doesn't provoke as negative a response). The color combination of red-and-white-and-blue, on the other hand, gives us equally strong positive reactions; notice how many countries use it in their national flags.

An interesting point is the modern science of color psychology's support for traditional beliefs about colors in our culture, as well as its recent findings about color and color-combination attitudes and reactions. Blue, for example, has always been associated with the emotions, psychic phenomena, and religion. Then we find out that successful executives and hunch players prefer blue and green, that schizophrenic patients are quietest in blue or blue-gray rooms, and that subjects score higher in ESP tests where blue is particularly in evidence. Note that the color combination most associated with the Virgin Mary, to many the supreme embodiment of benevolent motherhood, is always blue-and-white. The United Nations' flag is blue-and-white, as are many peace flags. I'll predict that Zener cards printed in blue on white will bring higher scores.

Subcultures, however, can have exactly the opposite attitudes from their mother culture. To many young men of draft age, the red-and-white flag of Canada is a joyful emblem of hope; while to others who consider nationalism barbaric and repugnant, the combination of red-and-white-and-blue is associated with oppression and stupidity.

In the West, the victory of the Christian religion over those of the pagans could be considered a victory of the *achromatics* over the colors with *hue* and *chroma*. Thus, the rich cultures of yellows, oranges, reds, blues, browns, greens, and purples were trampled into the dust by a simplistic culture of "black or white" values.* This victory of the *achromatics* quite literally ushered in the "Dark Ages." Dullness was virtuous and bright colors were sinful.** Out of this came the myth of the existence of Black Magic and White Magic, as well as farcical and vicious tales about "witchcraft."

A lot of the old books on Western occultism emphasize the Right-Hand Path and the Left-Hand Path as the only two ways to occult knowledge. Since 80 percent of the species is

* The interplay throughout European history of *hue, value,* and *chroma* can be studied by a careful examination of the paintings and murals of various eras. It is only recently that our Western culture has dragged itself out of the dreary black-white bag and gone back to the fresh, human, pagan colors of Life.

** Only in the "worldly" courts did clothing and tapestries become colorful; where the Church was strong, colors were weak.

right-handed and since the majority always thinks itself morally superior, the Good Guys were those on the Right-Hand Path and the Bad Guys were consigned to the left. A similar consignment was made in language; our word "dextrous," meaning skillful, comes from the Latin *dexter* meaning "right-handed," and our word "sinister" or "evil" is actually the Latin word for "left-handed." Note that those who are "correct" are "right"; those who are otherwise or isolated are "left." Once again the bigotry of the majority prevails.

The old books often show a picture right out of the *Baltimore Catechism* (one of the most simplistic collections of pseudo-theology ever shoved down the throats of innocent children in the history of education). I have even seen the picture in modern books published by supposed "Mystery Schools of the Right-Hand Path."

There is a tall mountain in the distance, with a beautiful and glorious city shining on the summit. Leading in its direction are two Paths. The one on the right is steep, narrow, rocky, full of thorns and pitfalls, uncomfortable and dangerous; it is shown leading gradually to the mountaintop. The Path on the left, on the other hand, is shallow, smooth, clear, easy and safe; it is shown leading to the bottom of the mountain and then going around behind it where some not-too-subtle hellfire flames upward. There is a young person at the fork in the road. The implication is obvious and heavy-handed; he can go the long hard route and get to his goal or he can take the easy way out and suffer for it later. Bah, humbug!

Let's use our heads, people! Imagine that you are the student at the crossroads. If you knew anything at all about mysticism, you would know that there was a "Middle Path" hidden somewhere right in front of your face. If you knew anything at all about magic you certainly wouldn't *walk;* you would teleport or levitate to the mountaintop. If you knew anything at all about science, you would take a helicopter. And even if you knew absolutely nothing about any of these areas, but just had some guts and a sense of adventure, you would refuse to use a Path at all and would carve out your own Way!

This is a picture and a doctrine to scare children and crush innovation. The Puritan Ethic demands that you work very hard and do things in the most difficult manner possible, especially if an easier way is available. They forget that every kind of progress in every human endeavor has been the result of someone *working hard to figure out an easy way to do something.* Then, too, skilled occultists, mystics, and magicians tend to be very egotistic and elitist (it's almost a requirement for success in these fields, but some people overdo it). They hate to think that anyone might make it to where they are by an easier route. So with the typical conservatism of the elitist and the religious zeal of the moralist, they deliberately make it as difficult as possible for newcomers to topple them from their thrones. Progress in occultism is rough enough without these people pouring sand into the gears.

Now magicians and witches who are doing Black Magic are using magic for whatever purposes their society has decided are "evil." These can run anywhere from murder, adultery, and theft, to treason, sedition, or spreading heresy against the established gods or politicians. In the West, people doing Black Magic are supposedly working, implicitly or explicitly, for the Devil.

The history of the myth of the Devil is worth a book in itself.* In the Old Testament there is a personified abstraction in the Hebrew cosmology called Satan. The name means "the accuser" or "the tester," and his function was to act somewhat like a prosecuting attorney for YHVH's "court" of judgment. If you read the *Book of Job,* I believe you will understand how he operated: His characteristic question was, "How do you know he's moral if you haven't tested him?" To the Hebrews, he wasn't so much a personality as an idea,

---

* *See* Tractenberg and Schonfield in Bibliography.

that of temptation and self-discipline. Even in the New Testament, he appears only to test Jesus to see how strong Jesus' resolve is after fasting in the desert. Unfortunately, Satan, the accuser, got mixed up with Sathanas from the Latin word meaning "slanderer." While I'm sure that many people may feel that way about the D.A., they have no right impugning his character.

The Jews were often referred to in the New Testament and the writings of the Christian theologians as the "children of Satan" or the "people of Satan." In fact, even their meetings were called synagogues of Satan. And in a sense I believe they were; it's just that non-Jews did not understand who or what "Satan" was. Hebrew attitudes to the Torah and the Talmud were far different from Christian attitudes to the Bible. The writings were never generally accepted as Absolute Truths With Only One Meaning. On the contrary, Hebrews were never supposed to study their scriptures alone, *for Jewish study consisted mostly of discussion and debate ("Pilpull"). Every line and every law was considered something to be tested and tried in the crucible of argument, which in a philosophical and symbolic sense could be called the Principle of Satan.* No wonder the violently anti-intellectual Christians considered the Jews to be the children of an "unspeakably Evil" anthropomorphic personification of the Satan Principle (even though *this* personification was made by the Christians, not the Jews), for if the Truth was debatable then the Church could conceivably be wrong!

The concept of a supreme deity of Evil was common throughout the Mediterranean during the Hellenistic Age; it had been imported from the Persian Zoroastrians.* The Good God was nonmaterial and the Bad God was the physical world; to a certain extent it was even believed that the Bad God made the world during a time when the Good God

---

* Zoroastrianism was the first of the monotheistic /dualistic faiths (which later included Judaism, Christianity, Islam, Marxism, etc.) and seems to be responsible for their adoption of genocide as a conversion technique.

wasn't looking. It was an intensely puritanical, antiphysical religion. Thus, the local gods of fertility and sensuous pleasures became minions of Evil.

Now the word "devil" is related to *"devi"* or "godling," and at one time was used for the followers of the "Good God." Our word "demon" comes from the Greek *daemon* meaning "spirit"; the *daemons* could be good, bad, or neutral. With its usual contempt for reality, Christianity put together a conglomeration of local nature spirits (evil by definition since the physical world was evil), fertility gods and goddesses, godlings of the woods, the wine, song and joy, and called the whole conglomeration demons and devils led by the most evil of all: Satan, or the Devil.

Anyone who has studied Greek and Roman Mythology will recognize this figure: half man, half goat, with hairy legs, horns, cloven hooves, and huge genitals. He was Pan, he was Silvanus, he was king of the satyrs, pans, and fauns. He was half the nature and fertility spirits of Europe. He was the Serpent (a common symbol for wisdom, knowledge, immortality and power, used by the other gnostic sects with which early Christianity had to compete). Above all, and most unforgivably, the Horned God was far more erotically attractive than Christ was. He had to be destroyed, as quickly as possible.

The Devil became the emblem of all those gods and religions competing with Christianity. Obviously since he hated Christ, he hated mankind and would do his best to hurt all and sundry. Since he was a supernatural being, he could of course grant supernatural powers to his followers. This meant, of course, that he could help people to do Evil Black Magic.

In actuality, this charge of Black Magic or "Devil Worship" was leveled against anyone not worshiping the Christian God in the Christian Way (which differed according to local politics), especially Jews, heretics, pagans, and anyone else who was unpopular, eccentric, held property wanted by the Church, or wouldn't sleep with the Inquisitors.

Before we can go much further we are going to have to make another side excursion to discuss the differences between magicians, wizards and the various sorts of witches. The topic is extremely confusing, so I have had to develop a classification system for types of witchcraft in order to at least make the dimensions of the problem clear. These classifications are tentative, but will have to do until more data becomes available.*

The meaning of the word "witch" has changed several times throughout European history and there are numerous partisans around today to claim that each and every one of these varying meanings was and is the One True Right and Only Definition. My current conclusion is that the word "witch" is utterly useless for communication without qualifying adjectives to indicate which of the different kinds of witches it is that one is talking about. In the following pages we will meet: Classic, Shamanic, Gothic, Familial or "Fam-Trad," Immigrant or "Imm-Trad," Neopagan, Feminist, Neoclassic, Neogothic, Neoshamanic, Ethnic, and Anthropologic Witches.

We can begin, as usual, with some etymology. I seem to have been the first modern occultist to point out that the Old English words *wicce* (feminine) and *wicca* (masculine) and *wiccan* (plural), from which the Modern English word *witch* derives (via the Middle English *wycche* and *witche*) are based on the Old English root *wic-*.

This in turn seems to be based (Russell tells us) on the Indo-European root *weik*, some of the meanings of which involve (a)magic and sorcery in general and (b)bending, twisting and turning. Which of these meanings is the true origin of *wicce(a)* remains to be settled, but it is fairly obvious that those practicing *wiccian* (or *wigle*) were considered to be magicians and/or benders

---

* Those of you who have read the first edition of *Real Magic* will notice that this section has been drastically rewritten. Fortunately I have been able to meet a larger spectrum of witches and witchcraft scholars over the last few years and they have helped me to correct the errors in my previously printed discussions of this topic. Thanks are particularly due to Margot Adler, Deborah Bender, Gavin Frost, Aidan Kelly, Sybil Leek, Jeffrey Burton Russell, Tim & Morning Glory Zell, and numerous others whose names must be kept private. They gave me a great deal of information and advice, but should not be blamed for my conclusions.

of reality (or ones who could "turn aside" as in the Old Norse *vikja*). Equally obvious to any etymologist is that *weik* is not related to any of the various words (such as the Old English *witan*, "to know") involving knowledge or wisdom. The words *wicca(e)*, *wycche* and *witch* never meant "wise one" as many modern witches claim. The real Old English word for "wise one" was *wys-ard*, which we now spell "wizard." Not until the late Middle Ages was this word used to refer to male witches.

When *wicca(e)* was translated into other languages at the time, the words chosen in those other tongues were usually ones with these meanings: sorcerer, magician, singer, healer, midwife, charmer, drugger and diviner. Frequently the translation words had a feminine gender, but this seems to have depended upon the cultures involved. Almost none of the foreign terms (except in Ireland) had any specifically religious meaning—a very important point to consider for those who wish to claim that the earliest witches were the clergy of one or more prechristian religions.

We know almost nothing about the social and cultural patterns of the tribes in prechristian Europe. Guesses can be made based upon archeological data and anthropological research but it must be remembered that these *are* only guesses.

By the beginning of the feudal period, most European cultures seem to have had similar ideas about the people I will call "Classic Witches." The functions of the male and female practitioners of Classic Witchcraft seem to have included midwifery, healing with magic and herbs, providing love potions and poisons, weather prediction, blessing and cursing, etc.

But what did these people do when there were still Pagan priests and priestesses around during the tribal days? Did they exist side-by-side with the clergy (the famous Druids in the Celtic and Germanic territories), handling some matters while the clergy handled others? Was there any clear-cut distinction between witches as healers and clergy as general purpose magicians? Did the witches merge with the Pagan clergy after the Christian conquests, or replace them entirely? Did the witches only begin to exist after the clergy had been overthrown, because the witches *were* the remnants of that clergy and their descendants (which is quite possible in Ireland)? Nobody really knows, though lots of people have theories.

And where do the "wizards" fit in? The term of "wise one" could have been a mere compliment, applied to anyone showing extraordinary wisdom. Contrary to the fond beliefs of many occultists and theologians, such a category is not now and never has been limited strictly to people involved in magic and religion. The major folkloric figure of the wizard is as late a development as is our knowledge of witchcraft in the early Middle Ages, yet it too may point to an earlier truth. The Wizard is usually described as a loner, a stranger who wanders about performing wondrous deeds with little equipment save a staff or a sword. Could it be that the term "wizard" became attached to various Pagan clergy who had gone into hiding, and who traveled from village to village, providing some of the old priestly services to people now no longer able to get them? We shall probably never know.

What we do know is that for several centuries people practicing Classic Witchcraft were pretty much ignored by the Church and civil authorities, except when specific crimes-with-victims were suspected. In fact, it was official Church dogma during the early Middle Ages that all magic produced by non-christians was illusionary, and that belief in the ability of anyone to fly through the air, cast spells, etc., was a Pagan "and therefore heretical" belief.

Ah, but maybe there *were* some people flying through the air (or at least thinking they were) including some who were later to be executed as "witches." Michael Harner (see Bibliography) has pointed out that the "flying ointments" referred to in many medieval documents as being used by witches seem to have contained as parts of their standard recipes several powerful hallucinogenic herbs, including belladonna, henbane, various members of the *Datura* genus and others of the *Solanaceae* order. These drugs can give an illusion of flying as well as images of wild orgies and dancing.

An interesting note is that many of the women interrogated

claimed to have been accompanied on their nocturnal flights by a Moon Goddess named (by them or the Church is unclear) Diana. Morning Glory Zell has pointed out to me that, just as users of peyote from many different cultures will often see the "same" green vegetation deity ("San Mescalito"), users of belladonna around the world frequently report seeing the same "White Lady," whom they associate with various Moon and Sea Goddesses. Zell believes that it is entirely possible that independent but highly similar cults (usually run by women) of belladonna users could have sprung up all over Europe before the conquests, and could have survived, perhaps in fragmented form, into the medieval hysteria period. Since this seems plausible to me, I am including this idea in the classification system under the name "Shamanic Witchcraft "(see Chapter 8).

But what most people think of when the word "witch" is used is neither Classic nor Shamanic Witchcraft, but something else entirely: "devil worship." While it is true, as Russell has pointed out (see Bibliography), that a number of dualistic heretics such as the Cathars *did* actually worship the Christian Satan, these people were wiped out by the Church *before* the main period of witchcraft persecution (1450-1750). A number of the accusations made against the Jews and Gypsies (poisoning wells, sacrificing babies and eating them, cursing enemies, blasphemy against the Church, etc.) were dusted off and used against these gnostic dualists and later against "witches."

By the middle of the 14th century, Europe began to run out of heretics. The solution was to turn local Classic (and Shamanic?) Witches into heretics by inventing a new form of witchcraft, one I am going to call "Gothic Witchcraft." Manuals on what questions to ask accused witches were written and distributed throughout Europe, so that similar "evidence" would be accumulated everywhere (which makes things tricky for modern scholars trying to base theories on those confessions). Gothic Witchcraft was said to be basically a reversed version of Roman Catholicism, in which worshippers of Satan were granted magical powers to harm those around them.

I still tend to believe that Robbins' book (see Bibliography) is one of the best summations of this period, at least as far as facts are concerned. Somewhere between 250,000 and several million women, children and men were executed for the thought-crime of Satanism. Although it's possible that some of the victims were midwives or belladonna eaters, most of them seem to have been crazy old women, pretty young women, or just plain "uppity" women.

A number of theories have been offered to explain the persecution of the Gothic Witches: The Church needed an "enemy" to distract the attention of the masses; the Inquisitors and witchfinders wanted more power, sadistic sex and money; the Pagan customs were being kept alive by some of the peasants as a cover for grassroots revolutionary movements; the women of Europe were starting to demand a return to their prechristian rights (and rites?) and this budding feminism had to be crushed; there was a continent-wide underground of secret worshippers of "Diana" who were organized into a unified "Old Religion;" there really were devil worshippers (descendants of the gnostic dualists) scattered throughout Europe and conspiring against Christendom. Take your pick, each of the theories has points in its favor and sound arguments against it as well.

Throughout European history, the ceremonial magicians seem to have had things comparatively easy, as far as persecution was concerned. They did their best to keep their religion separate from their science, though they were of course safer if they claimed to be Christian. Magicians were always scarce and usually of the nobility, as it took both brains and money to become one. Medieval magicians were expected to learn Hebrew, Latin, mathematics, philosophy and astrology. They had to have enough wealth to afford special equipment and to live without earning a traditional living. Thus, they usually had the cash and the cunning to remain free and healthy. Occasionally though, one would become careless and have to run for his (they were almost all male) life.

But other users of magic could use money as well. It now

appears that many aristocratic families in Europe may have kept alive old Pagan customs of magic and religion as part of their "private family business." As the centuries rolled by, members of these families studied the Kabbalah, Rosicrucianism, Freemasonry, Theosophy and other movements in the European occult scene. Many of these families heard their activities referred to as "witchcraft" and began to call it that themselves. These "Familial Witches" were able to use their wealth and power to protect their privacy and survival for many centuries. They may or may not have included members of the other flavors of witchcraft in their ranks, depending on the family and country involved. Today there are said to be scores of Familial Witchcraft groups alive in Europe and the British Isles, though only recently have they started to communicate much with each other.

Later, some of these "Fam-Trads" (from "Family Traditions") immigrated to the Americas, as did entire villages of peasants (some of whom were keeping alive fragments of their Paleopagan customs). In the New World these people often practiced activities which they and others called "witchcraft." Thus was born what I call "Immigrant Witchcraft."

Meanwhile, back in Europe, the "Age of Enlightenment" was happening and the general public was becoming less and less interested in witches of *any* sort. In the late 1800's various scholars began to publish speculations about a "Matriarchal Golden Age" that supposedly had predated the Christian conquests. In the early 1900's, anthropologists and folklorists such as Margaret Murray (see Bibliography) published theories about a universal "Old Religion of Goddess Worship" which had supposedly hidden underground to this very day, and which they felt had been the real reason for the medieval persecutions. Robert Graves published *The White Goddess* and all of academia became aquiver about the new theories.

Sometime around the late 1930's or early 1940's, a Britisher named Gerald Gardner, according to his later claims (and those of others), came into contact with a British Fam-Trad group in England. Feeling that their tradition was fragmentary, he began to use his anthropological training to "restore" what he thought was the original faith. The result was a brand-new religion, calling itself "Wicca," using a relatively new system of group magic (although the "Key of Solomon" cribs are obvious in the earlier versions), and worshipping a Moon-Sea-Earth Goddess and a Horned God of the Hunt-Vegetation-Sun. Because this new religion bears far more resemblance to the various "Neopagan" faiths invented in the 1960's than it does to anything ancient, I refer to it as "Neopagan Witchcraft."

Aidan Kelly (see Bibliography) has done a brilliant job of analyzing Gardner's papers and proving that 99% of "Wicca" was the creation of Gardner and several friends. Many current Neopagan Witchcraft "traditions" are based on Gardnerian materials, but just as in Zen Buddhism or Christian Science, tales by or about the founders are irrelevant to the magical and spiritual power of this religion. New Neopagan Witchcraft sects have been created, with no claims offered.

In the early 1970's yet another kind of witchcraft was invented. Many women involved in the feminist movement belonged to "women's spirituality groups" and were looking for new or old religions centered around female energies. Eventually some of the women ran into some of the Neopagan Witches. In fact, Morning Glory Zell turns out to have been the first priestess to have presented Neopagan Witchcraft at a feminist convention, to a tiny but extremely influential audience. Since many of the Neopagan Witches considered themselves to be feminists already, a merging of the two movements was inevitable. Soon independent feminist magicians began to join them and the result was "Feminist Witchcraft"; a new religion in which the Horned God was booted out entirely (thus turning a duotheistic system into a heno- or monotheistic one), the local groups consisted of all-women covens (instead of the Neopagan mixed ones), and entirely new and eclectic magical techniques were invented and experimented with.

While the Neopagan Witches have tended in the last few years to drop various dogmas about their supposed antiquity, these same dogmas about "an unbroken tradition going back to the Matriarchal Golden Age" have been continued (and even in some cases inflated futher) by most of the Feminist Witches. Charismatic leaders invented enormous amounts of "politically correct" theories about anthropology, archeology, folklore, history and biology, along with the now traditional stories about being initiated by their grandmothers. But despite some confusion in the scholarship department, Feminist Witchcraft has become one of the most rapidly growing, creative and spiritually exhilarating religions on the modern scene.

But there are plenty of other kinds of people now who still call themselves (or are called) "witches." A lot of individuals are studying herbology, midwifery, divination and simple magic, with varying degrees of seriousness, and they can be termed "Neoclassic." Naturally, we have a few modern Satanists trying hard to be everything that conservative Christians say they should be, and these we can term "Neogothic." A tiny handful (mostly from the Neopagan ranks) are trying to rediscover the old ritual uses of hallucinogens, and these I'm going to call "Neoshamanic Witches."

Mind you, this entire discussion of witchcraft in the 20th century has been limited to those individuals and movements which speak English or American English as their mother tongue. There are thousands of people using various systems of magic and religion in their own ethnic neighborhoods, who are called "witches" by most English speakers. In their own languages (Spanish, Portuguese, Chinese, Japanese, Hawaiian, etc.) they are called various names which translate out as "priest or priestess," "healer," "magician," "sorcerer or sorceress," and so forth. These often bear a minor or major similarity to those we have already discussed, but in order to keep them clearly distinguished from those of European ancestry, I prefer to call them "Ethnic Witches" if they absolutely have to be called witches at all.

We can close out this listing of various sorts of witches by mentioning the "Anthropologic Witches," who are those persons whom anthropologists like to call "witches." Usually these are independent magicians in tribal cultures who are outside of their societies' accepted behavioral norms, and/or they are suspected of being monsters who can curse others with the "evil eye." They are usually considered by their tribes to be menaces. This helps keep witchdoctors in business hunting them down.

At this point we should probably return to the Middle Ages and our discussion of "White" and "Black Magic."

Most medieval magicians claimed (publicly at least) to be White Magicians. Perhaps a few exceptionally rich and powerful noblemen may have called themselves Black Magicians, but that term was usually applied by enemies. Many of them simply did not believe in the reality of Satan (despite the fact that they summoned up entities they called "demons") and they were in any event too intelligent to worship him.

But whether they were thaumaturgically or theurgically inclined, most medieval magicians threw a lot of Hebrew and Christian prayers into their ceremonies. There were a variety of good reasons for this practice.

To begin with, magicians as philosophers were by definition going into territory staked out (!) by the Church as its own. Magicians as scientists examining the mind and body of humanity, and their relations to the environment, were certainly trespassing on sacred ground. Even if you were an atheist, it was safest to pray long and loudly during a ritual or experiment, just in case someone was listening. Then too, it is always a good idea for a magician to stay on good terms with whatever deity-circuits (see Chapter 6) are strongest in his or her geographic area, especially one as dangerous as the Christ Circuit.

Furthermore, as we shall see later, prayers (especially when prolonged and montonous) can be very useful for building up a properly dramatic and hypnotic atmosphere. Finally, magicians consider sacred names and phrases much as mathematicians consider x's and y's—as variables to be manipulated as needed.

One obsession of the occult community has been the organization of hundreds of groups calling themselves Great White Brotherhoods, Black Lodges and miscellaneous Secret Mystery

Schools of mysticism, both Right-Handed and Left-Handed. The White groups are mostly Secret Societies of amateur magicians and occultists who get together to compare recipes and exchange gossip. They borrow their terminology from badly garbled Egyptian, Greek and Hindu sources. These White Lodges are often theosophical clubs of self-appointed "adepts," who believe it their duty to save the world, usually through the process of fighting magical wars with groups they consider Evil (usually each other).

Those of the Right-Hand Path have many quaint and curious beliefs. They seriously think that a spell won't work unless it consists of nine parts prayer to one part just plain Goodness. Anyone of a different religious or ethical opinion is automatically doing Black Magic. Pleasure and the physical world are evil; pain and the spiritual world are good. All progress must be expensive, psychologically and monetarily; the emphasis is upon sacrifice, deprivation, Gestapo-like discipline and (above all) the avoidance of thought and reason on selected topics as "inferior" and "limiting" (somehow they never get around to simply saying that there are times when reason is appropriate and times when it just gets in the way—something every magician would agree with).

According to the Right-Handers, if you want to become a powerful magician, you must spend all of your time trying to be Good. If you cast a curse, it will always miss your intended victim (some say only if she or he is "innocent") and instead come back three times as strong, "home to roost." This would seem to make it impossible for the Left-Handers to ever cast curses at all (supposedly their main activity) but then, I guess they must have "the Devil" protecting them. I have, however, seen "White Magicians" and "White Witches" casting curses with no backfires at all. They invariably "explain" this by claiming that the curses were "justifiable self-defense."

As for followers of the Left-Hand Path, we have them around as well. Self-styled leaders of "Black Covens" (of Neogothic Witches) and "Satanic Churches" are thicker than uniforms in the Pentagon (the mentalities involved are also quite similar). Although they are outnumbered by the Good Guys ten-to-one, they are also quite religious in their outlook. But usually they are willing to admit that they are more interested in personal power than they are in personal enlightenment. The more gullible of their followers quite seriously believe in and worship the Devil in ceremonies composed of bits and pieces of ripped-off Pagan, Catholic and Masonic rituals.

Here in the San Francisco Bay Area, for example, an ex-circus odd-jobber jumped on the occult bandwagon and came close to making a fortune. Knowing just enough about occultism to impress the ignorant, he plagiarized Nietzsche and Hitler to put together a philosophy that appealed to Fascists countrywide. I've often found it interesting that leaders of the Left-Hand Path attract mostly "Right-Wingers"—this would seem to make the rabid conservatives the "demonic" and "Satanic" ones, rather than the "Left-Wingers" and Communists. However, this man soon had members of the KKK, the American Nazi Party, local police departments, the Mafia, and ordinary socialites and jetsetters in search of a new thrill all flocking to his meetings. Those without money or influence never got through the front door. (How did *I* infiltrate then? That's another story.)

This man had a rather monotonous repertoire of six or seven routines he performed weekly. These included prayers to Satan for blessings on the members, "incantations" of pure gibberish, ceremonies stolen from the Masons, the wearing of black KKK sheets, and a nude woman for an altar.

Corny as he was, the rubes ate it up. He had absolutely no magical powers of his own; all he had was an incredible amount of charisma and pure *chutzpah*. But then again, there were fascinating deals going on behind his closed doors (in his "Inner Circle"), and his knowledge of the private lives of San Francisco's wealthiest and most powerful families gave him tremendous opportunities for extortion and blackmail. In short, like most Black Magicians, his powers were not magical at all.

This man was an exception in that he was so successful.

Nevertheless, we still have quite a few groups of Black Witches and Black Magicians running around trying to be Evil (a task just as boring as trying to be Good). I have never found any evidence of the existence of actual Black Lodges, though I have no doubt that many White Lodges are labeled as such by their competitors.* So we are now ready to sum up the differences between modern practitioners of Black and White magic:

The first have the only system that works. The second have the only system that works.

The first bless their own and curse their enemies. The second bless their own and curse their enemies.

The first are destined to prevail and fate is with them. The second are destined to prevail and fate is with them.

The first have The One True Right and Only Way. The second have The One True Right and Only Way.

The first are self-righteous, power-hungry, and Fascist. The second are self-righteous, power-hungry, and Fascist.

The first know that the others are cowards and weaklings without the guts to accept the Truth. The second know that the others are cowards and weaklings without the guts to accept the Truth.

The first are very "different" from the second. The second are very "different" from the first.

I have tried very hard to find a difference between the two groups, other than religious bigotries. I have failed. Both sides practice methods that are supposed to belong to the other. Both perform acts that are supposed to be done by the opposition. Both draw their traditions and rituals from the same major sources. Both sides are very much anti-life; one through an obsession with puritanism disguised as good taste, the other through an admitted and cultivated obsession with

---

* But considering the Infinity and Paradox Laws, there is bound to be at least one genuine Black Lodge, and since there are always "sickies" in any field of study, there are probably many such groups.

skulls, graves, and death. Members of both groups eventually destroy themselves with their own negativism,* simply because skill in magic requires a sane and well-balanced personality powered by a mature and intelligent mind. To become an "adept," to develop your *talents* to their fullest, you must have a positive attitude to life. Remember that it is your physical body, modulated and controlled by your personality, that is responsible for your *talents*. If you hate your body and mind, if you are unbalanced and without self-discipline, if you are unable to retain sanity and flexibility, if you cannot adapt to sudden changes, you will kill yourself. The fact that you are *talented* will only speed the self-destruction process. I have met many members of the Right- and Left-Hand Paths who were very powerfully and skillfully tearing themselves to shreds. The very few pro-lifers that I have met in these groups have actually been practicing Green, Red, or Brown Magic.

It is easy to see that there is no difference between the concepts of "Black Magic" and "White Magic" as schools of thought, but what about individual acts? Let's pick something easy like the murder of the Pope with magic. That is definitely Evil Black Magic, right? But what if the victim was Adolf Hitler in 1935? Or Joseph Stalin before his purges? After all, murder is murder, isn't it? Well?

You can see that we will soon get bogged down in a morass of conflicting ethical and religious philosophies. *There is nothing that we as scientists (and all magicians are scientists) can label "Black Magic" or "White Magic" just as we cannot as scientists label anything "Good" or "Evil." That is the job of ethics, not science.* And I am *not* saying that scientists should not have ethics, in fact, we need them today more than ever.

Morals and magic do not mix. Magic is a science and an

---

* In theory the White Lodges are supposed to be fighting the Black. But since they spend 90 percent of their time in internecine warfare, the Black Lodges (and the far more dangerous Red Lodges) have nothing to fear except *their* internal warfare.

art, and as such has nothing to do with morals or ethics. Morals and ethics come in only when we decide to apply the results of our research and training. *Magic is about as moral as electricity.* You can use electricity to run an iron lung or to kill a man in the electric chair. The fact that the first is preferable does not change the laws of physics. It would be nice if the words "destructive" and "creative" could be interchanged with "Black" and "White" when describing acts of magic, but the facts of history will not allow it.

However, there are sound reasons for the use and growth of such phrases as "The Black Arts," "The Powers of Darkness," "Creatures of the Night," and "The Witching Hour" of midnight. They have to do with the psychology of darkness, and night.

Go back, for a moment—back a million years. We cannot see in the dark. Darkness is scary because it is the home of the Unknown. In daylight we can see dangerous things far away before they can get to us, but at night they can creep up and be upon us before we know it. We go outside and see the stars looking so far-off and alone. Just as lonely as we are. We know the sun brings warmth and safety, but at night it goes away. Light is rare just as life is. Darkness is the rule, and death is hidden in the darkness. Light is an alien entity in a cold, dark, hostile universe; just as life is. Therefore, darkness is death is evil and light is life is good.

Thus our earliest ancestors reasoned, but we now know that life is *not* alien, that it is scattered throughout the universe. We know that those tiny, lonely lights up in the sky are actually huge suns, many of them blazing in the skies of life-filled planets. Recent discoveries of complex molecules in intergalactic space are indicating that life may be an *inevitable result* of stellar evolution. Neither light nor life is really alien and alone in the universe. Such realities will, however, take long to alter inbred attitudes to light and darkness.

But there are more realistic reasons to connect magic with the night and with darkness. There is much less psychic "static" at night, since most people are sleeping; it is, therefore, a good time for doing your spells. Also there is less chance of discovery or of disturbance at night, something very important during the Middle Ages. There is less visual distraction at night or in a dim room; thus, darkness makes it easier for your *talents* to operate (this is the reason why even honest mediums prefer to work in dim surroundings). Thus, ordinary practicality makes nighttime ideal for magic.

Sex and attitudes to it have a great deal to do with concepts of Evil Black Magic and of the darkness as evil. To the Church, sex was a "necessary evil." The orgies and fertility rites of the peasants (later confused with witchcraft and magic) were definitely even more evil than usual. Orgies were generally held at night, to avoid discovery and disturbance. In fact, many sinful things happened at night and were never found out. Darkness protected evildoers. Therefore, darkness was evil, and magic, generally done at night back then, was also evil.

There are other connections between sex and magic, all of which seemed only to make magic more evil. Consider the fact that most RSPK activity is connected with adolescents experiencing the awakening of sexuality. Note that most psychics first get their powers at puberty. Note that the sex drive is one of the most powerful of all in its affects upon the human metabolism and personality. Note that in many schools of occultism, people are advised to practice chastity in order not to dissipate their energy. Note how many tribal cultures demand sexual abstinence before the performance of magical rituals, many highly sexual in nature. Note that sexual power and control are the major aims of most of the rituals available to us from around the world. Note that the two items I am asked about most often are sex magic and curses (usually against sexual rivals). Sex and magic are here to stay.

But, as we all "know," sex is evil (except when done by man

and wife, in the Missionary Position, for the express purpose of having children—and even then you must avoid enjoying it, for pleasure is also evil). Therefore, since sex and magic and darkness are so interwoven, they are all evil. Sure. And of course women are evil too, * because they tempt men to enjoy sex, which is why most evil witches are women.

So we can see that most of what we have been taught about Black Magic and White Magic is pure nonsense, and bears little, if any, relation to reality. But there is much writing in the occult literature on a subject most people never hear about, "Gray Magic." This was the title reserved for acts which were considered ethically neutral or at least wishy-washy.

Since we've tossed out Black and White magic, we can hardly have Gray magic, so why not get rid of this whole *achromatic*-moralistic-bigoted-anti-life scheme of classification of magical acts and organizations? Let us return to the vibrant colors of the spectrum and use another system based on pagan, nonliterate, and associational classification of colors.

In fact, since the system we will be using is very similar to that traditionally used to judge auras, we'll have to detour for a page or so to discuss this phenomenon. Auras are supposed to be fields of energy surrounding the body. Those who are *talented* can observe these fields and make judgments about the physical, mental, emotional, and psychic state of the person being examined.

We already know from physics and physiology that the human body puts out all sorts of energy along the electromagnetic spectrum, from the lowly infrared of body heat to the radio waves of telepathy. Whether these auras are actually energy fields of this sort or are merely *input mechanisms* for handling telepathic data as if it were visual, is impossible to tell at this point and is probably irrelevant anyway.

---

* It has been suggested that since *some* women generate large amounts of catapsi energy during unpleasant menstrual periods, this may be a legitimate excuse for barring them from *some* sorts of rituals.

Everyone, we are told, has three different auras in layers surrounding the body. The first two are very close, while the third extends several feet. The innermost aura is said to be yellowish in hue and supposedly indicates the state of the nervous system, while the second aura is normally red and indicates the person's bodily health. When people and books talk about "the Aura" though, they are referring to the third layer, which unlike the "nerve aura" and the "body aura" has many possible colors.

It extends for several feet in all directions, surrounding the body with a sort of shell of energy. Within this shell colors swirl and pulsate, revealing the person's character and thoughts. Often the colors are said to be layers, one upon the other, with the innermost layers revealing the deepest characteristics. Others say that the colors shoot out in rays from the body, as sudden moods and emotions occur. Usually one color predominates, dwarfing all others, and this indicates the basic personality (see page 121).

I have had my aura examined many times, with curious results. Though usually gold and copper predominate, I am told my aura occasionally has an "Aurora Borealis" aspect— for once no pun intended—that every color in the spectrum as well as a fantastic amount of ultraviolet light is constantly shimmering away from my body in a rainbow pattern. The "readers" have all told me that they have never before encountered such an effect, and so far, none of them has been able to figure out how to interpret it. Whatever its explanation, my aura frequently winds up freaking out people who try to judge it.

Now all the different colors of the spectrum, the *achromatics* and ultraviolet are supposedly visible in the human aura. (Did I mention that plants and animals are said to possess auras, too? They are usually green and red, in that order.) All the colors show up in varying proportions, tones, shades, and changes. Moral value is accorded clear, bright, and intense hues. Black is, of course, evil. Brown, or dark

Psychic Energy Fields

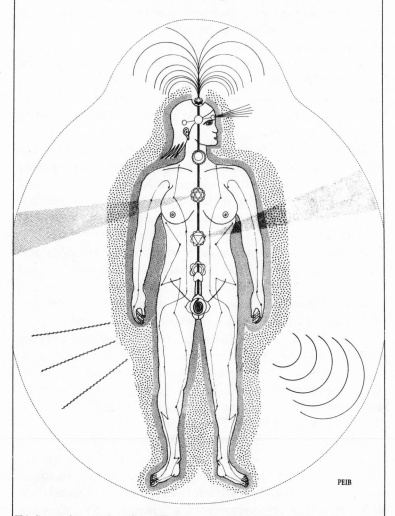

PEIB

This diagram shows (1) the traditional Western concepts of the swirling, multi-layered human aura; (2) one possible arrangement for the Tantric system of "chakras" or psychic centers and the rise of the "Kundalini Serpent" through the body; as well as (3) a suggestion of a few of the "meridians" of "Ki" flow and their associated acupuncture points.

orange if you prefer, is considered bad especially if it "muddies" other colors, as this implies a "sensual" nature. The system we will be using to classify different areas of magic can, by a chicken-or-egg process, also be used to judge auras if you should have the *talent* for "seeing" them. As to the actual existence of auras: Insufficient data!

We will now begin to list different types of magic, by color. After each one will come those areas of activity, normal and magical, which would come under the heading of that "color" magic. Naturally, magic itself has no color; these are merely associational devices.

Red Magic: Has to do with matters of the body, both human and animal. The association is obviously derived from the color of blood and therefore involves both healing and killing. Thus, this color includes: the medical sciences and the military sciences, blessings and curses, matters of physical strength and power, and the zoological sciences.

Orange Magic: Deals with matters of ego-strength and materialism, of pride and self-confidence, of courage and security, and of the physical and economic sciences. The derivation of these associations is not clear, until we note that orange stands between red and yellow in the spectrum.

Yellow Magic: This is the magic of the mind and nervous system. It includes, therefore, matters of the mental sciences, such as mathematics, logic, and philosophy. Also included are learning, organization, and theorizing (now you finally understand why this book is an introductory treatise to *Yellow Magic*). It is the color of Thaumaturgy.

Green Magic: Now almost obsolete in America, it was originally the magic of agricultural fertility, and we are no longer a rural nation. It includes, naturally, the botanical sciences, fertility and creativity, beauty and art. I'm sure we all know at least one person with a "green thumb"; they are often unconscious practitioners of *Green Magic*.

Blue Magic: We all know what "having the blues" means, and this is the basic association of this color: emotions. Therefore, we logically and traditionally include religion, ESP, other psychic phenomena, spiritualism, fortune-telling, theology, and the social sciences. This is the color of theurgy.

Indigo Magic: This is at once one of the oldest and newest of all the colors of magic. Originally it was the color of rain-making and weather control, and thus of meteorology. It has since been extended to other sciences of the sky, including astronomy, astrophysics—ruled by the Angel Nasa, remember?—and matters of space and time travel.

Purple Magic: This color of magic is rarely, if ever, referred to as "Violet Magic," perhaps because violet just does not coincide with this color's main association: violent and physical passions. Remember the phrase "purple passion"? Well, the color purple is a mix of red and blue, so we could expect physical emotions to be the result. Thus, we have matters of love, lust, hate, fear, anger, and ecstasy. Strangely enough, matters of power and the political sciences are also traditionally linked with this color. Is it only because of the purple cloaks of royalty? Not necessarily, for purple is the only way we can normally view. . . .

Ultraviolet Magic: This is the traditional color for the crackling flashes of pure power in the psychic realms. Often the color is confused with black (you've seen "black lights"?) and since power is often considered evil, here was yet another reason for calling evil magic Black. Thus, this is the proper color for matters of power and politics, yet we will normally let them retain their attribution of Purple Magic. Additional support for our theories comes, though, from the fact that the color of strong emotions is also the color of psychic power. Ultraviolet Magic by itself is somewhat useless, not to say suicidal.

Brown Magic: Brown is not technically a *hue,* neither is it an *achromatic.* It is, instead, a mixture of red and yellow with medium to low *value* and *chroma.* In short, a dark orange. Remember the attributes of Orange Magic—well, brown is even more materialistic. As we mentioned before, in "auric readings," brown indicates a sensual nature. For our purposes we can consider it the primitive and animal color. Brown Magic then easily earns its traditional place: the magic of the woods and glens, of animals and hunting, of the wilderness, and of the ecological sciences.

As you can see, all these color classifications overlap and interact. You will notice that they match fairly well with those of Tantra, as well as those popular with nonliterate tribes worldwide. But one thing to remember is that, should something feel better to you if you put it under a different color magic, then do so! It is always best if one uses the associations that work most effectively for him personally, even though you may occasionally run into *circuits* of the *Switchboard* that disagree (which won't make any sense until after the next chapter). The listing provided is merely the most convenient color classification I have been able to devise.

You may have noticed that while the *achromatic* colors were used to refer to the abstractions of pure "good," pure "evil," and "wishy-washy," our system refers to concrete and living things that we all know and interact with, and without the moralistic overtones. That is why I call them the Living Colors.

The magicians (and witches and wizards) of Living Color are the magicians of the modern age. The bright, splashy colors of modern fashions and art are only symptoms of this move away from the *achromatics* of anti-life. I personally know three Red Magicians, three Indigo Magicians, and a dozen Green and Brown Magicians, Wizards, and Witches. Their numbers are growing every day, and I can only advise you, if you plan to practice magic of any sort, to try the Living Colors.

Recently (1979) I have been told that some people using this color coding system have started referring to *Infrared Magic* as being the appropriate category for various forms of Psychopyresis and "fire magic" in general. It sounds to me like a workable idea, so you may want to try it. But it brings up the question of what colors people should use for the other "elements" of Earth, Air and Water. Different magical systems use various colors for these purposes. The commonest systems seem to be: orange or red for Fire, brown, black or green for Earth, yellow or blue for Air, and blue, green, grey or silver for Water. I've never made up my mind, myself, and use different colors on different occasions.

So I'll repeat myself here: *use whatever colors seem right at the time,* and don't worry about whether or not they violate mine or anybody else's system. I think you'll get better results if you stick to the same system most of the time, but you should follow your own intuitions. After all, that's a large part of what this so-called Age of Aquarius is all about.

CHAPTER SIX

Placebo Spells, the Switchboard, and Speculations on Explanations

By this time there will no doubt be some people who will think that I'm just plain batty, what with my talk of spells and incantations actually working. To placate them a little and to dampen my more enthusiastic followers we will now proceed to examine a slightly more "down to earth" way in which magic can work; that is, the *placebo effect*. This chapter will have a nice, quiet, and sedate opening but things will get freakier as we approach the end.

"Placebo" comes from the same Latin verb as the word "placate" or "please." Most people will be familiar with the "sugar pills" that doctors often give hypochondriacs. Indeed, though, you will find out if you start asking around that placebos are being used to an ever-growing extent in modern medicine. If you give someone a pill and tell him that it is a new wonder drug, this treatment will often be as effective as if the placebo really *were* an actual drug.

In 1965, Theodore L. Thomas described the placebo effect in the February edition of *Fantasy & Science Fiction*. Perhaps because it was printed in a science fiction magazine his article was considered "unscientific" and therefore ignored. However, consider what he had to say:

> When a patient responds to medication or treatment that cannot have a direct effect on his illness, you have the placebo

effect. Healers have used the placebo effect for thousands of years. When stomach cramps are cured with ground bat hair, when a backache is cured with a sugar pill, you have the placebo effect in operation. A placebo may consist of a dose of harmless vitamin or an active drug in an amount too small to be of direct medical value. It may be a harmless injection, or sham electric treatment, or even fake surgery. It could be the laying on of hands. A recent guess says that forty percent of medical prescriptions are placebos.

Research on the placebo effect shows remarkable results. Placebos controlled the sugar level in the blood of over half of a group of diabetics. They improved almost all of a group of peptic ulcer patients. They reduced the pain in patients after major surgery. They brought about symptomatic relief in rheumatoid and degenerate arthritis. Up and down the line, placebos have done the work of the actual drugs, even better, in some instances. The inevitable happened, though. Placebos sometimes had the same side symptoms as the drugs themselves, dizziness, nausea, fever, swollen ankles, and all the rest.

It was found that the conditions under which the placebo was administered to the patient were important; a white coat—or no coat—on the doctor would have a bearing. A myriad of factors was uncovered. Even animals responded to the placebo effect. Something certainly was at work, something beyond the patient's imagination.

Well, it is obvious to suggest that the placebo effect could conceivably cure cancer. Or, give a man a shot under the proper circumstances and tell him he will live forever, and see what happens. The placebo effect would seem to have far greater possibilities than these. Why waste money on the search for actual drugs and vaccines and improved surgical procedures? Put the money in research on the placebo effect. If the mechanism of the placebo effect could be understood, there would be no need of anything else, not really. Any man could be cured of anything so long as he was administered *something* under the proper circumstances.

Is it possible that the mechanism involved is personal Cellular Psychokinesis? All we can say at this point is "insufficient data." But suppose we look at something closer to our official field of magic. Claude Lévi-Strauss, in an article referred to earlier, "The Sorcerer and His Magic," showed how a person could die from a curse *that he was aware of*.

For a while now try to imagine yourself to be a member of a nonliterate "primitive" society. A local sorcerer has just told you he has put a curse upon you. Everything that you have ever learned tells you that you are doomed. Your friends and neighbors avoid you and begin to refer to you in the past tense. Perhaps they even hold your funeral! People begin to resent you for still being alive. The result is a condition called thanatomania (preoccupation with death). Lévi-Strauss says:

> How are these complex phenomena expressed on the physiological level? Cannon showed that fear, like rage, is associated with a particularly intense activity of the sympathetic nervous system. This activity is ordinarily useful, involving organic modifications which enable the individual to adapt himself to a new situation. But if the individual cannot avail himself of any instinctive or acquired response * to an extraordinary situation (or to one which he conceives of as such) the activity of the sympathetic nervous system becomes intensified and disorganized; it may sometimes within a few hours, lead to a decrease in the volume of blood and a concomitant drop in blood pressure, which result in irreparable damage to the circulatory organs. The rejection of food and drink, frequent among patients in the throes of intense anxiety, precipitates this process; dehydration acts as a stimulus to the sympathetic nervous system, and the decrease in blood volume is accentuated by the growing permeability of the capillary vessels. These hypotheses were confirmed by the study of several cases of trauma resulting from bombings, battle shock, and even surgical operations; death results, yet the autopsy reveals no lesions.

In short, you've got all this adrenaline running through your body and no way to release the energy it triggers. Per-

---

* Lévi-Strauss forgets here that dying from a curse *is* an acquired response!

haps you will go mad and run amok, in which case your fellows will be forced to cut you down. Perhaps you can go to a rival sorcerer and he will give you confidence and cast a countervailing curse himself against the first sorcerer. If you have no other recourse though, you will simply find that your metabolism is tearing you apart from the inside out!

Here, suggestion is being used to kill instead of cure, and what has happened is comparatively easy to explain by modern psychophysiology. It is clearly a different mechanism from that involved in "faith healing," or in curses where the victim is unaware of the attack (except perhaps through unconscious telepathy?).

There is ample evidence in occult literature to confirm that simply telling a person you have cursed or cured him is often sufficient to do the job. The person proceeds to do all the work himself, either by the procedure outlined above or by Cellular Psychokinesis.

Personal experience has borne this out. I have often had people come up and ask me for a spell to help them. Sometimes they are worried about their job, or their lover, or their health, or just plain "bad luck." Often I decide that they don't really need a spell at all or that the situation is far too complicated for me to tackle. In such cases, I may use a *Placebo Spell;* that is, *I tell them I will cast a spell but I actually don't* (sometimes I make the promise in good faith and something interferes, so that even though I wanted to do a spell, I couldn't).

The strange thing is that *such placebo spells usually work!* Days later they will come back to me and say, "Oh, what a great spell you cast, it all worked beautifully," or words to that effect, and I actually haven't done anything at all. Or have I?

Many possible explanations arise. Maybe all they needed was a little self-confidence to work things out themselves, normally or magically. Or there may have been some garden variety hypnosis involved. Perhaps in those cases where I wanted to cast a spell but couldn't, I may have done something subconsciously, if only the releasing of their own latent powers. Insufficient data!

Remember, *it's the thought that counts.* This is something that works on many levels, from the physical, emotional, and mental to the psychic. If I sincerely believe that someone can curse or cure me, then he can. Period. It does not matter whether my reaction is conscious or not, it is there nonetheless. Conversely, if someone (whether doctor or magician) sincerely believes that he can curse or cure people, and they have no defenses up, then he probably can!

Please note here that the placebo effect can interweave and mingle with actual spells performed. When you consider how much suggestion and association control magic it should not be surprising if every spell had a little placebo mixed in. The window dressing and props used in rituals rarely have power in themselves initially—they usually have placebo power.

To the person using the placebo effect, whether doctor or magician, the Law of True Falsehoods offers some explanation; though not for the recipient, since to him there is nothing false going on.

But as Theodore Thomas said, this is one area that demands investigation by the medical profession. The power of "the will to live" seems to be responsible for almost all cures short of surgery.* However, I doubt if the American Medical Association plans to invite any witch doctors (other than the psychiatrists) to its next convention. Pity.

Now we are going to return to the arena of "pure" and real magic to discuss a theory I have long held. It raises nearly as many questions as it answers, but it opens the way for much research and the questions raised are ones that can eventually be answered. *This theory is pure speculation on my part,* but I have found it useful as a working hypothesis and a highly convenient research tool. Additionally, it allows for the

---

* I have received recent estimates of the total number of medical cures brought about by psychosomatic means, ranging from 72 to 95 percent.

copious use of Occam's Razor amid jungles of conflicting and chaotic concepts. It is the theory of the *Switchboard.*

We start with an assumption that is well on its way to final proof and now accepted by many parapsychologists around the world; that is, *every human being is constantly broadcasting and receiving on telepathic wavelengths* (remember Kogan?). From the moment of your birth (or even before?) every thought you have ever had has changed your neural balance and thus modulated your broadcasting. The theory in its purest form follows logically from this:

My entire memory has been broadcast to all the world and it is now a part of your memory. Conversely, somewhere down deep inside, I have all of *your* memory as a part of *my* memory. Now, when I die, you will still have all my memories intact inside your head; and when you die, others will have your memories of my memories, *ad infinitum.*

The final result is that *each of us has, buried deeply, the memories of every living human being as well as all the memories of those who are now dead.* The vast net of billions of interlocking metapatterns with their innumerable subpatterns is what I call the *Switchboard,* for reasons which will soon become obvious.

I am very far from the first to come up with this concept; you have possibly read much of the Hindu ideas of the *Akasic Records* as the repository of all knowledge of lives past, and of Carl Jung's writings on the *Collective Unconscious* as a repository of memories that we all have in common. However, I think that the concept can be usefully stated in baldly rationalistic and mechanistic terms.

Even if we accept this theory as "true," quite a few questions and problems remain. Is there a spatial effect involved? As Kogan and others found out, distance seems to diminish the amount and quality of data received. Perhaps only those physically close to me will pick up all of my memories. This might help account for so-called race memories of isolated peoples and the fact that *psi* phenomena are much more common in such isolated groups. For that matter, there is no one person who has been near me constantly since I was born (thanks to modern mobility). Possibly my memories are deposited in chunks in the minds of hundreds of people scattered around the world. Remember though that every new datum that you receive, including presumably the memories of others, changes you and thus modifies your own broadcasting. Therefore everything is constantly rebroadcast over and over again, and eventually this would mean that the entire globe would be covered. Yes? Since the range of waves broadcast by the human body is capable of almost infinite modulation, it does not seem unlikely that overlaps and re-transmissions could occur.

We also have to ask if there is a historical variable involved. How far back does the *Switchboard* go? Does it stop with Cro-Magnon, Neanderthal, or Pithecanthropus? Does it stop with man at all? Could it go all the way back to the first animal to have a nervous system capable of transmitting and receiving? Also, as long as we're into zoology and evolution, we might as well consider the subject of mutants. It might not be necessary for *everyone* to be a member of the *Switchboard*. If even one in a million were specially talented at telepathy, we might still have a good size *Switchboard* of several million memories. We could still have these mutant metapatterns as a part of a larger *Switchboard*.

We have yet to discover what combination of variables determines the strength of a particular pattern or *circuit* within the *Switchboard,* and tracing the circuitry patterns themselves is an incredibly complicated task.

For example, suppose that a hundred men die, each believing in the Great God Irving; then a new *circuit* of "Irving belief" is formed. In time, perhaps millions of Irving worshipers may die and their memories join the *Switchboard.* They are dead, but their memories live on. It seems likely that the number of metapatterns connected by a *circuit* may be an important variable determining the strength of the particular *circuit*. Thus the more people who die believing in Irving, the stronger the "Irving belief" *circuit* would be within the *Switchboard*.

And now we have yet another time variable to consider. Is the belief *circuit* of one billion Christians stronger than the belief *circuit* of three billion worshipers of the Earth Mother, simply because the former are more recent additions to the *Switchboard?* Or is it just that the recent ones are easier to contact? Or, dropping from the level of a *circuit* to an individual metapattern, does the metapattern of your great-grandmother have more power and/or is it easier to contact than that of your great-great-great-grandmother?

Another variable that we must consider is one that traditionally has always been very important, the state of a person's metapattern at time of death. Does the memory of a very vital man who fought death all the way differ from that of one who resigned quietly, as far as the number and strength of *circuits* formed? Remember that the extra adrenaline secreted during the death crisis would drastically modulate and intensify your telepathic broadcasting; this is probably why victims of violent or sudden deaths are the most common "ghosts." * What effect do the strong passions of rage, love, fear, lust, hate, or courage have upon the subsequent *circuitry* formed within the *Switchboard?* Do people with strong egos and wills differ from those with weaker egos and lesser wills, when elements of their metapattern begin to interlock after death?

Certain logical outcomes from the acceptance of the *Switchboard*'s existence are going to have to be examined, especially since such terms as "living" and "conscious" are still so loose and undetermined.

Let us go back to our previous example of religious belief patterns. There are going to be very large groups of people

---

* This also explains why deathbed curses are the strongest. If a person decides to use all that energy in cursing, instead of fighting to live, he can have devastating results.

in the *Switchboard* (that is, very strong *circuits*) that believe that there is a real god Thor, and a real god Jehovah, and real demons, Ymir and Satan. Remember that each individual metapattern included these belief patterns as a part of that considered "true" by the person involved, and that they acted upon these beliefs in universes where these beliefs were "true" (because they worked). We therefore have very strong *circuits* in the *Switchboard* that say these gods and demons are "real." The final result, which fits in nicely with the Law of True Falsehoods, is that *every god, demon, and spirit ever believed in may actually exist.*

We must also ask whether or not the *Switchboard* is conscious or alive. Many mystics and magicians would say yes, that it is indeed "alive" in its own special way, because you can interact with it just as you could with other entities. And of course, by the Law of Personification. . . .

Some even claim that the *Switchboard* is very much alive and is evolving as Man evolves; it may even be trying to control human evolution by introducing new ideas and concepts, especially of a religious or ethical nature. I personally *feel* that the *Switchboard* has a sort of "quasi-life" of its own, as a totality and in many of its stronger *circuits*, but I cannot say for sure.

Another thought occurs. Is it possible that other species, here on Earth or elsewhere, might have *Switchboards* of their own? The dolphin, remember, has a brain and nervous system just as complicated as our own and no doubt just as capable of broadcasting and receiving energy. There is a vast realm of lore about human-dolphin relationships throughout history. Just a few months ago there was another report about a Greek fisherman who was shipwrecked in the Mediterranean Sea and carried twenty miles to land by a school of dolphins, who were fighting off sharks half the way. Some scientists "explained" that the dolphins were "playing" with the man, though they lost several of their number to the sharks in order to continue their "play." For that matter I am inclined to think that dolphins may be smarter than men. Not only do they have more brain convolutions (wrinkles in the brain that seem correlated with intelligence), but have you ever heard of a dolphin building an atom bomb or creating poison gas? This is usually "explained" by the fact that dolphins don't have hands. Additional proof of their inferiority is that they don't even try to exterminate their own kind! But unless some ecologically active magicians start casting spells on the tuna industry, we may never find out.

However, imagine if you will, two massive *Switchboards* hanging around the planet Earth (they are after all "merely" modulation patterns of energy generated by our physical bodies—and dependent upon us for their physical survival). As they grow stronger they reach out toward *Switchboards* on other planets in other stellar systems, forming, in time, a huge *Galactic Switchboard*. And why stop there? As these reach out toward each other we might finally have a *Universal Switchboard* linking every galaxy in our physical universe. Perhaps this *Universal Switchboard*, with uncountable quadrillions of minds, might in time figure out a way to reverse entropy and create a new universe, by saying something like —"let there be light!"

However, we have now entered the realm of science fiction and fantasy, but you can see how a simple theory can be the basis of incredible extrapolations. Let us now once again return literally back to Earth.

Some of you may have wondered why I refer to this collection of metapatterns generated by human bodies and shared by all living minds as the *Switchboard*. Since I know you can't stand the suspense, I will tell you that I call it that because some people seem to be able to *plug-in* to parts of it, accidentally or on purpose.

Plugging-in to the *Switchboard* would seem to be a type of *psi* phenomena, in that the same variables are involved. You could conceive of this *plugging-in* as a kind of telepathy with the *Switchboard* or as a kind of "super introspection." Once again, association powered by emotion seems to be the key, and, as in other kinds of *psi*, it happens more often by accident than design.

Suppose, for example, you are praying in ,a church with many of your fellow believers. Not only may you become a part of a small localized "group-mind" or mini-*Switchboard* generated by the thoughts of those present, but you could also find yourself *plugging-in* to a *circuit* of the *Switchboard* composed of all believers of the same faith.

Then again, suppose that you are living in the South a few years ago and hear that a black man has just tried to marry a white woman. A large crowd gathers in the center of town and every mind is consumed with hate and bigotry. Suddenly a *circuit* is formed and the crowd turns into a mob. As a part of that mob you are swept along with the miasma of hate, and you may find yourself doing things that, as an individual, you would find appalling. Many people who study mob psychology have noticed that a mob seems to act as a unit, as though some primitive bestial mind were directing its action. If there is within the *Switchboard* a *circuit* corresponding to the feelings of the mob, a connection may be made, and members of the mob will be "possessed." If ever Black Magic was done, it was by "men" wearing white sheets who knew how to whip up lynch mobs and cause them to perform hideous atrocities, usually in the name of Christianity.

Or suppose you are walking through an old and crumbling ruin of a house. Your perceptions begin to form patterns in your mind. Somewhere in the *Switchboard* there are metapatterns of memories about that same house and deeds done within those walls. Emotional associations may be strong enough on either side of the gulf, and the patterns of associations now forming in your mind may be similar enough to one or more within the *Switchboard,* that suddenly a *circuit* is closed and you have *plugged-in* to the *Switchboard.* Memories begin to flood your mind, memories not your own. The data received begins to be interpreted in unfamiliar ways.

Perhaps you will "see" a "ghost" or "hear" strange voices or noises, telling you things you could never normally know. You are not insane and these are not ordinary hallucinations. You have merely accidently *plugged* yourself *in* to the *Switchboard,* and you are inputting the data you are receiving as if it were visual or aural sensations. You may even hold a conversation with the "ghost" as many spiritualists have done. For that matter, if your conscious mind refuses to understand and stubbornly clings to disbelief, your subconscious mind may begin to use psychokinesis to convince you. Lamps may suddenly go out, doors slam, mysterious lights appear and disappear, furniture fly across the room. You have just experienced a full-fledged "haunted house," and there wasn't a single bit of the "supernatural" there. But there were some rather *unusual* things going on!

Perhaps, though, you are just at home sleeping in your bed, and some unsuspected pattern in your metapattern meshes with one in the *Switchboard* and you are *plugged-in* without knowing it. You just happen to have *plugged-in* to the memories of a very vital individual of several hundred years ago. As his or her memories flood your sleeping mind, they may be so strong that they seem to be yours, and so you input the data as though it were personal memories of a "previous life" that your personality once lived. The problem is that although the *Switchboard* does indeed consist of the memories of people who are now dead (as well as those now living), they are the memories of *other* people, a distinction easily blurred. For once the physical body is dead, it ceases to broadcast, and the personality survives *only as a memory* within the minds of those still living.* It may indeed be a very strong memory and easy to contact (*plug-in* to), but, except in *very* rare cases, it will *not* take over a new body and continue to grow. In fact there is every reason to believe that most metapatterns begin to break down after death and degenerate (witness the fact that

---

* It becomes yet another autobiography in the Akasic Public Library.

even in genuine spiritualistic contacts the mental organization of the "spirit" contacted is usually very poor). Probably it is merely the desire for personal immortality caused by the healthy instinct of fear for death, combined with accidental *plug-ins,* that is responsible for the entire concept of "reincarnation." Also, one hates to think that nasty people who do well in this world won't get their just deserts in some other existence; thus, the idea of karma can be used to provide emotional shoring up for moralistic concepts of reincarnation. As those of you who believe in these things can tell, I am indeed a materialist.

I am, however, very familiar with the literature of reincarnation, and I have yet to find a case where my theory of the *Switchboard* does not provide both an alternate explanation of greater simplicity and less insult to common sense. However, I could be wrong. The Earth could be flat, too, but present concepts are much more useful.

It has been pointed out to me by more than one occultist that although materialistic electromagnetic theories may account for telepathy, they cannot explain the various *clair senses* or *precognition.* I think they're wrong. Given the existence of telepathy as an electromagnetic phenomena, the theory of the *Switchboard* follows, as we have seen, quite logically. I find it perfectly possible that all the *clair senses and* possibly even the various forms of hypercognition may all be functions of the *Switchboard.* Perhaps we merely *plug-in* to the *Switchboard* to pick up the data we then interpret as clairvoyance or clairaudience. It may be that part or all of the *Switchboard* is acting constantly as a giant "computer," figuring out probabilities about the data on hand. With that many metapatterns involved, a great deal of high-class calculating could be going on (stuff that would make the latest HAL 9000's look like abacuses). Occasionally you might accidentally *plug-in* and pick up a bit of data, consisting of a prediction or probability calculation about the past, present, or future. Notice that this does *not* mean that the *Switch-*

board does this consciously; any more than a modern computer, which is only a big-dumb-stupid-but-*fast*-adding-machine, has to be conscious or "intelligent" in order to function.

What this could mean, of course, is that there may be *only one kind of ESP,* that is, telepathy, which is probably electromagnetic in nature (sorry). Paraphysics, on the other hand, seems to have little or no connection with the *Switchboard,* except possibly where the latter may provide extra power to the *agent.* But then, since (a) all matter is energy, and (b) paraphysics involves the manipulation of matter and energy, and (c) the *Switchboard* . . . wheeee!

As we have seen, the theory of the *Switchboard* can be used to explain many different unusual or "supernatural" phenomena in terms somewhat more palatable to the modern mind. Remember, though, that *all this has been speculation,* following logically from the premise that we do indeed use telepathy constantly without knowing it. This premise is a modern translation of universal mystical beliefs about how every thought, word, and deed is recorded *somewhere.*

It looks like we may at last be getting some scientific verification for this ancient belief, *but if Kogan and the others are wrong, we will have to start all over again and discard this theory mercilessly.* Such radical surgery upon the body of my magical beliefs will hurt, but if such surgery is not done when it is needed, the result will be a festering cancer that will eventually destroy everything.

Then again it may be that new research will only require modifications in theory. This, of course, would be preferable since the theory is so very useful. We might just find that though telepathy exists, it is not electromagnetic; in that case, most of the theory of the *Switchboard* could be retained. However, since it is so *very* useful, for the time being and as far as this book is concerned, we will consider the theory of the *Switchboard* to be "true."

Now we have already discussed many things in this book

that many people would call supernatural, and by waving our linguistic wand and changing the word to "paranormal" we have been able to consider sane, rational, and natural explanations for all of them. This has been one of the major purposes of the book—to give you a system of organizing your data about magic and the "supernatural" in a way that will not insult your mind. Many years ago this was the way in which the mystical Kabbalah was used; it provided a set of interlocking pigeonholes for data organization. Today, however, complex philosophical systems that require metaphysical gymnastics are not suited to our world of hurry and scurry. Thus, this little tome is designed to provide twentieth-century pigeonholes for twentieth-century magicians.

We have been gradually noticing the usefulness of the interdisciplinary approach for explaining unusual or bizarre happenings. Provided that we take everything with a small Siberian salt mine, we will find that many bits of "folklore" and "superstition" have at least a smidgen of truth to them. Pick a superstition, any superstition, and we'll see what happens:

How about "werewolves"? They are people who are supposed to be able to change into wolves, a process known as lycanthropy (shape changing into many different animals has been believed in for thousands of years, and the term "lycanthropy" has been extended to cover all of these). If an injury is done to the werewolf after this *metamorphosis,* the marks would supposedly show on his human body when he returned to human form. If killed while in animal form, the human body would perish. As mentioned just above, wolves were not the only animals involved; some people became werebears, werelions, wereboars, weredeer, and just plain weredoes. Such transformations were also stock in trade for traditional "witches," who supposedly could turn themselves into animals and prowl around picking up information or doing miscellaneous bits of mischief, *or they could "borrow" the bodies of their "familiars"* and do the same things.

Ninety-nine point ninety-nine percent of the stories about werewolves, like those about witches in the Middle Ages, were outright lies and fabrications by the Catholic and Protestant churches. They were designed to keep the Inquisitors and "witch-finders" wealthy and powerful, and they succeeded quite nicely. But we still have that 00.01 percent of medieval tales, plus all the non-Western ones, to consider. The process works like this:

First and always, we try mundane explanations. For one thing, it has been a worldwide custom throughout human cultures for individuals to dress in animal skins and imitate animal actions; usually in an attempt to invoke the Law of Association. Remember the Cro-Magnon cave paintings, and the myths of "the horned god" of the wildwood, not to mention various initiation and fertility rites. Also the Vikings used to dress in bear skins in order to freak out their enemies in battle (thus giving us the words "bear-sarker" and "berserk"). All of this comes under the heading of illusion, suggestion, and fraud. Insanity must also be considered; it is quite possible that a man might go mad and believe that he has become some other wild animal, even going so far as to attack cattle, sheep, and people, and rip out their throats with his teeth (just as a mammal, man is a much more dangerous animal than we usually think). I'm sure that most of you are also familiar with stage hypnotists who convince people they are cats or dogs; self-suggestion and insanity is much more powerful than this. It is notable here that most werewolves were supposed to change at the full moon, the traditional time of madness and "lunacy" (but even though experiments have been reported showing that mental patients are most active during the full moon, modern scientists "know" there is no such connection). Also note that the condition was believed to be spread by *biting* (Law of Contagion) at a time when little or nothing was known about medical infection or contagion.

Only after we have taken each case through these previous

possibilities are we ready for some unmundane explanations. What if such activities were *psi* phenomena?

Suppose, for example, that I were to establish *full telepathic rapport* with my cat, Bubastis. Since I have (I hope!) the stronger personality, I could possibly move right in and take over her body (utilizing the Law of Identity, etc.). I could then go about looking through her eyes, hearing through her ears, and so on, though the sensory scanning range might seem weird to my human mind. However, if an injury were done the cat's body while we were in such strong *rapport,* the shock would probably drive me "back" into my own body. Now, since innumerable experiments have shown that hypnosis and other forms of suggestion can cause wounds to appear or disappear on the human body (probably by CPK), it is not totally improbable that injuries sustained during *rapport* with an animal might be reflected upon my own body. Remember, when the cat was hurt the mind inside the cat was *mine;* thus, when the cat's paw was cut off, it was *my* paw being cut off. I then become a being with a missing paw. When I return to my normal body, I would still carry this concept, especially since it was associated with a great deal of pain and thus thoroughly branded into my metapattern. Back in my human body, I would find that the concept was still strong, and would proceed to carry it out upon my present body; thus, I would lose (by paralysis or CPK) one of my hands or feet. Probably if the cat was killed while I was "inside" it, the shock would be enough to kill me too!

Personally, I lean toward this theory of real lycanthropy as telepathic *rapport* much more than I ever could toward those that would allow a man to transform every molecule in his body while still retaining enough of a human mind to effect his return to normal. Then again, if you were skilled enough at psycholuminescence, you could manipulate the light around you so that you *looked* like a wolf. Easier still for an illusion would be the use of telepathic hypnosis to fool your audience. Now I will admit that the whole subject is pretty farfetched, but there are two nagging thoughts that keep recurring. One is the ever-growing number of experiments demonstrating animal-human telepathy. The second is that it was *silver,* an excellent conductor of electromagnetic energy, that was used to destroy suspected werewolves.

As long as we are on the subject of old Hollywood horror movies, we might as well discuss Dracula, Frankenstein's monster, and zombies.

Dracula (Slavic, from the Greek *dragula,* meaning "dragon" or "monster") was supposed to be a vampire. Vampires were devoutly believed in during the Middle Ages and were supposed to be dead men and women who rose from their graves to attack the living and suck out their blood. Unfortunately for the romantics, there are perfectly mundane and satisfactory explanations for the origin of these beliefs. To begin with, there is a rare form of madness that causes a craving for blood. Remember also that the blood has always been associated with life, and that it is almost always what ghosts are said to feed upon. And during the Middle Ages, there were many people who were buried while they were still alive, simply because medieval doctors knew little about comas and the like. If one of these victims of premature burial were to wake up and try to get out of the tomb or grave, a not uncommon occurrence I am told, anyone who saw him would freak quite royally. The bit about how vampires change into bats is a late addition to the myth and belongs in the realm of lycanthropy. However, I place little Woodstock in the image:

© 1970 United Features Syndicate, Inc.

Psychic vampires, however, are horrors of a different color (caller, choler, collar, culler) and do exist, though they are far rarer than most occult gossipers would admit.

Frankenstein's monster was simply a modern version of the "golem," or a primitive idea of a robot. The golem was an artificial manlike being created either by carving wood, wax, or metal, or by sewing together pieces from various dead bodies. The golem was usually given life by carving a sacred name into his forehead. The golem had no mind and was a perfect slave for the magician who could create him. The concept of the golem played a big part in Jewish mysticism and magic, but I doubt if anyone ever succeeded in creating a working model.

As for zombies, or "the walking dead," they are a part of "Voodoo." The myth is a combination of the vampire and golem myths, since zombies were resurrected dead people used as slaves. Other than the points noted above about these myths, consider the fact that Voodoo witch doctors supposedly had a drug that could induce an artificial catalepsy that so closely counterfeited death that the victim was usually buried quickly. Days later the witch doctor could return and administer the antidote. But the combined effects of oxygen starvation and the drug would thoroughly melt the mind of the victim who was then set to work doing simple tasks in the fields of the witch doctor, who thus received a handy labor supply, powerless to rebel. This, at least, is what my research indicates. I just wish that some botanist would find the plant from which this drug was apparently extracted.

Now, as a rule, I am not overwhelmingly interested in werewolves, vampires, golems, and zombies; but would any book on occultism be complete without them? Besides, if I omitted them, I would probably be kicked out of the ranks of occult authors, and we wouldn't want that to happen, would we?

Got a stubborn *poltergeist* bothering you? In nine cases out of ten there's going to be a teen-ager involved, and he or she is going to be very frustrated about something, usually sex. Problems with authority are often the other cause of frustration; try some psychological counseling for *both* parents and children.

How about problems with a ghost haunting your house? Well, as we saw earlier, ghosts are the result of accidentally *plugging-in* to a *circuit* of the *Switchboard* that remembers the same perception patterns you are then seeing; you input this as a vision or voice, and presto! Instant ghost! To get rid of one, you must break the connection between your meta-pattern and that of the ghost. If either you, the ghost, or the priest happens to believe strongly enough in Christianity, you could have a Catholic or Anglican priest perform an exorcism. I *have* done pagan exorcisms with great success, but this was because both my clients and I believed that I could. Sometimes a complete remodeling and painting of the haunted house will do the trick, because it will change your perception pattern and thus break the link, but you must avoid thinking about the ghost from then on, because your memories can *plug* you right back *in*.

If you can manage to engage the ghost in conversation, you can ask it how to break the connection, though it will probably speak in terms of "being released from earthly bonds," etc. For that matter, since they do not grow, such metapatterns when contacted often do not know that their bodies are dead! Inform them of this as tactfully as possible.

If nothing else works, call up a parapsychologist or two who will bother the ghost so much that it will probably refuse to show up at all, at least for as long as the scientists are there. Come to think of it, you might invite the most skeptical person you know, and have him spend a few nights. Such people give off so much Catapsi static that they can often sever the connection permanently.

CHAPTER SEVEN

The Fundamental Patterns of Ritual

In all the reading that you do in the occult you will find many descriptions of religious and magical rituals for varying purposes. If you look closely, you will begin to notice haunting similarities lurking behind the authors' highly spirited arguments for the uniqueness of their claims. In this chapter, we will examine a few rituals closely to see if we can make some of these common elements materialize.

To begin with, the same basic patterns run through both those rituals labeled religious and those labeled ceremonial magic in Western culture. In fact, the word "ritual" comes from a Latin root related to "number" or "counting," the way things are to be done (that is, "one after another"). Since "ceremony" is equivalent to "ritual" for our purposes here, ceremonial magic is just magic with the emphasis on the ritualistic aspects. In all rituals the crucial point is to do things in the proper order in the proper way, usually as prescribed by custom or tradition. As we shall see, the rituals to be presented are yet further examples of how people can try to get one thing and wind up with something totally different.

Despite their more abstruse theological differences, most of them totally unknown to their believers, the churches known as "Protestant" (Mahayana) have retained for the most part the basic order of worship perfected by the early Greek and Roman Catholic churches. Let us attend one now.

We see the priest or minister entering upon the sacred area at the front of the church. He goes before the altar and begins to address prayers in the general direction of various geometric shapes or statues. In Catholic churches, these are often pictures or statues of Christ crucified, Mary, Joseph, or other saints; for ritualistic purposes, these are far superior to the more bare (and often barren) symbols that others use. These opening prayers usually consist of confessions of past offenses and requests that the deity addressed will (a) not hold it against them, and (b) listen to the prayers to follow. The congregation often joins vocally or silently in these prayers.

Passages are then read from various books, most presumed with brave and noble disregard for facts to the contrary to be the handiwork of the god in question. Thus, the deity in effect replies to the prayers just offered.

Then a sermon is preached emphasizing some theological point deemed of interest or importance, but requiring neither intelligence nor action from the congregation. Here of course the basket is passed.

The officient returns to the altar and resumes his dialogue with the god, presenting him with gifts, especially bread and wine. In the early centuries c.e., all the members of the congregation would have marched up and presented actual loaves of bread and jugs of wine. It was also at this point that new converts would have been dismissed * because they were not worthy to witness the miracle to come. But back to the twentieth century.

The priest now identifies himself with the god by repeating the incantation that turns the bread and the wine into the body and blood of the god. It is very important that we note that the priest says, "This is *my* body . . . this is *my* blood" and not "This is *your* body . . . this is *your* blood" as would be the case in a mere commemoration. If you are a Catholic,

* This first part was known as the Mass of the Catechumens.

this is a literal change called *transubstantiation;* if you are a Protestant, this is a symbolic change called *consubstantiation.* Somewhere there is a very important difference between these two terms; you can tell because millions of men, women, and children were maimed, mutilated, and murdered over it (here you see the "Three *M*'s" of Western religion).

Now the congregation and the priest consume the now tangible god, believing that in doing so they will absorb his powers and characteristics (this is in addition of course to the virtues of sharing food with one another). After the meal is over, the deity is thanked for coming down, and his presence in the communion is reaffirmed. Final prayers and requests are made by the now powerful and god-filled congregation. The minister tells the people that their prayers will be granted, that the god is with them, and then dismisses them.

Throughout the ceremony, all sorts of props, costumes, music, incense, and miscellaneous special effects are used to heighten audience emotions to a peak that culminates with the consecration and consumption of the god-food and subsequent wielding of his powers. Though some of the prayers are altruistic, most are for pragmatic everyday blessings upon crops, children, property, and so on.

At one time this mass was the most powerful ritual in the Western world. The Latin phrases were chosen as much for their sounds and rhythm as for their meaning, and a master of Gregorian chant could play the emotions of the congregation better than the organist could his organ. Now that the prayers have been translated into local languages, they have lost this power (not to mention the faulty theology that has been suddenly exposed to view). Most of the costumes have been eliminated and incense is rarely used except on special occasions. And there hasn't been what I would consider a decent piece of church music written for the last hundred years. For these and other reasons, the mass is no longer as powerful as it used to be (I must admit I have seen two or three priests who could still do it effectively, even in English, but they are very rare). Recent attempts at changing the mass may have been great for the theologians and for the ecumenical movement, but they've been murder on the ritual.

There has been no rain for a long time. The Hopi are beginning to get desperate. They decide to do a Kachina Dance, hoping that the Kachinas (semi-divine beings) * will bring them rain. Each dancer has an elaborate costume and mask.

The ceremony begins and continues with one long dance, with the prayers sung throughout. The opening prayers state that the Hopi have been sinful and wish to beg pardon. Bits of history are recited, both of the tribe and of the Kachinas being invoked. All the members of the tribe strive to keep their thoughts pure and faithful, concentrating only on the ritual.

The dances are very elaborate and formal, for a missed step could mean failure. After a few hours, as they get more and more into it, the dancers find the barriers between themselves and the Kachinas dissolving. Each dancer *becomes* the Kachina he is dressed as. The rhythms and patterns of bodies and voices and rattles repeat over and over. Every once in a while a few dancers will pause to rest while the others continue. But once the point of identity has been reached, the dance speeds up as the Kachinas wield their powers and command rains to come. The dance is suddenly interrupted by a cold gust of wind, the sky darkens, and the clouds burst.

In Southern Tennessee an offshoot of the "Holiness Church" known as the White Pentecostalist Church or more commonly, The Holy Ghost People, is beginning its Sunday service (in a ritual largely borrowed from the Vodun of the Negro slaves, though of course the Pentecostalists neither know nor would ever admit this).

The congregation consists predominantly of adolescents and old people; they are already singing and clapping. The

* *See* Glossary for further information.

rhythm of the chanting has already succeeded in putting several members into a trance; they are swaying back and forth. Now the preacher enters and goes to a podium, Bible in hand, to begin his sermon.

It starts with statements about the sinfulness of the congregation and the even greater sinfulness of those not in attendance. The preacher's voice drones on rhythmically, soliciting cries of agreement from the audience, asking them questions and having them reply with ritual answers. He puts in a word about all races being equal, which receives enthusiastic agreement—there are only whites in the room.

Passages from the Bible are read, especially ones about the miracles possible for those who believe strongly enough. Stating "if you believe, then God is obligated to do something for you," he continues to whip up enthusiasm. His voice drones on, constantly repeating himself, reinforcing every statement many times, gradually increasing the speed of rhythm.

During this, one girl has fallen to the floor, twitching spasmodically; nobody seems to notice. One old woman goes up to the preacher, who begins to pray for her blind eyes. Men and women are kneeling on the floor crying. Soon everyone is moaning and shaking and many (predominantly adolescent girls) collapse to the floor in violent seizures, screaming out in strange languages. They are all possessed by the "Holy Ghost" (or the Devil, according to one Baptist witness). And things are just starting.

A large box filled with copperheads and rattlesnakes is brought in and opened. Acting on the Biblical promise that the faithful "shall take up serpents and not be bitten," they pick up the snakes and start tossing them around the room; apparently no one is bitten. The snakes have not been defanged and are just as dangerous as ever. (Note: this is not really very dangerous since only 3 percent of rattlesnake bites, for example, are fatal. Nonetheless, this whole snake-throwing bit is highly illegal in Tennessee.*)

* Fundamentalists have never had too much respect for law and order.

By this time, total bedlam has broken loose. People are thrashing on the floor, screaming at the top of their lungs, tossing snakes, speaking in tongues, and giving testimonies. A normal quiet Sunday morning service.

Finally the preacher resumes control, and the people follow his voice and begin to calm down; "the Spirit" is departing. The collection plate is passed ($44). The snakes are all returned to their box, except for one. The preacher holds it aloft as he preaches about faith. The Lord protects him because his faith is strong. Then the rattler bites him.

Rather embarrassed, the preacher tries to end the service quickly, presumably so that he can get a tourniquet (although this is a further sign of a lack of faith). The members of the congregation insist on praying over him and several girls decide to throw fits again. Finally he manages to dismiss everyone, telling them their prayers will be answered, and runs to his house. His "immune" arm is now swollen to twice its normal size (he lived).

We are in Haiti in a ramshackle building built to house ceremonies of Vodun (from the West African *wodun*, or "power," meaning a conscious power or entity; later confused with the French sect of Vadois, and evolved in America to "Voodoo"). Here we will see a less diluted (deluded?) ritual.

Lots of incense, liquor, and food have been brought ahead of time, as well as animals to be sacrificed. The preparations may take days or hours, depending upon the occasion. Today is not a high holy day, it is a normal small service.

People sit around on chairs and benches, chattering or singing, while the drummers get warmed up. Others are dancing lightly to the music. A pig or hen is sacrificed to the gods; libations of liquor and flour are poured on the floor. So far, it's not much different from an ordinary party. People are eating and drinking and having a great time. The priest acts as host, making sure that all goes well. Then one member of the group goes into the "*loa* crisis." He has been possessed by one of the gods.

His voice gets louder and shriller, the drummers hear him and pick up the speed and volume of their beating. The priest and his assistants begin to chant, but their voices are drowned out by the general chattering. Soon others are possessed, each acting out the personality ascribed to the god that has possessed them. Some limp around as if lame, others make lewd gestures, others stand stock still. They eat, drink, talk, and sing as the god they are. Occasionally one god "leaves" a person, only to be replaced by another.

It is important to have a good time, because the gods can only enjoy themselves if the persons they possess are having fun. So although the service is not the "Black Magic Orgy" depicted in Grade Z movies, it is one heck of a good party. Once in a while a god-man will get a little too excited and the priest will calm him down, or he may help another who is feeling faint. While possessed, a man will find his friends and neighbors addressing him and treating him as the god in question (though never in *question!*); they will ask for blessings and help.

The services can and do go on for hours and sometimes days, but eventually the food and liquor run out. The Vodun people have honored and worshiped their gods, and the gods have therefore agreed to reciprocate. Once the god has left the man or woman though, the person returns to his ordinary social roles. Most leave the service claiming to be invigorated rather than exhausted.

In Southern California the services at the American Head-quarters Temple of the Nichiren Shoshu are held in a huge room, the size of a cathedral, with thick carpeting and no pews. People take their shoes off when they come to the ante-room. Here they can purchase prayer beads, prayer books (in Japanese and in transliteration), make donations, make orders for home altars, and receive in general the same services available at any "religious articles counter" in any other church.

The people go into the huge temple, men on the left, women and children on the right. Everyone is already chanting the mantra *Nam-myo-ho-renge-kyo,* and some have been doing it for almost an hour. People sit or kneel as is comfortable. The priest's assistant asks the congregation to continue chanting for a while as he prepares the altar. Above the altar is a huge replica of the "Gohansan" (their sacred scroll) in gold and ebony. In fact the whole place has enough gold, silver, ivory, and ebony to feed thousands, or even to rival a cathedral.

Finally, all the candles and incense sticks are lit and the priest walks out in front of the altar. He rings a gong to alert the more glassy-eyed and begins the service. He starts reading from the prayer book, in Japanese, of course (why not? if the Catholics can do their stuff in Greek and Latin . . .); though most of the congregation hasn't the slightest idea of what he is saying, they docilely chant along with him. The opening prayers seem to be a confession of sorts rather than just prayers or praise. The major mantra is used as a common response interjected and sprinkled throughout.

The priest gives a sermon on some abstruse point of theology, but it is filled with enough glittering generalities and backpatting to make all happy. He then does a special blessing of the new converts, who march up to the altar rail in a procession highly reminiscent of a Christian Confirmation ceremony. After this, the priest returns to the altar and everyone starts chanting the mantra again; *Nam-myo-ho-renge-kyo, Nam-myo-ho-renge-kyo, Nam-myo-ho-renge-kyo.* . . . After about three minutes they are actually chanting *Yo-lingyo-nam, Yo-lingyo-nam* . . . but this doesn't seem to bother anyone. The congregation sways back and forth "possessed by the spirit of the Gohansan." The only other sounds are of the prayer beads rattling in time to the chanting, which goes on and on and on and on. . . .

The priest closes the service with a few more prayers and requests for blessings. The people chant for their private wishes to be granted, and then just for the sake of returning to the trance. Most of them leave, but many stay behind and will remain there for hours, still chanting: *"Yo-lingyo-nam, Yo-lingyo-nam, Yo-lingyo-nam. . . ."*

In the hills, lit only by the moon, the Reformed Druids of North America (RDNA) are celebrating *Samhain* (pronounced "so'ahn"). This is the night that others call Halloween and in the old Celtic cultures was the "day between years," or the beginning of the new year. The RDNA is a revival of old Celtic (especially Irish) religious beliefs and practices, |"reformed" in that it forbids the practice of blood sacrifice. The group was founded in the early 1960's and is not to be confused with other groups using similar names or claiming to go back in unbroken lines to prehistoric Ireland. The RDNA makes no such grandiose claims.

The service starts with prayers to the Earth Mother (the personification of the "Life Force"), to Be'al (the personification of the abstract essence of the universe), to Dalon ap Landu, Llyr, Danu, and other deities of ancient Ireland. Reciting hymns translated from old Celtic relics and manuscripts, these latter-day Druids send up their praise to Nature. They admit their human frailties and limitations.

Then passages from the *Chronicles* of the RDNA are read and meditated upon (the *Chronicles* are a history of the movement written in pseudo-King James style, plus the translations mentioned above, plus meditations and poetry. All is considered the work of men, though possibly written while inspired).

The members of the congregation are wearing ribbons around their necks; these are red, the color of life. As the ceremony continues, the "Waters-of-Life" (about 80 proof) are exchanged for the "Waters-of-Sleep (pure H_2O); and the red ribbons are exchanged for white ones, the color of death. This is to symbolize that the Season of Sleep has begun; the red ribbons will not be worn again until May 1, the beginning of the Season of Life.

A short sermon is given by the Arch-Druid upon the subject of man's constant destruction and defilement of Nature (the RDNA was into ecology long before it became a fad). The Earth Mother is asked to bless her children and fill them with her powers, so that they may do Her will. The participants identify themselves as a part of the Earth Mother and assert their interdependence with each other and with Her.

After a few more prayers of praise the service is over. The participants, feeling refreshed and strong, sit on the hilltop to finish the Water-of-Life and gaze at the stars and the city below.

But all is not yet quiet upon that hilltop, for after all it is Halloween and the night is still young. A warning is given, but all choose to remain. The thin line between religion and magic is about to be crossed. Still wearing their traditional tabards, the two leaders of the group prepare for a ritual of ceremonial magic.

The altar is a chunk of rock imbedded in the hilltop, once used by the Indians for *their* rituals. It now becomes the center of a "magic circle." Holes are dug by daggers and staffs are planted at the four points of the compass; a fifth staff (the largest one there) is placed at the base of the altar pointing to the evening's *target*.

A wandering hippy out for a stroll in the woods happens on the group. When they tell him what they are doing, he decides to leave quickly (in that area one knows better than to mess around in the affairs of magicians *). A stick is used to

* "Never meddle in the affairs of wizards, it makes them soggy and hard to light."

trace a circle around the staffs and altar, and they enter. Unlike most magic circles this one is not designed to keep anything out but rather to keep energy in until it is time to release it.

The members of the group are mostly professionals, specialists in Green and Brown Magic. The two leaders of the group, one a Green, the other a Yellow Magician, are neither ignorant nor gullible (in fact, most of the group are college graduates with years of training in magic). The leaders have designed a ceremony with great care to take advantage of every method in the books to insure successful spells. Two items are on the agenda—a curse and an exorcism.

The ritual begins with a circumlocution of the ring of staffs. Readings from the *Chronicles* follow. The ring is cleared of all hostile entities and thought patterns. They now begin to concentrate.

A series of litanies is read to all corners of the globe, conjuring and summoning gods, demigods, nature spirits, and the spirits of great men. They are called on to join the group and lend their powers. The language is flowery and emotional, the expression rhythmic; emotion is built up as the Druids feel *presences* outside the circle. The moonlight or *something* is doing strange things outside the ring.

An image of the *target* is built up until every member has it clearly in mind. The past history of the man is retold, his atrocities enumerated, his danger declared. The wishes of the group are announced to the beings assembled.

The *target* is not to be destroyed outright, for he is well skilled in repulsing ordinary attacks of Black and White Magic. Instead he will destroy himself by being forced to suffer personally and directly the consequences of his *every* magical act. An impenetrable shield is imaged around him, with a "psychic mirror" covering the insides. Every time he attempts to use magic for *any* purpose, his energy will bounce off this mirror and strike himself instead of his intended victim. This is known as the "Boomerang Curse," or as a variation of "the mirror effect," and it can be harmless or deadly, depending solely upon the future actions of the *target*. It is pure "poetic justice" in action.

Emotion has been aroused and the *target* visualized. The desire has been declared in detail. The group focuses its energy with another extemporaneous chant and *fires!* More than one member sees amorphous shapes winging across the sky toward the *target*.

The second ceremony is an exorcism of the area. Using similar techniques emotion is once again raised and brought to a peak. Incantations are read declaring the intent. All great violence both physical and psychic is forbidden. Neither right-wingers nor left-wingers will be able to sway crowds into rioting; all White Witches and Black Witches who attempt destruction will find their powers neutralized. Once again it is not destruction that is done, but rather a stripping of power from those who would destroy. Peace and quiet are to reign, at least until the next High Holy Day. With grand and sonorous tones the Druid magicians *fire* the energy produced.

After both ceremonies a statement of success or "follow through" is made, asserting that all has gone and will continue to go as planned.

The second ritual finished, the assembled entities are thanked and dismissed. The circle is broken and the hilltop cleaned of litter. The Druids head home satisfied, leaving the hilltop to the moon and the rabbits.

They have used principles unknown to establishment occultists. They have mixed Yellow, Green, and Brown Magic as well as the roles of magicians, wizards, and witches. The *targets* were unprepared for anything but traditional attacks.

Extensive postmortems are later done, with interesting results. Shortly after the rituals were done, the first *target* lost the best sensitive in his coven; not long afterward his entire group had fallen apart and he was close to bankruptcy. The exorcism seems to have been a rousing success, as well; reports from various covens throughout the area revealed total confusion and consternation. As for the politicians, despite the fact that excuse after excuse popped up, they were unable to stage one riot in the next three months, not in fact until after Candlemas!

It was, of course, sheer coincidence. Naturally.

Note the pattern so far: Supplication-Introduction, Reply from the Deity (or personified group-mind), Identification of Participants with the Deity (same note), Statement of Requests and Statement of Success.

The opening prayers at the Christian altar, the opening dance steps of the Hopi, the clapping of the Pentecostalists and Vodun people, the chanting of the Buddhists, the singing of praises to the Earth Mother, and the Conjuration of Beneficients; all these are Supplication-Introduction.

The readings of sacred scriptures, whether the Bible, the *Chronicles,* or incantations written for the occasion, or the recital of histories; these are all in effect a Reply from the Deity or Power being addressed.

The priest consecrating the Host, the Druids changing their ribbons, the Hopi, Pentecostalists, Vodun people, and Buddhists "possessed" by their deities; all have achieved Identification with the Deity concerned.

And every single group asks for specific benefits and ends with a positive assertion that their requests will be granted; thus, we have the Statement of Requests and Statement of Success.

Grab a scrapbook of comparative religions, and I'm sure you will be able to find more examples of this pattern. But what is the basic theory behind it and why is there so much diversity in its realization?

Almost every magical-religious ritual known performs the following acts: Emotion is aroused, increased, built to a peak. A *target* is imaged and a goal made clear. The emotional energy is focused, aimed, and fired at this goal. Then there is a follow-through; this encourages any lingering energy to flow away and provides a safe letdown.

How do the rituals we have seen so far reflect this pattern of emotional catharsis? As you can see there are actually two different but interlocking emphases going on in these rituals. Where the stress is upon achieving the *plug-in* to the deity we label it a "religious" ritual, and the *target* is a *theurgic* one—that of the ecstasy of possession. When the stress is upon wielding the powers obtained by a *plug-in* or by the creation of a *mini-Switchboard,* we call it a "magical" ritual, and the *target* is usually a *thaumaturgic* one—a particular objective result. As you have seen, it is often hard to separate one from the other.

Why so much diversity if everyone is after the same things? Simply because different people in different cultures, times, and places have different reactions to emotional stimuli. Something that makes one person cry may make another laugh. Something that makes one person feel sexy may just bore someone else. Remember the Law of Infinite Universes.

One of the basic stimuli used around the world to arouse emotion is singing and clapping. The chanting of words fraught with sacred meaning can inspire and arouse, or just the droning rhythm and vibrations of a mantra can hypnotize the singer or chanter. The use of rhythmic clapping, drumming, piping, singing, foot-stomping, dancing, chanting, or rattling can be highly effective in inducing hypnotic trances (not to mention direct associational effects). Don't forget that a hypnotized or entranced person is very easy to stimulate emotionally.

Some find that high and mighty phraseology, playing alternately on fears and hopes, despair and joy, is the stimulus that builds and releases emotion. But in a well-run ritual, *all* the senses are employed.

The clothing, altar, chalices, wands, mandalas, mudras, mantras, incense, wine, singing, music, candles, emblems, relics, foods, and the very familiarity of the ritual itself—all are important ingredients. Taste, touch, smell, hearing, sight, and memory are all manipulated by these props and window dressing to create the desired atmosphere. Every item should remind you of every other item, there must be no jarring notes in this symphony of mutually reinforcing stimuli, all must be associated with the emotion and goals aimed after. Thus the desired emotion can be easily built up, directed, and discharged.

Why bother? Granting that there are universal methods of controlling and discharging emotional energy, what good does it do?

On one level, the one most modern social scientists take, religion and magic serve useful social and psychological purposes by channeling powerful emotions and dissipating them "harmlessly," though they are quick to agree that these institutions can be dangerous as well, sending out hordes of Crusaders to destroy the Infidel Commies (excuse me, Saracens).

On another level, we all saw what Hitler and Stalin managed to do with their massive rituals of state-worship. We have a need to know the rules and techniques governing this kind of behavior, especially today when the truly demonic, rabid superpatriotism and ultranationalism that is sweeping the globe threatens the very survival of man.

But there is yet another way to look at all this, one which "respectable" scientists have always refused to consider: *What if magic really works?!?*

You will remember earlier how we showed that *any* change in the electrochemical balance of the human metabolism affects and modulates the radio waves broadcast and received by the nervous system, thereby affecting other patterns of energy whether minds or matter (this at least is our working theory so far). And emotions as we all know have a tremendous effect on the workings of the body and its nervous system. Therefore, a ritual (that is, *an order*) for the manipulation and control of emotions is really a ritual for the manipulation and control of changes in the neural system, and therefore . . . ?

Add something else here. A procedure has been noted which seems to accompany successful ESP and PK experiments. The subject gets very emotional either about the test or some aspect of it, increases this emotion along with self-confidence in a visualization of a successful test, then discharges this emotion either by calling cards or by throwing dice or some other device. The particular emotion involved is not at present correlated with success; apparently any strong emotion will do. Someday emotions will not be necessary at all; injections of adrenaline or other hormones may suffice. More experimentation with selection and control of emotions will probably have "amazing" results on test scores.

At this point I am invariably asked which rituals work best and can I recommend a good book of spells? After a great deal of study and practice, I am forced to stay that *the best spells and rituals are modern ones, written by yourself and designed to affect you personally, with your twentieth-century mind.*

As it was with different sects of beliefs, so it is with different times. A ritual which worked splendidly in 1580 probably won't work very well in 1980—simply because the things that aroused emotions and associations appropriate to the task at hand back in 1580 are not going to arouse the same emotions and associations in 1980. It's like trying to wear the same clothes from two different eras; people have grown about a foot taller and styles have changed. You would be both ludicrous and uncomfortable if you didn't modify the fit and cut of the clothing. And even if the stuff could be altered to fit, you would hardly be acceptable in public walking around in medieval clothing in 1980. Unless, of course, you belonged to some club or organization that habitually endorsed such anachronism; even then you would want it to be a Society for Creative Anachronism. Many of the Secret Mystery Schools you will run across are just such specialists in anachronism, without even the saving grace of creativity.

What they *will* do is attempt to train your mind to react to *their* rituals, and only theirs.

The study of rituals from alien cultures is useful mainly because it reveals the basic patterns that shape magic. To continue the clothing analogy, studying the fashions of other cultures would show that most clothing is designed for beings with four limbs and one head. Once you know this and have mastered the techniques of needle (the laws) and thread (the Three *M*'s), you are ready to begin designing your own garments to suit your individual taste and fancies.

Reciting old incantations from dusty books and following hoary rituals are likely to produce absolutely nothing in the way of effects (unless you accidentally *plug-in* to the *Switchboard*). While it would be worth your time to study the *theoretical* works of Crowley, most of his baroque-rococo rituals have rotten stage directions, along with the usual sexual references and occasionally dangerous practical jokes* that permeate the rest of his writings. And rituals from Africa, India, Tibet or South America may be unsatisfying unless you can establish a strong psychic link to the cultures involved.

So what kind of ritual *will* work? Here we find ourselves entering into the subject of *Thaumaturgical Design*. The phrase as you can probably imagine refers to *experimental design for Thaumaturgical Magic*. By this time everyone should remember what this word means, so I won't repeat the definition.

Thaumaturgical Design is a matter of designing magical rituals and techniques that will (a) work, (b) be easy to evaluate, and (c) not backfire; as well as solving the associated problems of creating proper evaluation techniques for feedback and correction. In short: how to make magic more useful and "scientific."

As you have seen throughout this book, magic is a very complicated subject, primarily because it deals with powers

---

* They are not booby traps for the experienced, who can understand the paradoxes involved, only for the beginner, who will take things literally.

of the human mind, an unruly beast at best. As soon as you begin to delve into Thaumaturgical Design you will begin to notice a bewildering number of apparently unsurmountable problems. So you won't feel like you're in the middle of a cliff-hanger, let us now grab our mountaineering equipment and get picky-picky-picky.

The first major problem is the Variable Problem. In most experiments you try to keep all variables constant except for one special one; in theory you can then separate its results from the others. Even in the other sciences this isn't as easy as it sounds, but in magic things get even stickier. For one thing, just *how many* variables are involved in magic, and when, and in what combinations? For that matter, how do we find out? Is it possible to separate some or all of these variables from one another? Right now, behind closed doors, unknown to the public, people are beginning to ask if it is *ever possible to isolate any variable in any science* without automatically warping the variable under consideration. Can we actually control any of these magical variables at all? Should we just ignore those we can't control or qualify?

Now in this book we have examined quite a few variables, including: emotions, associations, cultures, sensory stimuli, individual personality traits, conditions of the Ionosphere, bodily health of *agent* and *target*, distance between *agent* and *target*, training and skills of *agent* and *target*, patterns of ritual, drugs in the system, intelligence and flexibility, and many others. It should be clear by now that we will never know *all* the variables involved in magic; and by the Law of Infinite Data we should have figured this from the beginning. But by examining traditional occult beliefs and training methods, modern anthropological research and the findings of parapsychology and other Establishment sciences, we have been able to come to some tentative hypotheses and theories.

For example, we have found out that all magic and *psi* phenomena seem to be the result of *associations powered by emotions*. Whether you accept Kogan's work or not, it is clear that the associations modulate and direct the energy generated by strong emotions, sending this energy to affect other energy-patterns whether minds or matter. Thus, we have both internal and external variables involved.

We have all these variables inside the minds and bodies of the *agents* and *targets*. We have even more variables in the (postulated) physical universe between the two. In neither of these areas is sufficient data known. For the time being we are forced to adopt the position of professional statisticians who say, "Any variable that cannot be known, measured, or controlled should be ignored over the short run, but recorded as well as possible for later long-term analysis."

There are other problems though. There is that monster bug-a-boo, the Repeatability Problem. The ability to repeat an experiment and consistently get the same results has always played a major role in the myths of science. It is a test procedure based on the Law of Cause and Effect. Since the same actions under the same conditions should always be associated with the same results, therefore, if you cannot repeat an experiment exactly and get exactly the same results every time, then you are violating this law. All of which is perfectly true, except . . .

No experiment has *ever* been repeated under *exactly* the same conditions simply because the Universe(s) is constantly changing. For things like chemistry and physics this constant change is far too subtle and unimportant to affect their experiments (except in quantum mechanics, where Unrepeatability is *de rigueur*). But when you move into the biological and then the social sciences, this constant change begins to show up as a problem. When you get to the inner realms of the mind and of magic, this never-ending change becomes so gross in comparison to the subtle variables being studied, that you are virtually overpowered. When you are dealing with human minds, you can never exactly duplicate conditions from one experiment to the next.

What I had for lunch today will probably have little effect

upon my results when doing a chemistry experiment. But it will have an increasingly greater effect upon my digestion, my general body tone, the way I treat my colleagues, and my ability to make observations of a subtle nature. And if I tried to guess Zener cards on an upset stomach—forget it!

Should we bother worrying about the Repeatability Problem at all, then? Yes, we should. Not because, like J. B. Rhine, we are still trying desperately to prove something to the world; but because, like progressive scientists around the globe, we have left that problem behind and are trying to prove things to *our own satisfaction.* We need to try to control and repeat experiments in magic simply to increase our own efficiency in researching the subject. We need to attempt to repeat experiments so that we can receive feedback from our failures and occasional successes, so that we can make needed corrections. The fact that there are far too many variables for easy control and repeatability doesn't mean that we can't *try!* After all, we have to start somewhere. Let us begin by repeating those variables that we *can* control and eventually we will get enough data to control new variables.

Then there is the "This Experiment Will Self-Destruct In Ten Seconds" Problem. How can we be strongly emotional and believing during an experiment and still retain sufficient scientific detachment to make necessary observations? Both of these are absolutely vital if we are ever to make magic a truly experimental science, which we must do at least privately if we expect to get any practical use out of it.

One solution is the "hang your intellect at the door as you come in" approach known in literary criticism as the "suspension of disbelief." Basically this means that you arrange everything carefully beforehand, then do the experiment without a scientific thought in your head, then perform extensive postmortems afterward. This requires that the Thaumaturgical Design be absolutely foolproof.

Another method works well for those who are good at achieving artificial "disassociation" or a temporary "split personality." If *most* of your mind can concentrate on the experiment, while a tiny part remains aloof to observe, you might be able to generate enough emotion in the one part without affecting the other. This, however, is very difficult to do and takes years of training.

Another solution is to have hidden cameras, mikes, and other recording equipment running during the experiment so that (a) you don't have to think about it yourself, and (b) you have additional substantiation for subjective experiences or results. This begins to get us into the Equipment Problem. It is very difficult to devise equipment for measuring thaumaturgical variables without interfering with the experiment itself; because most measuring equipment in the field destroys what it measures, much as rabid skeptics can destroy ghosts by the generation of *Catapsi* static. In fact, the very knowledge that they are being measured is often enough to cause participants to revert to *Anti-psi* defenses.

This of course is a matter of technological progress in the production of proper observational equipment. There is also the problem of getting the proper ritual tools in this century, but we will discuss that shortly.

As you can see we have been heading so far into the general direction of the Evaluation Problem: What constitutes a success in a magical experiment? For example, suppose you cast a spell to make it rain next Monday and it did indeed rain. Most people might be satisfied with just that. But the thaumaturgist would want to know *why* it rained. Was it because of his spell? Or was it sheer coincidence? If it was because of the spell, what parts of the ritual were vital and what parts were irrelevant? Unfortunately, we do not as yet have the necessary statistical tools for handling such numerous, subtle, and interwoven variables and probabilities as occur in thaumaturgical experimentation. We will eventually though, and I'm not about to sit on my duff waiting for them.

Now comes the hairiest problem of all, the Twentieth-Century Problem: or, how do you do *magic*—of all things—

in a technological age? It's bad enough that nonmaterialistic concepts are derided nowadays, but when you add to this the fact that faith, emotion, and imagination are considered anti-social and "counterproductive" then you really start to have headaches. Magic and religion are considered "superstitions" and those who speak out in favor of either are quickly labeled "nuts" or "fanatics."

Also, where in the twentieth century are you going to come by swords, chalices, wands, altars, and all the other tradi-tional "tools of the trade" so useful to the old-time magician? All this ritual equipment has always been hard to get, but never more than now (have *you* tried to find a genuine virgin for a ceremony recently?). It may be for these reasons that so many are switching to modern systems of symbology in their spells and incantations, especially symbology from cybernetics and electronics. The thought of a "psychic magnet" or "psy-chic thunderbolt" is intriguing enough; have you ever seen a "psychic laser" in action? I have; it worked quite nicely.

Another solution for the practicing magician is to put together a small, portable "Instant Wizard Kit," consisting of a suitcase or carpetbag with various incenses, candles, candle holders, amulets, rings, dagger, chalice, wand if you have one, and whatever personal books you may use (it's always best to write your own *Grimoires*). Mine includes a small, collapsible table plus varicolored cloths for use as an altar when necessary. As for robes, simply get a bolt of rain-bow cloth and make a tabard out of it. All this should be more than sufficient for emergency house calls or for hikes into the hills for rituals of Green or Brown Magic. Remember that, if at all possible, the items used for rituals should be used for nothing else; this is the only way to build up the necessary associations in your mind between putting on your robes, raising your wand, using a special talisman, and so forth, and *doing Magic and nothing else*. After a while, even if you are tired, the mere unpacking of your equipment will strengthen you, and what was originally only placebo power will eventually become seemingly "inherent" power. Obviously for full-scale rituals you would need fancier equipment and a full lab, but your "Instant Wizard Kit" will come in quite handy on a surprising number of occasions.

Just remember, though, that *your most powerful weapon is your mind!* With training and experience, you should be able to perform any magic spell while stark naked, without a bit of equipment other than your will and imagination.

The mention of a lab, though, brings up another aspect of the Twentieth-Century Problem—distraction and noise. In today's crowded cities you can hardly go about raising demons in your living room without the neighbors complaining of the noise (I wouldn't recommend it anyway; demons are rarely housebroken). Not only that, but you can go crazy trying to tune out all the noise your neighbors are making, and the traffic outside, and the fire sirens on the other side of town. And you can't smell your incense over the smog, and you can't see your *target* building three blocks away for the pollution, and your constant coughing interrupts your concentration. Even if you live near hills, as I do, you can rarely escape the evidence of modern man—if it isn't city lights against the horizon, it's beer cans along the trail. Thus, it is advisable that you make concentration and hypnosis exercises the principal part of your training.

Then there is the fact that the population bomb has meant an incredible increase in pure static in the psychic realm. As far as we can tell, *psi* powers were originally evolved in cultures with low population densities; you can see from Chapter Three that dense urban areas severely limit possible telepathic communications. Cities are deadly in more ways than the obvious. A *total empath* must literally avoid cities like the plague; they are hellish cesspools of psychic pollution. Thus it is advisable that you find a place away from large numbers of people when you plan to experiment. If the *psi* researchers in Australia would bother to go a couple of hundred miles into the Outback to set up their labs, they would probably increase their results tenfold. I am personally planning on finding some cheap land in the Sierra or Rocky Mountains, setting up a home-lab combination that can only be reached by helicopter or horseback, with a view that reveals not a single trace of humanity. All this, just to get some physically clean air.

A minor aspect of the Twentieth-Century Problem, but perhaps a major one to you, is the finding and training of suitable partners or assistants. Though more people are willing to admit to an interest in the occult these days, most of them make poor helpers. For my part, I rather doubt that a magical worker of any sort really needs or deserves an assistant until he or she has been in the field for several years, so that they can actually offer their would-be assistants something solid in the way of training, instead of just passing on their own ignorance. Be wary of the one who walks up to you leering and saying "Hi there! How'd you like to be a High Priest(ess) and study *under me* ?" They are usually far more interested in exploiting their "assistants" than in teaching them anything about magic, mysticism, witchcraft, or anything else psychic.

If somebody shows up who wants to help you and you haven't the time (or confidence) to give them some quick basic training, just send them off to Silva Mind Control or some other clean system of magical technology. These days I'm recommending Silva highly since even though they hardly ever mention the word "psychic" (and never the word "magic") they give very good foundation work in psychic and magical techniques, in a brief time and at a cost (!) far below that of Scientology, Est or other such groups. You can send a student to Silva and have them return with body and soul intact.

You will have to track down your own colleagues. It will probably be a long and hard hunt before you finally find suitable associates. Your best bet is to get together with a small group of from two to ten others and have everyone train together, exercise together, study together (though you should of course have specialties), work and play together (after all, magic *is* fun, or I wouldn't bother with it). In short: try to live together with the rest of your "coven" or "commune." *Never, never, never use a partner you can't trust 100 percent.* Remember, you may be entrusting your body, mind, and soul to him.

But we still have the biggest problem of all: How to Design a Spell That Will Work! And I said, "Patterns," plural, in the title of this chapter, and so far we seem to have examined only one pattern. Let me hasten to correct the situation.

Start by reviewing the major purposes of the magical rituals we have seen so far: build-up of emotion, imaging of *target,* focusing, aiming, *firing,* follow-through. Is it as simple as it seems? No.

Most magical rituals that you may be familiar with are *active rituals* (curses, cures, rain-making, etc.), all involving the build-up and *discharge of energy.* But there are also little known, perhaps because less dramatic, rites called *passive rituals* for the build-up and *transference or storage of energy.* The rituals at the beginning of this chapter for *plug-ins* are mostly of this sort; people go to them because they feel depleted and in need of energy. Due to a lack of research, *passive rituals* are much more difficult to explain in mechanistic terms, but we will try. First, however, to make sure you understand the basic principles of *active rituals,* we will now design a few examples. This is what you have all been waiting for, so here goes:

How to Cast a Curse:

You have just decided that a local dictator has got to go. You had better have your mind made up for sure that you really want to kill him, because at this elementary stage of learning you don't have the skill to cause anything but unsubtle effects, if any.

The emotions will probably be hate and righteous anger. Therefore, you think of everything you hate about him, building up your anger, cherishing it. Obviously you already have associations involved (or you wouldn't be bothering) but start making a collection of everything you can that reminds you of (a) your emotions and (b) your *target*. If the colors red and black are appropriate, use them. If chartreuse and puce seem better, use them instead.

Get a good mental image of the *target* and what you want to have happen to him. Photographs are very good for this; you can burn them, stick pins in them, tear them, etc. Surround yourself with stimuli for every sense, using the multimedia approach. Write yourself an incantation that expresses your thoughts and desires for his welfare (I'm assuming throughout, reasonably I think, that most dictators are males). Fill your mind with only one thought—destruction to the evil one. Repeat it over and over again, keeping these things in mind simultaneously: (a) your anger and hate, (b) the image of the target, and (c) what *is* going to happen to them.

Once you can concentrate 100 percent upon these thoughts, they will begin to feed upon each other, spiraling upward in power, getting stronger and stronger until you can no longer suppress them. Wait as long as you can and then *consciously force the curse out of your mind and at the target.* This is the "firing," and unfortunately I know of no more accurate way to describe it. But you'll know it when it happens.

Quickly do a follow through, telling yourself that the curse has been successful, and then clearing and cleansing your mind of the whole subject. If the dictator is head of a country with a strong magical or psychic technology available, it might be a good idea to set up some shields to prevent backlash.

Naturally, this curse is included here only for the purposes of theoretical instruction. We wouldn't want dictators to become an endangered species, would we?

How to Cast a Garden Blessing:

You've just planted a garden and you want to make sure that the vegetables will be big and healthy. The most traditional color for this is green, but purple is often used as well. You should lie out in the garden, between the freshly planted rows. *See* how plump the tomatoes will look; *taste* how delicious the carrots will be, *smell* how pungent the herbs will be; *hear* the breezes blowing through the healthy leaves; *feel* the onions as you pull them from the ground. Shift the pseudo-sensory images from the future tense to the present.

Happiness, anticipation and love are good emotions to use for this kind of magic. If you have someone available, make love to them in the garden. Build up your emotions with rapid breathing or other activities until you can no longer control them. *Fire* your purple-green energies slowly and steadily into the ground beneath you. Do a follow-through, concentrating on your images and your expected success.

How to Cast a Cure:

These are tough, as you have to affect a body as well as a mind, but they can be done. Normally the emotion will be one of compassion, sympathy, or sorrow; all basically passive emotions and hard to work actively with. However.

As before, you get a good image of the *target* and the *target*'s present condition. Change that image until you have one of the way you want the *target* to look.

Collect the props and window dressing that remind you of curing, health, the body, etc. Fill your entire being with compassion and resolution that the *target will* be healed. Build up everything to the utmost peak and *fire!* Do a follow-through, repeating your conviction of success.

Cures often require multiple casting, and you should not expect overnight results. Often it takes as long to effect a recovery as it took for the *target* to get sick in the first place.

In all these various spells, you may find it useful to invoke the names of gods and goddesses traditionally concerned with the matter at hand. Thus, you may find yourself *plugging-in* to the *Switchboard* and picking up a little extra power. As you no doubt noticed, the spells were highly similar. To cast a spell involving something not mentioned, just pop the appropriate variables into their places in the pattern. Thus a desire for rain, with the sky for a *target* and rain for the intent would do quite nicely to raise a storm.

As I mentioned, though, some emotions are hard to handle in an active ritual. Sheer "tiredness" is probably an emotion, but if you're that tired, you won't be in any condition to do an active ritual. This is the point where meditation or your religion would come in. I usually go up to the woods to recharge my psychic batteries, and the passive ritual I use is very simple. I just sit there and concentrate on *absorbing energy*, from the trees, from the Earth Mother, from the *Switchboard*. I open all gates for positive Life-filled energy to fill me. Many people do this sort of passive ritual when they go camping, though I doubt if they do it consciously.

Curing offers us another area where passive rituals come in handy. Suppose the patient is very far away, or else is unknown to you—even though a friend may be vitally concerned. Obviously if you cannot teach the friend how to cast a cure, you can always *transfer energy from him to the patient*. After all, he has the emotions and associations; you need only tap and focus *his power*. In this sort of thing a mandala helps.

This is because we have two different spells going on, the one you are doing to guide your friend and the one your friend is doing to cure the patient. So it is your duty as the magician to form a linkage between the three of you. I have done it successfully, so it is not actually impossible. Difficult, yes . . . very.

In two of the cases of this sort I used the modern symbology of a "lens," generated by my mind to focus the energy that the patient could use. Whether *I* cured the patient, or my

Typical Passive Ritual Mandala
for Healing of a Stranger

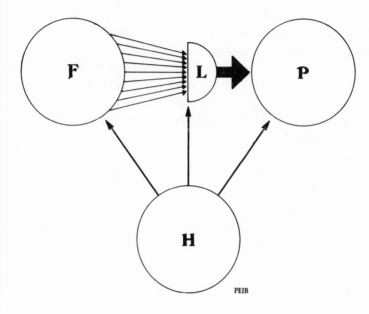

The circle with the letter "H" represents the Healer, that with the letter "F" represents the Friend(s), that with the letter "P" represents the Patient. They should be yellow, blue and red in that order. The half circle with the letter "L" represents the Lens and should be purple, as are all the lines coming from the Healer. The lines from F to L are blue, and the arrow from L to P is red.

friend cured the patient, or the patient used our energy to transfer to cure *herself* (normally, or by CPK); I haven't the slightest idea, *yet!* But these two patients are still alive, when they were supposed to be dead a year ago! And one of them lives 400 miles away and hasn't the slightest idea that I am doing anything!!!

In most passive rituals I find it useful to create a mandala of the emotion-target-desire and to quietly meditate upon it. But the whole subject is one I will have to look into more deeply in the next few years. I rather suspect that there will be connections with methods of using ESP.

However, I hope by this time that you have some idea of what I have been talking about. By this time you should be ready and able to design and execute your very own, tailor-made spells. If you can't, don't blame me; just go back to the drawing board!

CHAPTER EIGHT

Miscellaneous Ologies for Fun and Profit-cy!

As long as anyone can research or remember, people all over the world have tried out all sorts of ways to find out hidden knowledge about the past, present, and especially the future. Astrology, numerology, phrenology, bibliomancy, cartomancy, rhabdomancy, hydromancy, oneiromancy, crystallomancy, and a host of other "ologies" and "mancies" have been the result.

Everyone knows that "ology" at the end of a word means "the study of"; so that "astrology" means "the study of the stars" and "theology" means "the study of god(s)." But to find out why so many of these terms end in "mancy" and to find out some critical information about their origin, we are going to have to go back to Ancient Greece.

Way back then the word *mantis* first showed up, from the same root as "mania," and it meant quite literally what we call a "seer" or "prophet" of hidden things. The word "prophet" itself is Greek in origin (*prophetes* from *pro* meaning "forth" or "out" and *phanai* meaning to "speak"); it means a person who speaks out (usually for a god) or proclaims a revelation. Even though the two words can be equated today, back then a *prophetes* was not exactly the same as a *mantis*.

In any event, we soon had more specialists than you find at a convention of the American Medical Association. We had

"Iatromantis," or "healer seers," who could diagnose and cure illnesses. We had "Hieromantis," or "seers of sacred things." We had "Necromantis," or "seers of the dead." And no doubt many of them were Preyingmantis. All these forms of prophecy and divination (from "divine," a verb meaning "to find the godlike or sacred") became known as the "Mantic Arts," and as time went on and people discovered or invented new techniques of divination they would find a Greek or Latin word and tack "mancy" on the end of it to make a new term.

The study of ancient Greek religion (*do not, repeat NOT, confuse with the study of Greek Mythology*) is very useful to the student of magic. For example, it was in Greece that the arrival from Asia of *Shamanism* had an effect upon Western concepts of religion and occultism that radically changed the course of our entire civilization.

The evolution of the word "shaman" is fascinating in itself, but for those who are sick of linguistics by now, I will put the data in a footnote.* Shamans were predominantly the local witch doctors and medicine men for Asian cultures stretching from Finland to Indonesia. A shaman was usually a person of unstable mentality who received a "calling," customarily in a dream or vision, and often from some dead

---

* Shaman—Russian or Tungus *šaman* shaman. Buddhist monk, from Pali *samana*, Buddhist monk, from Sanskrit *śramana*, Buddhist monk, ascetic, from *śrama* fatigue, exertion, religious exercise—more at ASHRAM.

Ashram—Sanskrit *āśrama*, from *ā*, toward, near to + *śrama*, fatigue, exertion, religious exercise; akin to Sanskrit *śramyati*, *klāmyati*, *klāmati*, he gets tired, Old Irish *clam*, leprous; Welsh *claf*, ill; Breton *klañv*, *klañ*, Cornish *clāf*, ill, leprous—more at ACHARYA.

Acharya—Sanskrit *ācārya*, literally, one who knows the rules from *ācāra*, custom, rule of conduct, from *ācarati*, he approaches, proceeds, acts, from *ā*, toward + *carati*, he moves, goes; akin to Greek *o*— (in *okellein*, to run aground), Avestan and Old Persian *ā*, toward, Old English *ō*—, back, behind, Old High German *ā*—, Old Slavish *ja*— (in *jaskudī*, ugly)—more at WHEEL.

Wheel—Middle English *whel, wheel, whele*, from Old English *hweogol, hweohl, hwēol*; akin to Old Frisian *hwēl*, wheel, Middle Dutch *wiel*, Middle Low German *wēl*, Old Norse *hvēl, hjōl*, wheel, Latin *colere*, to cultivate, inhabit, Greek *kyklos*, ring, circle, cycle, wheel, *pelesthai*, to be, become, *telos*, end, Old Slavish *kolo*, wheel, Sanskrit *cakra*, wheel, *carati*, he moves, goes; basic meaning: to bend, turn. Does this remind you of *wicce*?

shaman who promised to bequeath his powers. The boy would then go into a retreat, fasting and performing ascetic exercises, and then seek out a master or teacher (dead or alive). His initiation often involved a change of sexual identity. By his training and renunciation of the flesh, he received many magical powers. The most important of these were (a) the ability to do astral projection at will, (b) healing of physical, psychological, and psychic illnesses, (c) obtaining knowledge of hidden things, (d) the attendant control of these things, and (e) an ability to compose songs, incantations, and poetry.

As the Greeks expanded along the northern shores of the Black Sea, practitioners and believers of shamanism began filtering into Greece from "Scythia" (the Greek term for everything north of Greece, which covers a lot of territory) mostly from about 800 B.C.E. to 500 B.C.E. This was the period when the most famous of the early *thaumaturgoi* made their reputations, with great miracles and wondrous prophecies. But it was what they preached more than what they did that had the greatest importance.

The idea that a man could separate his consciousness from his physical body and make journeys through the spiritual and physical worlds had a literally shattering effect upon Greek philosophy. All of a sudden man received an occult self of divine origin, and for the first time "soul" and "body" became separate and opposed. It was the impact of pure undiluted shamanism that set off the whole body-soul dichotomy that, combined with Greek concepts of pollution and blood-guilt, wound up creating the entire Puritan movement in the West. Ultimately the whole mess resulted in the warpings of St. Paul and the early Church Fathers. So, to a great extent, much of our modern religious and ethical system is founded upon what was probably misunderstood ESP.

Also the Greeks were among the first to clearly label and declare the connection between poetry and prophecy. Every *poietes* was considered a *mantis*, only in reverse. That is, a poet was a "seer" into the past, rather than the present or future. A poet was not just making up his stories; he was in contact with divine beings who revealed visions of past events to him, which he then turned into verse. The same word in fact is used in most Indo-European languages for poet and prophet; examples would be the Latin *vates*, the Gaelic *fili*, the Icelandic *thulr*. Throughout the Western world, Druids, shamans, and wizards were expected to be poets as well as prophets. Aristotle even went to the point of declaring *all* divination to be concerned only with the past.

Poets, like prophets, were often maimed or disabled, blind or deaf. This would seem to fit in well with the fact that people who lose one sense often compensate by developing their other senses, including ESP, to a very high degree.

We are told that the early Greek poets did not usually go into trance states, though some of the later ones did. When a poet was "inspired" ("breathed into") or "enthused" ("god-filled"), he would be possessed by beings who would reveal information to him. Many poets felt they did their best work while drugged or drunk (remember Coleridge and "Kubla Khan"?), but I'm not too sure of this, having seen some of the stuff I've produced while stoned (it *seemed* great at the time . . .). As it was, almost anybody bothering to write down a prophecy would do it in metrical form. It would seem, off-hand, that poets were merely(!) specialists in ESP and retro-cognition.

The Greeks also recognized different types of mantic trances, which will fit in well with what we already know. There was the "oracular possession trance" which was very similar to that of modern mediums and spiritualists; the breathing would slow and become husky, the voice would change in pitch, and the mantis would become "possessed" (that is, *plugged-in*) with some divine being who would then deliver messages. These were usually of such a cryptic nature that specialists had to interpret them to the customers, and often they were ambiguous or two-edged. But there are records of some very plain oracles given, which turned out to be exactly right. There was also the "frenzied hysterical possession trance" of the sort we have already met, with the Pentecostalists and Voduns. Those possessed were usually not professional *mantes,* but were mostly women and adolescents. The followers of Pan and Bacchus were the most famous examples. Then there was, of course, the "shamanistic" trance, involving meditation and astral projection. It was this last form of trance which Plato combined with his philosophy of "Rationalism," changing this disassociation-trance idea into one of mental withdrawal and concentration of the Socratic type, which fused with the so-called "Pythagorean" Mystery School which became a cornerstone of Western occultism. A serious reading of available texts concerning the early Greek, Egyptian, and Roman "Mystery Schools," by the way, will be an excellent antidote to a great deal of nonsense within Theosophy, Rosicrucianism and other esoteric groups.

All these different concepts of poets and prophets, divination and possession, healing and miracle working, spread throughout the Mediterranean during the Hellenistic Age (roughly 350 B.C.E. to 350 C.E.), mixing in with and absorbing those of Egypt, Persia, Rome, Babylon, Africa, and Germanica. The result was an incredible mishmash of different techniques for fortune-telling and divination (not to mention the incredible mishmash of religious concepts that eventually produced "Christianity"—not to be confused with the teachings of Jesus).

Astrology: Probably the oldest of the complicated Mantic Arts, astrology is still today fervently believed in and beloved by more people than any other method. There are tons of books on the market that will tell you more than you will ever want to know about the history and terminology of the science. And yes, we have to call it a science, since it is one of the most organized systems of knowledge known, though this does not necessarily imply its validity.

Astrology does not deal principally with the movements of stars; it actually is more a matter of the movements of various "planets" (including the sun and moon) through different constellations or star patterns. Honest astrologers will admit today that the stars and planets do not actually revolve around the Earth, and that the geocentric orientation of astrology is merely a convention.* As it was, they were thrown off by the discovery of Neptune, Uranus, and Pluto, and they are still trying to figure out how to fit these "new" planets into the schema. There is also the slight detail that in the past 5,000 years every single "Sign of the Zodiac" has fallen about one constellation behind its original position. As far as modern astronomy and physics are concerned, astrology has absolutely no connection with "reality," a point which may be totally irrelevant.

A "horoscope" is basically a picture of the way the sky looked at the time you were born, or at any other special moment. Very specialized books with reams of charts are necessary for all the calculations involved in casting a horoscope. This is because the variables involved include the precise locations and interrelationships between: the exact time of the subject's birth, down to the second; the precise longitude and latitude at the place of birth; eight planets, the sun and the moon; twelve "signs," or segments of the 360 degrees of the Zodiac; the "rising sign," or the sign that was coming over the horizon; the "midheaven," or the sign that was directly overhead; twelve "houses," or sections of the chart dealing with different areas of life; all the different angles between these variables (these are called "aspects" and can be 180°, 90°, 45°, 60°, 30°, $72\frac{1}{2}$°, etc.); different ways of dividing the chart into houses; and a few other *really* complicated factors. The mathematicians in the audience are welcome to figure out the total number of possible combinations of these variables. Each of these variables stands for

---

* There are heliocentric astrologers using various types of "sidereal" astrology, all of which are as confusing and contradictory as regular astrology.

different personality traits, expected events, and so on. So it would seem that we have a very exact system that could easily be tested for validity, right? Wrong.

This is because every planet, sign, house, and aspect has at least two, if not more, contradictory meanings that can play a role in the interpretation of the chart. Anyone can learn to cast a horoscope in a few hours with only two or three books and a lot of scratchpaper; I know because even *I* can do it. It's figuring out what the hell the chart *means* that gets tricky.

Many experiments have been done in attempts to "prove" or "disprove" astrology once and for all, and the results have been mixed, to say the least. I once handed the same chart to a dozen different astrologers and received descriptions of a dozen different people, not one of which came even close. But then experiments have been done in which the charts of selected individuals from widely different walks of life (including a streetwalker of life) were presented to professional astrologers to match with a list of the jobs; the success ratings were much higher than mere chance could account for. I have also seen astrologers give slanted interpretations of the same charts, depending upon whether they wanted to impress the customer positively or negatively. Charts drawn up for the week of the November 1972 elections indicate that a great deal of violence and skulduggery can be expected. I don't need astrology to tell me that.

If you are seriously interested in astrology, I would suggest you purchase a copy of Margaret Hone's *Modern Textbook of Astrology* (printed in England where astrologers are licensed by the government), and the *German* Ephemerides and Tables of Houses. Under no circumstances use those put out by the Rosicrucians; they are so full of misprints and mistakes that they are worthless. You might also invest in a computer; it'll save a lot of time in making calculations.

Ignore those mass-produced books that claim to give you a year's predictions based only on your sun sign, and this

includes those newspaper columns—no matter how pres-
tigious the authors. This is simply because there are more
than twelve kinds of people in the world. At the very least
you "need" at least three different things: your sun sign,
moon sign, and rising sign. You can also ignore those "Com-
puter-Horoscope" companies because even though it is easy
to program a computer to print out a proper chart, they are
incapable of interpreting *anything* properly. Remember that
computers are only the big-dumb-stupid-but-*fast*-adding-
machines we mentioned earlier. They are not as yet capable
of handling the paradoxes and contradictions inherent in
astrological interpretation. What some of these companies do
is to run up your chart, then go to a file where they have 366
sets of interpretations and predictions; they pick the one for
your birthday, type your name on top, and send it to you.
Just as with drugs, the old slogan applies: "Know your
dealer."

You might just have a friend (or even yourself) run up a
chart for you that you can carry in your pocket or purse. Then
the next time some nut runs up to you and says "Far-out-
Harvey-Krishna-What's-Your-Sign?" you can whip out your
chart and bury him with a long technical discussion. Once
will usually cure them.

Despite the many famous and intelligent people who
fervently "believe" in astrology, including famous scientists
all over the world, if we are to be fully honest in stating an
opinion about astrology it has to be: Insufficient data.

Bibliomancy: This is the art of opening books (Latin
biblus), especially sacred ones, at random and seeking out
special information from the lines first glanced at. This can
be done with any book: the Bible, dictionaries, encyclopedias,
textbooks, or works of fiction. Interpretation is solely up to
the bibliomancer. It can be fun, and as I am typing this
manuscript, I am now going to open some books at random

to see what I get in response to the question: "What about my book?"

"But the fish gate the sons of Asnaa built. They covered it, and set up the doors thereof, and the locks, and the bars."
—Second Esdras 3: 3
Douay Bible

"Lo! as for those who traduce virtuous, believing women who are careless, cursed are they in the world and the Hereafter. Theirs will be an awful doom."
—Koran, 24: 23

"For neither did his brethren believe in him."
—John 7: 5
King James New Testament

"Litharge: a fused form of lead monoxide."
—Webster's Dictionary

"One-sidedness means thinking in terms of absolutes, that is, a metaphysical approach to problems. In the appraisal of our work, it is one-sided to regard everything as either all positive or all negative."
—Quotations from Chairman Mao, Ch. 22, Para. 26

" 'Probably some of the professor's notes were stolen,' he said."
—Daughter of Fu Manchu

I was a little worried about the quote from the Koran, but it would seem that the last answer may come closest of all; which would lead to some interesting conclusions as to the superiority of Fu Manchu over the Bible, at least for bibliomancy. However, the reader is invited to draw his own interpretations.

Cartomancy: This is the use of cards for divination; fans of Tarot cards will find this their home. Theories about the Tarot are varied, but most occultists agree that whatever they were originally (probably a book of pictorial instruction in occultism for those who couldn't read) they were soon used for fortune-telling. Our modern playing cards were developed from the Tarot cards, and the use of modern cards in divination is primarily a cross between the old Tarot meanings and numerology. There are lots of new designs of Tarot cards and lots of books on the subject. I personally prefer Case on theory and Waite on divination methods.* If you really want to, you will have no difficulty finding out all sorts of ways to manipulate and arrange the cards for fortune-telling. The matter of their validity or value is another question entirely. Some people are very good; most are miserable at it.

Crystallomancy: This is "crystal-ball-gazing," or "scrying," pure and simple. You just take a sphere of glass or plastic that is perfectly clear and stare into it until you see something. Other devices used include curved lenses and mirrors ("speculomancy"), or bowls filled with water ("hydromancy"), ink ("atramentamancy"), blood ("hemomancy") or any other available liquid. Supposedly the sphere or pool will eventually get cloudy and murky after a while and you will see images within these clouds. This is the sort of "fortune-telling" most connected in the public mind with (a) the "Gypsies," and (b) fraud. The Gypsies were far from the first people to use this system (they get blamed for too much anyway—for much the same reason "hippies" and "bums" get put down—simply because they are a freewheeling subculture at odds with the established norms). Also I have seen crystallomancers come up with some very accurate results, while in my presence, even though I could not see a thing going on in the sphere (and without giving anything away myself). I have also seen quite a few people blow it entirely.

*   *   *

* *See* Bibliography

Dactylomancy: "Dactylomancy? Dactylomancy?" Here is one that hardly anybody has ever heard of, yet it is the ancestor of some of today's most popular methods: "Table-tipping" and the "Oui-Ja Board." Dactylomancy involved the erection of a tripod (supposedly to duplicate the famous one at Delphi) which was placed in a large basin. Around the basin were written the letters of the alphabet. After suitable prayers, consecrations, and rituals had been performed, the tripod would move (supposedly by itself) toward different letters to spell out the answers to questions, while the diviners rested their fingers on it. That is where we get the "dactyl" in dactylomancy, because the root is Greek for "finger" or "digit" (don't confuse with "dactylogy"—that's the hand-language used by the deaf and dumb—something worth studying just for the research into mudras). Or sometimes the dactylomancers would hang rings from the edges of the tripod top, and note which letters were struck by rings as the tripod twirled.

Most methods of "table-tipping" involve a group of people who sit around a table with their fingers resting lightly on the tabletop while questions are asked. The thumping of the table as it "moves" up and down, or the direction it may take off to, can be used as "answers" to the questions posed.

The most popular form of dactylomancy today is that of the Oui-Ja Board. The name comes from the French and German words for "Yes-Yes," and the board usually consists of a listing of the alphabet, the numbers from zero to nine, and the words "Yes," "No," "Maybe," and "Good-bye." A small triangular piece of wood or plastic with three very short legs (called a planchette) is touched by the fingers of those using the board and is allowed "to move by itself" over various letters, numbers, and words. Sometimes a small pendulum is held over the board for the same purpose; this has the extra advantage that the up-down, right-left, clockwise-counterclockwise movements of the pendulum can also be tossed into the interpretation pot. The Oui-Ja Board is quite plainly labeled today as a tool for the release of "psychic," "ESP," "supernatural," or "spiritualistic" powers—depending upon the manufacturer and buyer. It is often denounced as a "tool of the Devil" or "Black Magic" because the messages spelled out are often nasty, spiteful, or downright obscene. In my opinion, if genuine ESP is involved at all, all this proves is that the *users* have dirty minds, at least subconsciously.

Hepatoscopy: This is divination by examining the livers or other internal organs of living beings. When done with humans, it is often called anthropomancy. It used to be very popular, but is now out of vogue. This is a pity, as I can think of several people who have entrails I should like to examine.

Necromancy: This is one of the most romantic and famous words in all occultism. It is divination by "speaking" with the dead. Modern spiritualists are all necromancers, whether they know it or not. The word got its lurid reputation mostly because it was considered highly dangerous and sinful, not to mention impolite, to raise the dead just to ask them stupid questions. For some reason the dead have always been credited with having all sorts of knowledge; not only about the past, which would figure, but also about the present and future. It is interesting to note that the rituals for necromancy were always rituals for *plug-ins,* highly specific as to which person would be contacted and as to how the *circuit* would be input. The extraordinary knowledge ascribed to the dead fits in nicely with our previous discussions about the *Switchboard,* but all this stuff is just silly superstition and nonsense. Obviously.

Numerology: Now here's another biggie in the world of divination. The manipulation of numbers, and later geometric concepts, became as popular as astrology and soon was interwoven tightly. Because every society soon associates certain numbers with elements of its culture, and because the manipulations are arithmetical, and therefore, highly predictable, numerology has become an integral part of magic and mysticism. We are all used to saying that "good things come in threes" (bad things too) or "seven is a lucky number." Most books on occultism will give you a rundown on the "meanings" of the numbers from zero to thirteen and how to manipulate them.

All this would be great if it weren't for one small detail: Numerology's claims of "universal meanings" of various numbers just don't hold water. Modern numerology is a product of our Indo-Aryan culture and of our recent (about 400 years old) obsession with mathematical patterns as the ultimate proof of *anything*. To the Navaho, for example, it is the number four and not three that is the "magic number"; in some cultures it is six or eight.

Although the early Greeks were the first to be overwhelmed by the uses of mathematics, it was not until the late Middle Ages that philosophers began to insist that anything which could be mathematically proven *had* to be so in the physical world. There is, of course, no real reason why the universe should fit our human concepts of mathematics, except for our egos. The scientists soon restored mathematics to its proper place in scientific investigation; that of an organizing method for handling data received from observation and experimentation. But the occultists, with their normal disdain for "profane" science, puttered along several centuries behind, still believing that "reality" must be *made* to fit into their favorite mathematical patterns. Even today in the social sciences we have many researchers who get very upset when they find out that real people act as individuals instead of as elements in their equations. Here again we see the time lag between the sciences. As far as the use of mathematics is concerned, modern occultism is still in the Middle Ages, insisting that numbers have absolute meanings.

Western numerology also got very confused when we switched from Base-12 counting system to our present Base-10, or Decimal system. Have you ever noticed that we count in English "nine, ten, eleven, twelve, thirteen, fourteen . . ." instead of "nine, ten, oneteen, twoteen, threeteen, four-teen . . ."? It's the same thing in German and other Northern European languages; there are separate names for eleven and twelve that do not match the rest of the counting system. This is because we used to count from one to twelve instead of one to ten. The reason that thirteen was "unlucky" was because it was one more than the number of "perfection," that is, twelve (which is divisible by one, two, three, four, and six). For the same reason eleven was considered "unlucky" be-cause it was one *less* than perfection. Thinking about it logi-cally, you would expect that nowadays nine and eleven would be the "unlucky" or "evil" numbers because they are on either side of our present number of "perfection" ten. Some numerologists and occultists made this switch; others didn't. So now everyone is confused.

The nice thing about numerology, though, is that it is even more flexible than astrology. Any number can be made to mean anything, depending upon how you manipulate it. Get a book or two on numerology (or borrow your ten-year-old's arithmetic book which will have lots of "tricks" and "games" in it, most of which the numerologists have stolen), and a telephone book. You can have a lot of fun analyzing the "mystical" significance of various telephone numbers and addresses. We did it once with a computer-read-out of random numbers, and for a while the computer seemed to be giving us some great "revelation," but it turned out to be a demand for prettier programmers.

Provided that you don't go overboard, numerology can occasionally offer useful hints on window dressing for rituals

—for a ritual of unity you would burn one candle, for a spell of separation you might wear two different colors, etc.

Before we leave the subject, I should admit that I have met numerologists who made remarkably accurate statements "based" upon their numerology. I have met many more who were lousy.

Oneiromancy: This is divination by interpreting dreams, and goes way, way, way back. All sorts of systems have been invented for interpreting dreams, from those of the Egyptians and Babylonians to those of Freud and Jung. Since most spontaneous cases of ESP occur during dreams, it is not totally unlikely that oneiromancy may have some basis in fact. The problem, of course, is that no matter how important your dream may be, the way you interpret it will determine everything.

In this field, too, even more than in hepatoscopy, there is a lot of tripe on the market, ranging from a million versions of "Irving's Book of Dreams" to the latest soggy-dream theories of the Neo-Freudians. As mentioned before, anything can be made to correspond to anything; it is the usefulness of the associations that is critical.

It is said that one day Freud was giving a lecture to a group of his graduate students, puffing away upon a huge black cigar as he spoke. As he got into the subject of sexual symbolism in dreams, he began to notice every eye in the room riveted to his cigar. He then pulled it out of his mouth, blew a huge cloud of smoke at the class, and as they choked he held it up and said, "And another thing, gentlemen. We must always remember . . . that sometimes a cigar . . . is just . . . a cigar."

Then we have such things as *Palmistry* and *Phrenology*, involving the "reading" of palms or bumps on the head. My investigations into this show that the data received and reported is usually of the "Sherlock Holmes" variety, rather than anything psychic. Remember when Sherlock would look at the dirt on a client and then tell Watson where the man came from? Watson would always be astounded and ask Sherlock how he knew what kind of dirt it was. To which Holmes would reply, "Sedimentary, my dear Watson, sedimentary."

Rhabdomancy: This is divination by sticks or rods, and is also a method that goes back beyond the Egyptians. Most people are familiar with it under the name "water-witching," though forked twigs and pendulums have also been used for finding minerals and oil and a host of other items. We've come a long way from the old sticks and rocks on strings; today rhabdomancers use devices made of a multitude of different materials (ranging from complicated gadgets of copper and platinum wiring to bent coat hangers and thread spools).

Rhabdomancy has a fairly solid foundation of evidence by now, thanks to the efforts of especially *talented* people such as Henry Grouse and others. Some are even able to run miniature rods over *maps* of land and succeed in finding water and minerals. I have had many returning vets from Vietnam tell me how they would use coat hangers or branches as divining rods to hunt for mines, booby traps, ammo dumps, and underground shelters; often with the consent and help of superior officers (in fact, I was told that they even got help from occasional experts sent out by the U.S. Parapsychological Corps). The U.S. Department of Agriculture and other federal geologists are continuing a running battle with the "dowsers" that may never end, but members of the U.S. Army Corps of Engineers just continue quietly to use their rods. Sewage and electrical conduits in a dozen major cities across the country as well as in Europe are traced by rhabdomancers as a matter of course. All in all, it would seem that this is the one "mancy" with the most support behind it, primarily because it has results that are easily checked, highly practical, and obviously only examples of another way to use ESP or hypercognition. And it works, too!

Sortilege: This all-purpose term comes from the Latin roots for "a lot or gamble" and "to gather" (*sortis* plus *legere*); it now means divination by the casting of lots, dominoes, sticks, stones, dice, bones, and other small objects. This is really most common in nonliterate cultures where the patterns formed by the falling objects are given special meanings. A large number of gambling superstitions come from confusions with sortilege interpretations. For that matter, the use of dominoes for fortune-telling is still popular in some parts of the country.

Perhaps the best developed system of sortilege ever invented, and now becoming popular in the United States, is that of the *I Ching* ("Book of Changes"), a Chinese collection of interpretations for the patterns formed by falling coins or sticks. The book is actually a sacred scripture for many people, and bibliomancy can be done quite successfully with it, since it is full of good, common-sense advice. I myself often have used the *I Ching*, and I have kept a scrupulous record of my questions, interpretations, and later events. So far, over the past few years, the *I Ching* has a very high batting average indeed. There are many editions available now, complete with instructions, though I am told and believe that you should really learn ancient Chinese and read it in the original. My favorite translation is by Gia-Fu Feng, who also has a very nice version of the *Tao Te Ching* (see Bibliography).

About the only system of divination we haven't included so far is *Augury,* the art of taking anything and everything as a "sign" whenever you happen to be in need of a "sign." You trip over the dog on your way out the door; this is a "sign" that you will have a bad day. Or a new dog.

Now throughout this chapter we have examined various methods and techniques that have been designed to reveal the Unknown. In every case wishful thinking, fraud, hypnosis, hallucination, or cultural conceit can account for the majority of results. But we still have that small minority of situations where the "ology" or "mancy" seems to work! How?

It is my personal opinion that *none* of these systems has any value at all *in itself alone;* but rather that they provide props, window dressing, orientations, devices, and meditational techniques that a *talented* person can use, for the exercise of any *psi* powers he or she may have. *The value of all these methods lies in the users, not the method.* If you have genuine *psi,* then you can use anything: astrological charts, crystal balls, Tarot cards, willow wands, or entrails. If you have no *talents* then none of these systems will be of the slightest use to you. It's just that some *talented* people feel more comfortable with one kind of prop rather than another.

Then again, there is Carl Jung's "Principle of Acausal Synchronicity," explaining how similar but apparently unrelated events may nonetheless still be connected. There are enough different cultures in the world who have this as part of their magical systems that perhaps a *Law of Synchronicity* should be added to the other magical laws.

Remember the *Web.* The physical Universe (assuming it's there) is a huge *Web* of interlocking energy, in which every atom and every energy wave is connected with every other one. The farthest star in the sky has *some* influence on us, even if only gravitational; the fact that this effect is too small to measure with present equipment is totally irrelevant. All energy is interwoven with all matter; this is the *Web,* the pattern to end all patterns, continually changing and continually the same.

The noise I'm making while typing is changing the energy balance in my vicinity in millions of ways I can't even begin to guess at. The effect may only be "local" but is a part of the *Web.* Our minds, too, are a part of the *Web,* and huge as the *Switchboard* seems to us, it is only a very small pattern within the *Web.*

If you can use your innate *psi* to *plug-in* to either the *Web* or the *Switchboard,* you can then interpret it any way you want and still get valid results. It may be that someone thousands of years ago made a *plug-in* and returned with the information that charting the movements of the stars could be used to produce analogs to future human behavior, and thus astrology was born. The same may go for all the other Mantic Arts.

Or perhaps we should call them RoMantic Arts!

Indeed it would not be too bad an oversimplification to state that the major aim of mystics is not to "join" or "unite" with the *Web,* but to achieve full realization of the fact that *already* all of us are united within the *Web.* Similarly the major aim of a magician is to gain understanding (by whatever means necessary) of the structure of the *Web* and his place within it, so that he can manipulate strands of it to suit his purposes and produce desired results.

CHAPTER NINE

Conclusions and Suggestions for Future Research

> *"Laughter is not at all a bad beginning for a friendship, and it is far the best ending for one."*
>
> —*Oscar Wilde*

Magic we have seen is a very interwoven and complicated subject. In this book we were forced by the limitations of human language to present items one at a time, in isolation; * with the total interrelationships only hinted at. In the hope that it will help to tie things together a bit more, let us review each chapter.

In the Introduction I presented a bit of my personal history and qualifications. We made a fast survey of the field of books on occultism now available and found them sadly lacking. I told you about my attitudes toward secrecy and absolutism. We discussed Occam's Razor and the interdisciplinary method. Then the fun started.

In Chapter One we examined the Laws of Magic, worldwide principles of occultism. We found that most of them fitted nicely with what we know of the human mind, if not so neatly with formal Western Aristotelian logic. This chapter may offer some new insights to anthropologists attempting to construct theories of "primitive" magic and religion.

* *Dann haben die Teile wir in der Hand, fehlt leider nur das geistige Band?*—GOETHE, *Faust.*

In Chapter Two we started out with that master linguist, Professor H. Dumpty. By the end of the chapter he was still securely seated upon his wall; as I suppose should have been expected. We did some digging and saw that the words "occultism," "science," "mysticism," and "magic" were not so complex and opposed as most people are led to believe.

In Chapter Three we made a lot of conservative parapsychologists upset. We gave definitions for various types of *psi* phenomena that are today quite acceptable. Then we went into occultism, ethnography, spontaneous reports, and personal experiences and found all sorts of new phenomena; all of which could be fitted into the standard *psi* systems of classification, merely by extending those systems logically. We added the new concepts of Atomic-Psychokinesis, Hyper-cognition, and *Anti-psi*. We saw how the interdisciplinary method could be used to throw new light upon old problems. We discussed some of the more important variables involved in *psi* and noted that they were the same as in magic. Then we looked at some work by a hard-core physicist, indicating even more evidence for a mechanistic explanation for *telepathy* and other *psi* activity, with the critical variables being associations and emotions. Then we noted that almost every magic ritual is designed around these same two variables.

In Chapter Four we examined the Eastern system of occultism known as Tantra. After a short history lesson, we examined Tantra's major aims—control of emotions and associations. We looked at the "Three *M's*" and saw how the Tantrists used them to achieve their aims, as well as glancing at the Western analogs. We noticed that Tantra holds to all the Laws of Magic though it uses them for theurgic rather than thaumaturgic goals. We looked at some of the exercises and associated practices connected with the training and practice of Tantra, many of which can be done by Westerners. And we discussed how moralistic occultists and theologians smeared the reputation of Tantra.

Which led us into Chapter Five, a discussion of the myths

of "Black Magic" and "White Magic." We found that the distinction was not warranted, especially by thaumaturgists. We discussed the confusion between concepts of witches, wizards, and magicians, and saw again how meddling moralizers botched up the whole area. We saw that color associations are predominantly culturally determined and that there are no inherently "good" or "evil" colors. We saw how the Christian Church invented the Devil and later the myth of Satanism. We discussed various groups calling themselves Lodges, Brotherhoods, Covens, etc., of both the "Left-Hand Path" and the "Right-Hand Path"; those who were not fraudulent were confused, as were most of the concepts involved. We dabbled in the "psychology of darkness" and examined the "aura." We listed a different classification system of colors, based upon *acts* not *ethics,* upon areas of study, not religious or egotistical bigotries. This was the chapter that probably upset the most Establishment occultists.

In Chapter Six we went from the mud to the stars. The placebo effect was explained and its place in real magic delineated. Then, based on the one hypothesis of constant mutual telepathy, we built the theory of the *Switchboard.* By adding in bits and pieces from different sciences and schools of occultism, we found that the *Switchboard* could offer more plausible explanations for a host of "supernatural" phenomena and beliefs. I will repeat once again, that *this is only a theory;* it will be scrapped as soon as I find a more useful one. Then we went to the Horror Movies and, using both mundane and unusual explanations, found that traditional monsters weren't as horridly impossible (impossibly horrid?) as we might have thought. Once again the usefulness of the interdisciplinary method was shown, in sparking new *speculations on explanations.*

In Chapter Seven I gave away the "secret of secrets," or so some would think. We looked at several magical and religious rituals from majority and minority traditions. We noted a common pattern running through all of them, that of *control and manipulation of emotional energy and associations.* We then glanced briefly (due to a scarcity of data) at the differences between active rituals and passive rituals. We discussed some of the major problems of Thaumaturgical Design and hinted at the complexities involved (the hint was not because of a wish to keep anything secret—it's just that a full description would take another book, and probably will someday). For those who were really interested in such things we gave you simple, clear-cut instructions on how to cast various spells. *Until you have done your homework though, don't expect instant success.* The window dressing and props are completely up to you, and even though they are almost the most important part of the spell, *you will have to figure out your own personal versions, based upon your own personal association patterns.*

Chapter Eight was not really an integral part of the book. The only reason I included it was that the area of divination and "fortune-telling" is probably the murkiest in all modern occultism. There is more nonsense on the market about these subjects than about all the other areas of occultism put together. Hopefully, you learned one thing from the chapter, that the various "ologies" and "mancies" are merely props and window dressing for the operation of psychic or magical powers by genuinely *talented* people. Most of them seem to have no absolute validity in themselves (but then hardly anything does in the world of magic) but they are fun to play with and have been known to work with surprising regularity.

So now we are back to Chapter Nine. We have summarized each chapter and now perhaps we should make some conclusions about the book as a whole. This book is the sum total of my personal theories of magic; that is why it is subtitled as it is. It is only an *introduction* to Yellow Magic, simply because I am just beginning to get ready for *real* research. These are my *theories,* they fit my data received, they work for me. *They are not absolutes.* Neither is this a "fully scientific treatise" in the standard meaning of the phrase. In order to make it one, I would have to include enough footnotes and citations to double or triple the size of the book.

I do *not* hate Religion. But I do object violently to the abuses that have been committed in the name of religion. The fact that I have knocked Christianity more than the other religions around is due to two factors: (a) The Eastern religions have never been as violent as the Western religions, and (b) by various accidents of history it was the religion later called Christianity which, of all the Western religions, had the most opportunities for cruelty and destruction during the periods of history covered. It was not until the rise of the modern religions of Fascism and Communism that Christianity was surpassed in killing power, and that was only because the new religions were more efficient.

I am *not* anti-scientific either. I am fully aware of the tremendous advances in human knowledge made possible by modern scientific research. What I *have* objected to is the modern worship of science as an infallible source of truth endowed with "supernatural" powers over mortal men. I have attempted to show that science is as likely as any other human endeavor to make mistakes, though some people might think that I went a bit too far in my attempts.

Another point on magic and morals: I have not said that the use of magic should be amoral, but that the attempts to create a theoretical structure for magic should be. In any technology, we should try to keep morality out of our research and theorizing methods (though this does not give us an excuse to do immoral acts in the name of "pure science") and inject it as far as possible into the uses we make of the results of those methods. Only thus can we expect to get any sort of sensible and humane technology for handling the magical arts and sciences.

However, I hereby specifically refuse and disclaim all legal or moral responsibility for damages—mental, physical, emotional, spiritual or psychic—caused by the ignorant, clumsy or malicious use of any data contained herein. Evil acts cannot be prevented by keeping the public ignorant.

The "mechanistic," "profane," or "blasphemous" explanations I have offered still stand as my opinions. And I am not alone in thinking that this approach may be the best. At least one well known occultist, Sybil Leek, put it this way on one occasion:

Actually the best way for seeing psychic phenomena is without all this terrible veil of mysticism—when you don't have to put on a gramophone record with a hymn before you can get into a room to have a seance. In short, the time has come when we don't have to dress psychic awareness up in the guise of being a religion. It is *not* a religion. We don't have to dress it up as anything more than what it is—a part of you, or at least of some people. . . . But I do believe that I have a peculiar metabolism, something happens, which causes these phenomena. It's like setting a computer into action only I am the computer. . . .

And whether scientists like it or not, whether occultists like it or not, science and occultism are gradually going to get together until they are working in parallel. That's when we'll get some advances.

—Interview in *Psychic,* November, 1969

There are still more reasons why as many people as possible around the world should have access to the sort of information this book contains. Part of them have to do with a Top-Secret Government organization known, among other names, as the United States Parapsychological Corps. The Corps was an outgrowth of the teams of astrologers our generals hired during World War II to tell *us* what Hitler's astrologers were telling *him.* Then somebody found out that the Russians were doing experiments with telepathy between orbiting cosmonauts and the ground.* And the British had the head start on everyone in psychical research. Suddenly the idea occurred that *a spy who could read minds would be invaluable,* and the concept of "ESPionage" was born. Who came up with the idea first we will never know; but by this time, every major

* Something *we* just started in February of 1971.

nation in the world has a *Psi* Corps composed of researchers and "volunteers" working upon applying parapsychological phenomena to international politics and intranational control.

In the United States, for example (actually the United States is the country I have the most data about because it is within my range), "recruits" are made of various psychics, occultists, adepts at psychokinesis, and others with *talents* or knowledge wanted. The "volunteers" have little or no choice in the matter. Then they are trained, primarily by methods of hypnosis, sleep-teaching, and out-and-out "brainwashing," to increase their powers and to use them only for the United States. In the United States itself the major training centers are at the American University in Washington, D.C., the headquarters of the National Security Force (our internal CIA) known as the "Citadel" in South Carolina, some coal mines in West Virginia, and an ultrasecret training center in the Nevada desert, just outside the perfect town for testing psychokinesis and ESP.

The Russians also have an equivalent organization, "recruited" and trained by similar procedures. Their training centers are in Moscow, Kiev, Leningrad, and Stockholm. The British have been the most practical; their major center is near Monte Carlo. A point I find most amusing is that while Red China does not have a *Psi* Corps (and is looked down upon for that reason when it comes to ESPionage), it has some of the best, damned magicians in the world. The Chinese didn't invade Tibet and carry back scores of apprentices for nothing!

By the way, so that no government agents will be breathing down my neck, I will explain that there have been no security "leaks." The data I have has been picked up over the years from both published and psychic sources. It is all "hearsay evidence" if that comforts you. It doesn't comfort me, since I give it a probability rating of near 90 percent.

When I was small, my dad taught me never to trust a politician further than I could throw him. And I'm rather scrawny. I am aware of the fact that this information may only feed our national paranoia, but on the other hand, the price of liberty is still eternal vigilance. Today the battles are being fought for men's *minds* not their bodies. If an enemy spy or American traitor had a gun in his hand, you would not think of going up against him barehanded. The data and theories presented in this book should give everyone the necessary skills to defend himself.

That little spasm of paranoia over, we can now continue our summation and conclusions. Several interesting areas of new research have been proposed: What are the effects of physiological and glandular changes upon the electromagnetic waves broadcast by the human body, on various parts of the e-m spectrum? Why is there no unclassified research in the United States of the sort that Kogan has done? What is the real origin of the Indo-Aryan root *mag?* Exactly *how* is incoming sensory data transformed into patterns? What is the fundamental mechanistic basis, if any, behind the *clair senses?* Does astral projection involve real APK of subatomic particles? What determines the way incoming ESP data is input? Do bird and whale migrations involve *Animal-psi?* How do you separate CPK from the placebo effect? How about some more research into APK, Hypercognition, and *Anti-Psi?* Must we use emotion-free cards in ESP experiments? Why can't the application of Thaumaturgical Design to parapsychology give results 10–20 percent higher than chance, instead of 1–2 percent? Why are we twenty years behind the Russians in *psi* research? Can we narrow down the probable wavelength of telepathy? Will lead and mercury shielding stop Kogan's wavelengths? Why not go out into the country for researching instead of in the cities? Why no research into the psychology of shape? Can a red-blooded American boy perform *Kāma-kali* without blowing it? Exactly what *are* the electromagnetic properties of human neural cells? Exactly what *are* the full effects of drugs upon the mind and body? What is hypnosis really? How can we keep morals out of our theories yet in our applications? Exactly which items are associated in people's minds and for what reasons when they create demons (that is, why pick scales and fangs and furry legs)? How will we ever find out what psychic research our government has done? Why do we have the color associations we do in our culture? What is the exact nature of the placebo effect and how does it work? Why are no telepathy experiments being done with dolphins? What are the interrelationships between mob psychology and psychic *circuitry?* Why are "lunatics" most active during the full moon? How can we solve the various problems posed in our discussion of Thaumaturgical Design? Why do some divination props work better than others for particular people? And if you find these questions (or the book as a whole) confusing or disturbing, ask yourself two more questions: underneath all of your intellectual ideas and images, what are your emotional assumptions about reality? And why?

What then is our final conclusion about the meaning of the word "magic"? This: *Magic is a science and an art comprising a system of concepts and methods for the build-up of human emotion, altering the electrochemical balance of the metabolism, using associational techniques and devices to concentrate and focus this emotional energy, thus modulating the energy broadcast by the human body, usually to affect other energy patterns, whether animate or inanimate, but occasionally to affect the personal energy patterns.*

That's all!

I am most inclined to agree with the words of psychic researcher and author Allen Spraggett in a recent letter to me: "It may be, of course, that both our conceptions of matter and non-matter are naïve and that reality is something else altogether." I think he has hit the nail quite squarely upon the head, though few professional occultists would dare to be as honest. *We need more research!*

As I said in the Introduction, this book will have no real

meaning until it is obsolete. And the only way this book can get obsolete is if more research is done. I cheerfully invite all those who agree and all those who disagree with me to put their laboratories where their mouths are. I would be just as happy if every single idea in this book was disproved, as if they were to be supported, because the only way either one will be done is by massive, public research. I don't have that kind of money yet, but those who disagree with me do have that kind of money. And if we can light a fire under them they will *have* to do research, if only to try and disprove increasingly plausible evidence that the human mind is more powerful than any of their technological creations.

For several years now there has been a movement afoot known as "Science for the People." While this suggestion may upset many friends and foes, I say that we need a "Magic for the People" movement as well. It is time for the scientists and artists and poets and magicians and scholars and dancers and computer buffs and psychics and Zen Masters and astronauts and musicians and philosophers and lovers of the Earth *to get together!* We can exorcise the demonic barriers that have separated us from each other for so long. We can bring magic to the masses, and with it the discipline and freedom of the body, mind and spirit. Then earth and sky, love and joy, will marry, and hope will be their child, soaring to the stars.

Appendix

Corrections and Additions

or

Whatever Happened to the Good Old Days When Getting Out of Date Took a Hundred Years?

A lot of things have happened since the first edition of *Real Magic* was published, back in 1971, not only in my own life but in many fields of the occult and mundane arts and sciences as well. In this appendix I can only hit some of the highlights that are relevant to the topics discussed in the main text. For details, I suggest that you read carefully those books in the Bibliography published in recent years.

Introduction: As mentioned in the Preface, the "Occult Fad" is temporarily over, having been replaced by other fads. But the cycles are such that we can expect another round of occult chic (especially if more Arab magicians start publishing) in the mid 1980's.

Currently one fad has started to turn into an entire lifestyle (not to mention big business) for millions, and that's the "wholistic movement." The idea of viewing people and institutions as whole systems instead of as collections of individual units is revolutionizing medicine, architecture, psychology and many other sciences and arts. Although mysticism and "spiritual teachings" are often mentioned by the new leaders of the wholistic movement, the terms "occult" and "magic" are hardly even breathed.

Another effect of the wholistic movement has been a rapid rise in the numbers and prestige of interdisciplinary thinkers— generalists are once again becoming respectable. Unfortunately, not all of these new generalists have the intelligence or ethical sensitivities of Bucky Fuller, John Lilly, Charles Muses, or Gregory Bateson.

In fact the number of pseudoscientific rackets that have been started up under the umbrella of the wholistic movement has been astonishing. Apparently *anything* that challenges traditional scientific views of reality becomes instantly "true," regardless of how silly, inconsistent or downright dishonest it may be.

Theodore Sturgeon, one of the world's best science fiction writers, once coined a natural "law" which has since become known as "Sturgeon's Law." He was originally talking about the quality of writing in the science fiction field, but the law is perfectly adequate for various spiritual and occult topics as well. The law states that "90% of Everything Is Crap." At a lot of the "Wholistic Fairs" and "New Age Exhibits" the percentage would be better set at 95%. I advise you when going to these events to take every claim you hear with a small Siberian salt mine.

Naturally the crooks and the dingalings have been playing directly into the hands of various scientistic sorts, who have organized committees To Investigate and Disprove Everything We Don't Want To Believe In. An increasing number of honest scientists have been so repelled by the pseudoscientific abuses in the wholistic movement that they have joined forces with the not-so-honest ultraconservatives to denounce the entire field. This doesn't do anybody any good and makes it a lot harder for real scientists doing controversial research to get a fair hearing (let alone grant money!), or for people with genuinely new ideas to get anyone to give them an honest test.

Many people in the wholistic movement also exhibit a great deal of spiritual arrogance. Various "spiritual leaders" are often called upon to attend conferences and symposiums, in order to give lectures, run workshops, etc. It is quietly assumed that all of these leaders will be Christian clergy, Cabalists, Sufis, Hindus, Sikhs, Buddhists or members of other "respectable" faiths. Leaders of the Neopagan, Voudoun, Wiccan or Ceremonial Magick communities are simply "overlooked," since none of these systems is deemed to be a "real" spiritual movement.

But then, most of these overlooked movements are anarchistic and people-focussed, rather than being authoritarian and money-focussed, and so their leaders simply don't know how to get themselves into the public eye effectively. Hopefully over the next few years enough of their leaders will concentrate sufficiently on money making to enable them to get the slick four-color brochures, expensive clothes and whirling, buzzing, flashing gadgets to compete as equals in the spiritual marketplace.

Chapter One: Although I've rewritten my Two-Minute Sermon on Drugs, I did not have the space in the text to cover adequately the topic of shamanistic uses of drugs. I will take this opportunity here to direct your attention to the works of Eliade, Furst, Tart, Harner, Lamb, Wilson and Castenada in the Bibliography (all the other authors referred to in this Appendix will be found there as well).

What I have previously termed "anthropological" or "Third World" magical systems, I am now calling "Tribal" ones. In this way I am able to refer to defunct or disintegrated systems belonging to tribes in areas such as Europe that are no longer tribal. Thus the magical systems of the ancient Celts or Slavs are just as "tribal" as those of Native Americans or Africans.

I have decided in recent years to make a few additions to the Laws of Magic. Very briefly, here they are:

The Law of Synchronicity: two or more events happening at "the same time" are likely to have more associations in common than the merely temporal; very few events (if any) ever happen in "isolation" from other events; "there is no such thing as a *mere* coincidence." In point of fact, if you ever manage to pin a professional debunker against a wall (be careful, they get nasty when cornered), you will find that the word "coincidence" is a scientistic term of exorcism, which is used to banish away unwanted demons of implied causality. Naturally the word "synchronicity" is from Carl Jung's research, even though the concept shows up all over the globe.

The Law of Unity should have been obvious, but apparently it wasn't: every phenomenon in existence is linked directly or indirectly to every other one, past, present or future; perceived separations between phenomena are based on incomplete sensing and/or thinking; "All is One."

The Law of Personal Universes: every sentient being lives in and quite possibly creates a unique universe which can never be 100% identical to that lived in by another; so-called "reality" is in fact a matter of consensus opinions; "you live in your cosmos and I'll live in mine." This may or may not be the same as . . .

The Law of Infinite Universes (which I'm now rephrasing): the total number of universes into which all possible combinations of existing phenomena could be organized is infinite; "anything is possible, though some things are more probable than others."

The Law of Dynamic Balance is what I used to call just the "Law of Balance." I've changed the name in order to emphasize the dynamic qualities of the needed states of balance, since my references in the text may not have been emphatic enough on this important point.

The Law of Perversity: if anything can go wrong, it will — and in the most annoying manner possible; magical associations sometimes operate in the reverse of what was wanted; meaningful coincidences are just as likely to be unpleasant as they are to be helpful (especially if a lot of emotion goes into the related situations); even if nothing possibly *can* go wrong, some element of the universe(s) may change so that things will go wrong anyway; "whether we like it or not, the Gods *do* have a sense of humor!" This law is known in other fields as "Murphy's Law," "Finagle's Law," etc., and although humorous is meant quite seriously. It is probably based on the common occurence of countermagic done by one's own subconscious mind for whatever devious reasons it may have. My guess is that it also ties into the Anti-psi powers and can explain why some people's magic always seems to work backwards.

Chapter Two: Three points on the scientific method need to be added. One is that proving any given hypothesis does not *necessarily* prove whatever theory it may be part of (though sometimes disproving a hypothesis may *disprove* a theory, if it was designed for that purpose). All the bricks in a building may be sound, but if the architecture happens to be shoddy the building may still collapse. Secondly, researchers should try and remember that an experiment based on false premises and carried out in a sloppy manner can often be "successfully" repeated by other researchers sharing those same false premises and sloppy techniques. Thirdly, an obsession with getting "identical" results from supposedly identical experiments may or may not be appropriate for chemistry and biology; but it is clearly inappropriate for parapsychology and the other social sciences.

To paraphrase Blumer: the concepts and propositions of psychic research are devised for the direct (and indirect) examination of the empirical psychic worlds. "Their value and validity are to be determined in *that* examination, and not in seeing how they fare when subjected to the alien criteria of an irrelevant methodology." Or to put it another way, you don't use the techniques of zoology to examine volcanoes or Ming vases, nor the methods of pre-Einsteinian physics to study ESP.

For those who never got the joke: the original edition's blank page 29 was *supposed* to be blank, in order to represent the hypothetical definitions I "didn't get permission to quote." This time I've just inserted an illustration instead.

Definitions of magic in recent years have been getting further away from the physical realm and further into mysticism. Crowley started the mess by defining magic as "the art and science of causing *changes* to occur in conformity with Will;" Butler modified this to call it "the art of effecting *changes in consciousness* at will;" and Farren goes so far as to claim that "magic is not a way of doing things, but a certain mythic way of *seeing* them" (my italics in each case). There are a number of reasons for these somewhat cowardly mutations, beginning with the theurgical emphases that medieval ceremonial magicians began to spout as soon as the Church began murdering magicians. But probably the main reason for the extreme theurgic changes in the writings of twentieth century occultists has simply been that most Western magicians no longer know *how* to cause thaumaturgical effects and thus have to pretend that they aren't interested in such petty "low magic" methods. So it makes good sales sense to remove all of one's claims from the material (which is to say testable) realms. And the fact that magical training methods are usually superb psychotherapy systems gives "a certain touch of versimilitude to an otherwise bald and unconvincing narrative."

It should be noted that there are three main questions that have to be dealt with when one is attempting to define magic. The first is that of what the magician *thinks* she or he is doing when performing a magical act. The second is that of what the magician may "actually" be doing in some hypothetical "objective" reality. The third is that of what outside observers, qualified or unqualified (and always biased) may perceive or theorize the magician to be doing. I have dealt with all three of these questions throughout the course of this text, but perhaps without making these vital distinctions as clear as I should have.

These days, the definition of magic that I am starting to use is: "Magic is a general term for arts, sciences, philosophies and technologies concerned with (a) understanding and using altered states of consciousness within which it is possible to have access to and control over one's psychic talents, and (b) the uses and abuses of those psychic talents to change interior and/or exterior realities."

Chapter Three: The field of parapsychology has made a tremendous amount of progress in the last few years, mostly because (a) more researchers have become parapsychologists, (b) more physicists have started investigating the links between consciousness and quantum phenomena, (c) many of these researchers are "hip," and (d) most modern parapsychologists no longer limit themselves to the techniques pioneered by the ultraconservative "papa of parapsychology," J.B. Rhine. The "Rhine Foundation," by the by, is officially called "The Foundation for Research on the Nature of Man," although hardly anybody ever calls it that.

Let me emphasize that many of the psi talents I discussed are unrecognized by mainstream parapsychologists, though they are familiar to occultists and collectors of "damned facts" (such as Charles Fort). That's OK, they'll catch up eventually. In the meantime, here are some brief notes: *Telepathic Sending and Receiving* may be distinct, if not always separate, talents. I now use the term *Empathy* to refer to a type of Telepathic Reception involving emotions. *Mesmerism* is a perfectly good old term for the Telepathic Sending of hypnotic suggestions (something often done, like Empathy, by people who don't realize what they are doing). I've given up on getting people to use *Clairsentience* or *Clairempathy* instead of *Psychometry*. *Astral & Mental Projection* are now called *Out of the Body Experiences* (or "OOBEs"), and *Clairvoyance* called *Remote Viewing*, by fashionable parapsychologists.

One field of psychic research has boomed in recent years, and that's "paraphysics" ("psionics," "psychotronics" and "psycho-energetics" are also becoming popular — anything to avoid saying "magic"). Paraphysics is the study of (a) the overlaps between parapsychology and physics, and (b) the study of various forms of PK, including many of those mentioned in Chapter Three. I am no longer so attached to the "scientific" sounding names for the different kinds of APK, and am now referring to them by simple English names: *Mass Control, Density Control, Bonding Control, Gravity Control, Magnetic Control, Electric Control, Light Control, Temperature (Heat & Cold) Control, Radiation Control* and *Transmutation*. Not all of these are mentioned in the text, but it is easy to figure out what they mean. I suspect that the so-called "Geller Effect" of psychokinetically bending metal objects (which I have seen done by others than Geller, under unimpeachable circumstances) may well be a matter of Bonding Control in action.

Weather Control is probably not a distinct psi talent, merely an application of one or more of the APK talents. Similarly,

Arlynde d'Loughlan has suggested that a talent for using CPK to make people clumsy (or more agile, for that matter) could be called *Klutzokinesis*, but that's getting silly, isn't it? Well?

If we're going to stick with my four-part invention for orchestrating the classification of psi terms, then I guess that the talents of *Deflection* (or "bouncing"), *Filtering, Retuning, Damping* and *Amplifying* might as well go with the Anti-psi ones, especially since they are often used as protection against psychic attack. Note that different kinds of Anti-psi affect different aspects of incoming energies. *Catapsi, Splodging & Apopsi* affect the total structure of psi broadcasts (power, meaning & vector); *Deflection & Reddopsi* affect only the vector; *Negapsi, Filtering & Retuning* affect the meaning; and *Damping & Amplifying* affect the power levels.

As far as the Kogan materials are concerned, I would probably put them in an appendix if I were doing the whole book over again. It has been pointed out that if you use his figures without modification, you get an Information Transfer Rate so small that most well known magical and psychic phenomena become simply impossible. Kogan's research, like that done with plant telepathy, biorhythms, pyramid power and other stuff, seems to require faith on the part of the researcher in order to duplicate the results. Nonbelievers report much lower scores and/or different statistical results. So we have the old "Sheep vs. Goats" syndrome again. Kogan's theories must therefore be taken to be very tentative, but since he is neither the first nor the last researcher to suggest the idea of constant mutual telepathy, I think my Switchboard theory can stand without too much difficulty.

I have been criticized because my psi phenomena classification system does not include what many researchers consider a prime area for study: "survival phenomena" (this involves research into hauntings, mediumship, reincarnation memories, etc.). I think this was adequately covered in Chapter Six, but perhaps the order of presentation could have been altered, especially if I had been able to use a different medium.

William Roll has mentioned to me that in 1970 there were less than a dozen fulltime parapsychologists in the world, and that a large number of the experiments I suggested have since been done (with the results, let me add, supporting several of my theories). So I will apologize to the parapsychological community once again for my youthful intolerance of their previous snail's pace progress.

To help bring you up to date on recent psi research, I can especially recommend the works by Moss, Tart, White & Krippner, and Wolman, *et al.*

Chapter Four: Though some readers consider this the best chapter, I now consider it hopelessly inadequate. A lot of research has been done in recent years in both pattern recognition and the psychophysiological effects of mantras. Trance is, after all, only a subcategory of altered states of consciousness, a very complex topic.

If I were writing this chapter today, I would probably add references to such groups as the Moonies, Scientology, "est," the followers of various gurus, several charismatic sects of fundamentalist Christians, Crowleyites and Thelemites, miscellaneous modern Witchcraft movements, Sufi and Hasidic groups, etc. Many of these groups are dangerous and malevolent, while others are harmless and helpful.

Events in the last few years have clearly indicated just how dangerous some (usually called "cult") groups can be to their own members as well as to anyone else they can exercise influence over. Brainwashing, beatings, rapes and murders, mass suicides, military drilling and gunrunning, meddling in civil governments and other crimes have been charged against many groups, and in several cases those accusations have been true. Is there any relatively simple way to evaluate just how dangerous or harmless a given group is liable to be, without having to subject oneself to its power?

Perhaps there is now. I have recently constructed a crude analysis tool which I call my "Cult Danger Evaluation Frame," a copy of which is included in this edition of *Real Magic.* I realize its shortcomings, but feel that it can be effectively used to separate the sheep from the wolves. Feedback from those attempting to use the system would be appreciated.

CULT DANGER EVALUATION FRAME
by P.E.I. Bonewits©

1 2 3 4 5 6 7 8 9 10
Low   High

1. **INTERNAL CONTROL,** amount of internal political power exercised by leader(s) over members.

2. **WISDOM CLAIMED** by leader(s); amount of infallibility declared about decisions.

3. **WISDOM CREDITED** to leader(s) by members; amount of trust in decisions made by leader(s).

4. **DOGMA,** rigidity of reality concepts taught; amount of doctrinal inflexibility.

5. **RECRUITING,** emphasis put on attracting new members, amount of proselytizing.

6. **FRONT GROUPS,** number of subsidiary groups using different names from that of main group.

7. **WEALTH,** amount of money and/or property desired or obtained; emphasis on members' donations.

8. **POLITICAL POWER,** amount of external political influence desired or obtained.

9. **SEXUAL MANIPULATION** of members by leader(s); amount of control over sex lives of members.

10. **CENSORSHIP,** amount of control over members' access to outside opinions on group, its doctrines or leader(s).

11. **DROPOUT CONTROL,** intensity of efforts directed at preventing or returning dropouts.

12. **ENDORSEMENT OF VIOLENCE** when used by or for the group or its leader(s).

13. **PARANOIA,** amount of fear concerning real or imagined enemies; perceived power of opponents.

14. **GRIMNESS,** amount of disapproval concerning jokes about the group, its doctrines or leader(s).

15. **SURRENDER OF WILL,** emphasis on members not having to be responsible for personal decisions.

Low   High
1 2 3 4 5 6 7 8 9 10

The purpose of this evaluation tool is to help both amateur and professional observers, including current or would-be members, of various organizations (including religious, occult, psychological or political groups) to determine just how dangerous a given group is liable to be, in comparison with other groups, to the physical and mental health of its members and of other subject to its influence.

As a general rule, the higher the numerical total scored by a given group (the further to the right of the scale), the more dangerous it is likely to be. Though it is obvious that many of the scales in the frame are subjective, it is still possible to make practical judgments using it, provided that all numerical assignments are based on accurate and unbiased observation of actual behavior (as distinct from official pronouncements).

This frame can be used by parents, reporters, law enforcement agents, social scientists and others interested in evaluating the actual dangers presented by a given group or movement. Obviously, different observers will achieve differing degrees of precision, depending upon the sophistication of their numerical assignments on each scale. However, if the same observer used the same methods of scoring and weighting each scale, their comparisons of relative danger or harmlessness between groups will be reasonably valid, at least for their own purposes.

It should be pointed out that this evaluation frame is founded upon a) modern ideas of humanistic psychology concerning the nature of mental health and personal growth, and b) the author's twelve years of participant observation and historical research into minority belief systems. Those who believe that relativism and anarchy are as dangerous to mental health as absolutism and authoritarianism are, should count groups with total scores nearing either extreme (high or low) as being equally hazardous. As far as dangers to physical well being are concerned, however, the author feels that both historical records and current events clearly indicate the direction in which the greatest threats lie. This is especially so since the low scoring groups usually seem to have survival and growth rates so small that they seldom develop the abilities to commit large scale atrocities even had they the philosophical or political inclinations to do so.

Chapter Five: It has been suggested by Herb Goldberg that dualism may be based on male fears of ambiguity and irrationality, though this doesn't explain why Western males become dualists while the equally sexist Eastern males opted for polarity instead. I still think the blame has to be laid clearly at the doorstep of monotheism.

As the long footnote on page 104 indicates, the discussion of the various flavors of witchcraft is completely different from that in earlier editions. The numerous errors (based on the unrepresentative sample of self-proclaimed "witches" I knew) have been corrected and several gratuitous insults have been censored out completely. It is now obvious that "witchcraft" can no longer be defined as any one particular method of doing magic, since so many witches use so many different techniques.

It should be pointed out, that while Kirlian photography is a fascinating new research tool and one which may be useful for catching records of some sorts of energy flows around plants and animals, *there is absolutely no proof* that the energy fields photographed through the process are the same as the traditional concept of "auras." They may or may not be, the question is still very much open, despite what you may hear from salespeople at psychic fairs. *Caveat emptor!*

Chapter Six: Jack Schwarz and other researchers have proven by this time that people can exercise incredible amounts of control over their supposedly "involuntary" metabolic systems. He runs a fascinating research group called the Aletheia Psycho-Physical Foundation in Grants Pass, Oregon, where he collects and organizes results on biofeedback and metabolic controls research from around the world. His future books should be well worth watching for. Certainly, he makes my comments on the powers of the placebo effect look timid.

I'll also refer your attention to an article entitled "Language, Thought & Disease," by W. C. Ellerbroek, in the Spring 1978 issue of *Co-Evolution Quarterly* (which often has all *sorts* of occult materials under different names). Ellerbroek presents a brilliant discussion of the relationships between psycholinguistics and psychosomatic diseases, in a fashion that is directly appropriate to various Laws of Magic. However his suggestion that people say "I *should* have had this disaster happen to me today" as a method of avoiding stress can also lead to an unhealthy fatalism which might in the long run outweigh the positive therapeutic advantages of pollyanna perceptions.

On the topic of Placebo Spells, I would like to point out that nowhere in my original discussion did I state or even imply that I was in the habit of accepting money for spells not cast. However, the whole point is now moot (save for my honor) since I no longer have much time to do magic for strangers.

Many people have suggested that my theory of the Switchboard appears to violate Occam's Razor, since it seems to be far more complicated than merely saying "ghosts are real" or "reincarnation explains everything." So I'll point out that if a *seemingly* simple explanation for a phenomenon entails more complicated philosophical implications and the complete reworking of a science or three, that a researcher is fully justified in giving a higher probability rating to a superficially complex explanation involving fewer and less complicated hidden implications.

However, one piece of research has come out recently that may very well constitute major support for the idea of the Switchboard. I refer to the book, *Conjuring Up Philip*, by Iris Owen and Margaret Sparrow. This tells of how a group of psychic researchers in Canada managed to *artificially create the ghost of a man who never lived!* They put a lot of intellectual and emotional energy into inventing a complete personality for "Philip" and were rewarded with nearly all of the classic "survival evidence" in the mediumistic books. They had psychic phenomena coming out their ears, all supposedly caused by this "ghost." And as Jose Feola mentioned in his review of the book in the *Parapsychology Journal*, several of the Laws of Magic, as well as the theory of the Switchboard, are directly relevant to the results achieved by the researchers.

Even the recent books on reincarnation evidence (such as the excellent one by Fiore) fit nicely in with my theories. On the other paw, some of the work done by Elizabeth Kubler-Ross with dying and revived patients, in which they discuss their pleasant after-death experiences, may throw a complete monkey-wrench into the works. I will note, however, that at least one other researcher claims that many of the patients *he* talked to reported experiencing "hells" rather than "heavens." It may very well be that, if people do survive after death in some form, they go to the sort of afterlife that they *expect to*. In which case, I may arrange to have someone read to me from a *Book of the Dead* while I'm dying, so as to provide guidance just in case any might be needed.

Chapter Seven: There is so much new material that could be added here that I'm not even going to try and cover it all. To begin with, there are a number of techniques used by magicians to "raise" or "gain access to" psychic energy. These include: music, singing, chanting, dancing, meditation, various drugs, just about every known form of sexual behavior (eventually I'm going to have to do an entire book just on sex and drug magic), hypnosis and "tapping" from outside sources.

Music, singing, chanting and dancing are some of the oldest tools known to humanity for raising psychic energies, yet they are sadly neglected by most western occult groups, perhaps because western occultists are unwilling to take the time and discipline necessary to learn and perform these arts properly. The same comment could be made about meditation as a magical technique; it gives a distinct advantage in fine tuning but takes a long time to learn and use. Drugs, as I think I have mentioned several times in this text, are both dangerous and confusing to the beginner. Sex is difficult to handle while doing magic and conflicts over the topic can destroy a magical group faster than almost anything else. Sex magic should not be a group's prime focus unless all the parties involved are sexually healthy and psychologically well balanced.

Hypnosis is the basis of the entire Silva training system. They use it to teach students how to use self-hypnosis, so that the students can then "program" themselves in what is essentially a meditative magical system. They avoid calling what they do "hypnosis" by using a definition for the word that hasn't been used by experts in the field for thirty years. Probably they engage in this genial deception because they think the average American is scared of the word, though I would think "Mind Control" is a much more frightening term. But the Silva system is ethically clean and magically effective and is the *only* nationwide psychic training system that I feel comfortable in recommending.

"Tapping" is, in the "real world," a matter of gaining psychic energy (or "mana") from (a) the surrounding space-time continuum (what used to be called "the ether"), and/or (b) from other people or animals, and/or (c) from various "supernatural" entities, *probably* in the Switchboard. The ability to "tap" effectively may, in itself, be a critical psychic talent. Lack of this ability (or of training in it) may be one explanation why magicians with otherwise equal talents and training may get drastically different results. The major magical purpose of most "religious" rituals is to facilitate tapping from some diety, so that the clergy and/or congregation may cast spells (excuse me, "prayers") with the extra mana obtained.

Speaking of rituals, here's a definition I like to use these days: "a ritual is any ordered sequence of events, actions or directed thoughts, especially one that is repeated in the 'same' manner each time, that is designed to produce a predictable altered state of consciousness within which certain magical and/or religious results may be obtained." Thus, any spell, any religious cere-mony, any organized way of using sex or drugs or the other mana raising methods mentioned, when done for magical or religious purposes, constitutes a type of "ritual," "ceremony" or "rite."

Due to the thousands of physical, psychological, psychic and artistic variables involved in even the simplest use of a psychic talent, it should be remembered that no two rituals or their results are *ever* really "the same." Those who are obsessed with Repeatability in their research will find themselves repeatedly frustrated. Those who insist on performing written ceremonies word for word and gesture for gesture, without understanding the intellectual or artistic reasons for the original ritual designs, are also doomed to failure. In fact, a major problem of modern western occultism is that students are not taught to allow room in their rites for spontaneous changes and additions. This is a result of monotheistic theurgical attitudes ("there's only *one* way to do the ceremony"), white middle class biases ("only the ignorant or stupid lower classes have undignified rituals"), lack of experience with really intense energies, and traditional fears of unruly spirits, that is to say, the return of the repressed (something that terrifies intellectuals). But what good is a letter perfect ritual if it doesn't work very well (or at all)? Once you've got a couple of good exorcisms learned, you should try loosening up the rest of your ceremonies. You can have both discipline *and* creative freedom—ask any good jazz musician, or dancer, or painter, or scientist.

Readers of previous editions may notice that (a) the "How to Cast a Curse" sample has been rewritten to refer to dictators rather than mothers-in-law, and (b) the "How to Cast a Lust Spell" has been entirely replaced. The first was changed because I once had a perfectly delightful mother-in-law whom I do not want to offend, and because dictators make much better targets to practice on anyway. The second was changed because I got tired of lazy critics yanking it out of context and printing it in (or *as*) their reviews in order to discredit the entire book. Besides, the printers kept garbling my footnote about how I usually considered lust spells "unsporting" (I now think of them as unethical under almost every circumstance).

A few words on Aleister Crowley may be appropriate. He was a genius whose brilliance was matched only by his neuroses. The majority of his books are *not* suitable for beginners, despite his frequent claims to the contrary. I have decided after much thought and meditation that his Law of Thelema ("Do what thou wilt shall be the whole of the Law. Love is the Law, love under will.") is not, as he claimed, the "word of the New Aeon," but is rather the final crystalization of the word of the Old Aeon.

Crowley was not evil, but he was tremendously irresponsible. The Thelemic philosophy is one that only a saint can handle without causing great damage to those around him or her, and if one is already enlightened they probably have no need for it. Despite the best efforts of Thelemic organizations (such as the O.T.O. of which I am an initiate), the overwhelming majority of Crowley's followers still insist on interpreting it as "do whatever the hell I want shall be the whole of the Law. Lust is the Law, lust under any circumstances." While I am certainly a fond supporter of lust, I feel that the absolutist rightwing anarchism of Thelema, especially when exercised by many of Crowley's modern followers, is the complete opposite of the "Aquarian Age" ideals of cooperation, interdependence and mutual responsibility that I see as humanity's only salvation at this point in history. The "Age of Horus" is definitely not the same as the "Age of Aquarius," and I for one prefer the latter since it will probably be more conducive to human survival over the next hundred years or so. "Enlightened selfishness" works only when people really *are* enlightened, otherwise all it produces are more Hitlers, Stalins, Amins and Nixons.

Chapter Eight: I have done some detailed research into the scientific status of astrology (which I published as an article entitled "Does Astrology Really Work?" in *New Realities*, Volume 1, Number 2, April 1977). My results, after evaluating all of the pro- and anti-astrology research that I could find, was that some experiments seem to support and others contradict various astrological beliefs; while other experiments just produce results that are totally unexpected by any of astrology's friends or foes. It is definitely true, however, that the recently published attacks on astrology by conservative scientists have been replete with misinformation, deceptive phrasing, atheistic creedism and outright lies. Some astrological theories may be sound and others not, but we'll never know until more researchers start doing honest experimentation instead of shooting their mouths off on topics which they are clearly unqualified to discuss.

By the by, more research is appearing to indicate that the entire system of "biorhythms" is based on some extremely shaky statistics, not to mention some downright deceptive advertising methods. The final results are not in yet, but I'd advise not investing too much money or energy into the system for a while.

A magnificient book on the Tarot has come out, called *The Encyclopedia of Tarot*, by Stuart Kaplan. It looks as if it is going to be the definitive text on the history of Tarot, at least for a couple decades. I am currently working with a fine artist on a deck of "neotarot" cards, tentatively called *The Illuminated Tarot*, which are nondualist, nonsexist, nonracist, noncreedist, international in symbolism and multilingual in labeling. Also in the works is a book on "Do-It-Yourself Tarot" decks, discussing how people can design and produce their own decks of divination cards (something I encourage everyone to try if they are at all fond of using cards).

Chapter Nine: Some of the research I suggested has since been done, with most of the results supporting my guesses. The CIA, KGB and other espionage and military institutions are continuing to spend millions of dollars and rubles every year in order to investigate ways in which psychic powers can be used to enslave their own and each other's populations. More than one well known American parapsychologist is or has been (knowingly or not) on the payroll of the CIA and/or the U. S. Defense Department. Every parapsychologist in a communist nation is, of course, an employee of her or his own government; most are watched carefully when not actually helped. Many other countries have quietly set up psychic research programs, often while publicly ridiculing the entire topic.

I am not as much of a radical as I perhaps used to be, but I do believe that the final battles for human freedom and survival may very well be fought, not by soldiers and diplomats, but by magicians and psychics, witches and wizards, zen masters and taoist sages, sorcerers and shamans. And the war will probably not be a matter of competing governments, but of individuals of all nations seeking to defend themselves against their own would-be rulers.

It is my hope that this book, with all its faults, will provide individuals of all sorts with the basic knowledge they need to develop their own psychic talents to the maximum, without either help or hinderance from totalitarians of any stripe, political or religious. As I said in the Preface, with a little help from the Gods and a great deal of hard work, we may make it to the twenty-first century yet. I hope. And pray.

Bibliography

The following is an annotated Bibliography of books that the average westerner beginning to study magic will find useful, along with some fairly harmless advanced texts and a few lemons it is necessary to know about. Unless there is a note saying otherwise, it is safe to assume that most of an author's other works are also recommended.

I am no longer listing the publishing histories of each book, but instead am emphasizing paperback editions that may still be available. Library of Congress Numbers and Standard Book Numbers may, if needed, be obtained by looking up the works or authors involved in *Books in Print* (which will also contain the addresses of the publishers) at any large library or bookstore.

The listing is not, by any stretch of the imagination, a complete one. Naturally it reflects the interests and opportunities of myself and those who suggested titles. Nonetheless, the majority of those titles selected belong in any basic occult library. I am always open to suggestions for new titles to add, especially since I am considering someday producing a book-length annotated Bibliography of several thousand titles. That should keep me busy for a while. And reading the titles in just this brief listing should keep the reader busy (and fascinated) for quite some time as well.

Adler, Margot: *Drawing Down the Moon; the Resurgence of Paganism in America.* sc, Beacon Press, 1987. The best book ever written on the Neopagan movements.

Alhazred, A.; *Al Azif*, in Arabic. Translations: Philodius, Theodorus into Greek; Wormius, Olaus into Latin; Dee, John into English. hc, Starry Wisdom Press 1905. Standard Classic of Western Occultism.

Andersen, Marianne S. & Savary, Louis M.; *Passages: A Guide for Pilgrims of the Mind.* sc, Harper & Row 1972. Excellent exercises for altering states of consciousness without chemicals.

Anderson, Victor H.; *Thorns of the Blood Rose.* hc, Anderson 1971. Contains beautiful poetry of the Earth-Mother; very suitable for rituals. OP.

Anonymous; *Lost Books of the Bible & Forgotten Books of Eden*. sc, New American Library 1948. Apocryphal scriptures, will give you some things to think about.

Arbman, Holger, *The Vikings*. sc, Praeger 1969. Vol 21 in Praeger's "Ancient Peoples & Places" series. A basic text.

Arguelles, Jose & Miriam; *Mandala*. sc, Shambala 1972.

_____. *The Feminine: Spacious As the Sky*. sc, Shambala 1977.

Asprin, Robert: *Another Fine Myth—*. sc, Starblaze/Donning 1978. A profound introduction to the highest subtleties of magical theory and practice—and a hysterically funny fantasy novel.

Assagioli, Roberto; *Psychosynthesis*. sc, Viking 1971.

_____. *The Act of Will*. sc, Penguin 1974.

Avalon, Arthur; *See* Woodroffe, John.

Bachofen, J.J.; *Myth, Religion & Mother Right*. sc, Princeton University Press 1967. One of the speculative works that began the Matriarchy Theory in the late 1800's.

Bailey, Alice; *Treatise on White Magic*. sc, Lucis Publishing 1971.

Bandler, Richard & Grinder, John; *The Structure of Magic, Vol I & II*. hc, Science & Behavior Books, Vol I 1975, Vol II 1976.

_____. *Patterns of Hypnotic Techniques of Milton H. Erickson, M.D.* Two volumes. hc, Meta Publications 1975.

Bardon, Franz; *Initiation Into Hermetics*. English translation, hc, Osiris 1962. His theory did not survive the translation too well, but his training system is one of the very best available for mainstream Western occultism.

Barrett, Francis; *The Magus—A Complete System of Occult Philosophy*, sc, Citadel 1975. A classic summation of Western Occultism to 1800.

Bateson, Gregory; *Steps to an Ecology of Mind*. sc, Ballantine 1975. A classic of interdisciplinary thought.

Beane, Wendell & Doty, William, ed.; *Myths, Rites, Symbols—A Mircea Eliade Reader*. Two volumes. sc. Harper & Row 1976. Good selection of Eliade texts.

Bellows, Henry Adams; *The Poetic Edda*. hc. Biblo & Tannen 1969. One of my favorite translations.

Bentov, Itzak; *Stalking the Wild Pendulum*. sc. Dutton 1977.

Berne, Eric; *Beyond Games & Scripts*. Ed. by Claude Steiner & Carmen Kerr. sc, Grove 1977.

_____. *Intuition & Ego States: the Origins of Transactional Analysis*. Ed. by Paul McCormick. sc, TA Press 1977. Plus all of his other books.

Bettelheim, Bruno; *The Uses of Enchantment*. sc, Random House 1977. Except for the fact that the author is pompous, dogmatic, scientist and an orthodox Freudian, this is a very good book on the values of fantasy.

Blavatsky, H.P.; *The Secret Doctrine, Vols. 1 & 2.* sc, Theosophical University Press 1977.

_____. *Isis Unveiled: A Master Key to the Mysteries of Ancient & Modern Science & Theology.* Two volumes. sc, Theos-Univ 1972. These are two basic texts of the Theosophical movement.

Bloch, Arthur; *Murphy's Law and other reasons why things go wrong!* sc, Price/Stern/ Sloan 1977. Priceless materials relating the Law of Perversity to every human endeavor.

Blofeld, John Eaton Calthorpe; *Tantric Mysticism of Tibet: A Practical Guide.* sc, Dutton 1970.

_____. *I Ching: The Book of Change.* sc, Dutton 1965.

_____. *The Secret & Sublime: Taoist Mysteries & Magic.* sc, Dutton 1973.

_____. *Mantras: Sacred Words of Power.* sc, Dutton 1977.

Blumer, Herbert; *Symbolic Interactionism; Perspective and Method.* hc, Prentice 1969. A good book on basic methodology for the social sciences; very suited to thaumaturgical research. Should be required reading for all parapsychologists.

Bok, Bart J. & Jerome, Lawrence E.; *Objections to Astrology.* sc, Prometheus Books 1975. Superb example of deliberate lying by professional debunkers.

Bonewits, P.E.I.; *Authentic Thaumaturgy.* sc, Fantasy Games Unltd., 1988. How principles of magic can be used in Fantasy roll-playing games.

_____. *The Druid Chronicles (Evolved),* ed. sc, Pentalpha 1979. History, Theoilogy, Customs & Rites of the Reformed Druid movements.

_____. *Worshiping the Gods: Neopagan Liturgy in Theory and Practice.* In preparation. A complete guide to designing, preparing, and performing effective worship rituals.

Bonewits, P.E.I. & Odbert, James R.; *The Illuminated Tarot.* Deck & Book. In preparation.

Boyle, John P.; *ESP Research Equipment You Can Build Yourself.* sc, Prentice Hall 1977.

_____. *Psionic Generator Pattern Book.* sc, Prentice Hall 1975. Neat toys, and very useful for training.

Brand, Stewart; *II Cybernetic Frontiers.* sc, Random House 1974. An interview with Gregory Bateson, and one with several "computer bums."

Bristol, Claude M.; *Magic of Believing.* sc, Simon & Schuster 1967. Orange Magic.

Browning, Norma Lee; *The Psychic World of Peter Hurkos.* sc, Doubleday 1970.

_____. *Peter Hurkos — I Have Many Lives.* hc, Doubleday 1976.

_____. *Omarr: Astrology & the Man.* sc, New American Library 1978. Biographies, showing some of the psychological variables involved in psychic phenomena.

Broad, C.D.; *Lectures on Psychical Research.* hc, Humanities Press 1962.

Bruno, Giordano; *The Expulsion of the Triumphant Beast*, hc, Rutgers University Press 1964. Find out why he was burnt at the stake.

Buckland, Raymond; *Witchcraft from the Inside*. sc, Llewellyn 1971.

_____. *The Tree: Complete Book of Saxon Witchcraft*. sc, Samuel Weiser 1974.

Budapest, Zee: *Feminist Book of Lights and Shadows*. sc, Feminist Wicca 1976. Facts and fancies from and about a system of Feminist Witchcraft invented by the author. The lively rites, many adapted from Gardner's "Book of Shadows," can easily be used by either gender, but the herbal materials may contain dangerous errors.

Budge, E.A. Wallis; *The Egyptian Book of the Dead*. sc, Dover 1967.

_____. *Egyptian Magic*. sc, Dover 1971.

_____. *Egyptian Religion*. sc, Routledge 1972.

The works of Budge were done around the turn of the century, but they are still quite useful.

Butler, W.E.; *Apprenticed to Magic*. sc, Samuel Weiser 1970.

_____. *How to Develop Clairvoyance*. sc, Samuel Weiser 1971.

_____. *The Magician: His Training and Work*. sc, Samuel Weiser 1971.

_____. *Magic: Its Ritual, Power & Purpose*. sc, Samuel Weiser 1971.

_____. *How to Develop Psychometry*. sc, Samuel Weiser 1971.

The works of Butler are useful for their training exercises.

Byfield, Barbara Ninde; *The Book of Weird*. sc. Doubleday 1973.

Cammell, C.R.; *Aleister Crowley; the Man, the Mage, and the Poet*. hc, University Books 1962. Perhaps the worst of the serious Crowley biographies. NOT recommended.

Campbell, Joseph; *The Masks of God*. Four volumes.

_____. *Volume One: Primitive Mythology*. sc, Viking 1971.

_____. *Volume Two: Oriental Mythology*. sc, Viking 1972.

_____. *Volume Three: Occidental Mythology*. sc, Viking 1971.

_____. *Volume Four: Creative Mythology*. sc, Viking 1971.

_____. *Myths to Live By*. sc, Bantam 1973.

_____. *Hero with a Thousand Faces*. sc, Princeton University 1968.

The works of Campbell are highly recommended sources for research into mythical elements of magical traditions.

Carus, Paul; *History of the Devil & the Idea of Evil, from the Earliest Times to the Present Day*. sc, Open Court 1974.

_____. *Chinese Astrology*. sc, Open Court 1974.

_____. *The Religion of Science*. hc, Scholarly Press 1977.

Castaneda, Carlos; *Teachings of Don Juan: A Yaqui Way of Knowledge*. sc, Pocket Books 1976.

_____. *A Separate Reality*. sc, Pocket Books 1976.

_____. *Journey to Ixtlan*. sc, Pocket Books 1976.

_____. *Tales of Power*. sc, Pocket Books 1976.

_____. *Second Ring of Power.* hc, Simon & Schuster 1978. He's either a not-very-bright anthropologist or else a great fiction writer. You decide.

Cavendish, Richard; *Man, Myth & Magic; An Illustrated Encylopedia of the Supernatural.* hc, set in 24 volumes, Marshall Cavendish Corporation 1970. This material is much better in book form than the first few issues of the magazine form indicated. Belongs in every occultist's library.

_____. *The Black Arts.* sc, Putnam 1968. A classic text.

Chan, Wing-tsit; *Source Book in Chinese Philosophy.* sc, Princeton University Press 1963.

Ch'En, Kenneth; *Buddhism; the Light of Asia.* sc, Barron's 1968.

_____. *The Chinese Transformation of Buddhism.* sc, Princeton University Press 1973.

Church, Joseph; *Language and the Discovery of Reality.* sc, Vintage 1966.

Clark, Grahame; *World Prehistory in a New Perspective.* hc, Cambridge University Press 1977.

Clark, Grahame & Piggott, Stuart; *Prehistoric Societies.* sc, Penguin 1970. Should be required reading for those trying to build theories about pre-Christian Europe.

Clebert, Jean Paul; *The Gypsies.* sc, Penguin 1969. A nonlurid introduction to one of the world's most oppressed peoples.

Conze, Edward; *Buddhism: Its Essence and Development.* sc, Harper & Row 1959. Buddhism and Tantra.

_____. *Buddhist Wisdom Books: The Diamond Sutra, the Heart Sutra.* sc, Harper & Row 1972.

Conze, Edward & Horner, I.B. & Snellgrove, D. & Waley, A.; *Buddhist Texts Through the Ages.* sc, Harper & Row 1964.

Cox, Harvey, *The Feast of Fools.* sc, Harper and Row 1972. About festival and fantasy and the uses of ritual.

Critchlow, Keith; *Islamic Patterns; an Analytical and Cosmological Approach.* sc, Schocken, 1976. Theory and practice of mandala construction.

Crowley, Aleister; *Aleister Crowley's Astrology: With a Study of Neptune & Uranus.* hc, Samuel Weiser 1974. OP.

_____. *Book of Lies.* sc, Samuel Weiser 1981.

_____. *Book of the Law.* sc. Samuel Weiser, 1976.

_____. *Book of Thoth,* sc, Samuel Weiser 1974.

_____. *Diary of a Drug Fiend.* sc, Samuel Weiser 1970.

_____. *Eight Lectures on Yoga.* sc, Samuel Weiser. OP.

_____. *Energized Enthusiasm.* sc, Samuel Weiser 1976. OP.

_____. *Gems from the Equinox.* (Israel Regardie, ed.) hc, Llewellyn 1974.

_____. *Magick in Theory & Practice.* sc, Dover 1976.

_____. *Magick Without Tears.* hc, Llewellyn 1976.

_____. *Quabalah of Aleister Crowley.* hc, Samuel Weiser 1973.

————. *777* facsimile edition of original. sc. O.T.O. Grand Lodge 1979.

————. *777 Revised.* sc, Samuel Weiser 1986.

————. *Tao Teh King.* sc, Samuel Weiser 1976. OP.

————. *Thoth Deck.* Samuel Weiser.

Culling, Louis T.; *Manual of Sex Magick.* sc, Llewellyn 1971.

————. *Complete Magick Curriculum of the Secret Order G.B.G.* hc, Llewellyn 1971.
Information on the magical theories and practices of a Western lodge.

Daly, Mary; *Beyond God the Father: Toward a Philosophy of Women's Liberation.* sc, Beacon 1974.

————. *The Church & the Second Sex.* (with a New Post-Christian Introduction). sc, Harper & Row 1975.

David-Neel, Alexandria; *Magic and Mystery in Tibet.* sc, Penguin 1971.

————. *Secret Oral Teachings in Tibetan Buddhist Sects.* sc, City Lights 1967.
These started a lot of nonsense about Tibet.

Davis, Wade; *The Serpent and the Rainbow.* sc, Warner 1987. The book that reveals the secrets of the zombies!

Davison, R.C.; *Astrology.* sc, Arc Books 1967. Introduction.

De Bary, Wm.; *Sources of Chinese Tradition.* Two volumes. Columbia University Press 1960.

————. *Sources of Indian Tradition.* Two volumes. Columbia University Press 1958.

————. *Sources of Japanese Tradition.* Two volumes. Columbia University Press 1958.

DeCamp, L. Sprague; *The Ancient Engineers.* sc, Ballantine 1977.

————. *Lost Continents: The Atlantis Theme.* sc, Ballantine 1975.
Will both clear up a lot of nonsense.

DeCamp & Pratt; *The Compleat Enchanter.* sc, Ballantine 1976. Includes the entire "Incomplete Enchanter" series of fiction novels.

Denning, Melita & Phillips, Osborne; *The Magical Philosophy.* Five volumes. *Volume I: Robe and Ring.* hc, Llewellyn 1974.

————. *Volume 2: Apparel of High Magick.* hc, Llewellyn 1975.

————. *Volume 3: Sword & Serpent.* hc, Llewellyn 1975.

————. *Volume 4: Triumph of Light,* hc, Llewellyn 1979.

————. *Volume 5: Mysteria Magica.* hc, Llewellyn 1979.
A more or less complete outline of a modern Western magical lodge.

Deren, Maya; *Divine Horsemen.* sc, Dell 1972. One of the two or three best books on the subject of Haitian Vodoun.

DeRopp, Robert S.; *Master Game.* sc, Dell 1969.

————. *Drugs & the Mind.* sc, Dell 1976.

————. *Sex Energy,* sc, Dell 1971.

Dodds, E.R.; *The Greeks and the Irrational.* sc, University of California 1968.

_____. *Pagan & Christian in an Age of Anxiety; Some Aspects of Religious Experience from Marcus Aurelius to Constantine.* sc, Norton 1970. Will help you understand the formative influences of the Hellenistic Age on the Western mystical traditions.

Donnison, Jean; *Midwives & Medical Men: A History of Inter-Professional Rivalries & Women's Rights.* hc, Schocken 1977.

Dostmann, Otto; *Remnants of Lost Empires.* hc, Drachenhaus Verlag 1809. You might have trouble finding a copy, and should you succeed, it is *not* recommended that you use it. OP.

Ebon, Martin; *Atlantis: The New Evidence.* sc, Signet 1977. Good summation of recent research.

_____. *Prophecy in Our Time.* sc, Signet 1968. Sensible discussion of modern prophets.

_____. *The Amazing Uri Geller.* (ed.) sc, New American Library 1975. Possibly the best compendium of serious data on Geller.

Ebon's books tend to be very good or very bad. These are some of the good ones.

Eddy, Mary Baker: *Science and Health with Key to the Scriptures.* sc, Christian Science Pub. Society. A basic text on magical healing through the use of hypnosis and psychic shielding, though the author and the average church member would deny it vigorously.

Edmunds, Simeon; *Hypnotism and the Supernatural.* hc, Aquarian 1961.

_____. *Psychic Power of Hypnosis.* sc, Samuel Weiser 1975.

Ehrenreich, Barbara & English, Deirdre; *Witches, Midwives & Nurses.* Feminist Press 1973.

Eiseley, Loren; *Notes of an Alchemist.* sc, Scribner 1974.

_____. *Unexpected Universe.* sc, Harcourt Brace Jovanovich 1972.

_____. *The Firmament of Time.* sc, Atheneum 1972.

A naturalist's view of the universe.

Eisenbud, Jule; *The World of Ted Serios.* sc, Pocket Books 1967. Biography of a "thoughtographer."

_____. *Psi & Psychoanalysis.* hc, Grune & Stratton 1970.

Eliade, Mircea; *Yoga, Immortality and Freedom.* sc, Princeton University Press 1970.

_____. *Shamanism: Archaic Techniques of Ecstasy.* sc, Princeton University Press 1972.

_____. *Myths, Dreams and Mysteries.* sc, Harper & Row 1967.

Eliade is unreservedly recommended, for the above books and all his many other works on mythology, comparative religions and psychology. *See* Beane & Doty.

Evans-Wentz, Walter Yeeling; *The Tibetan Book of the Dead.* sc, Oxford University Press 1970.

_____. *The Tibetan Book of Great Liberation*. sc, Oxford University Press 1968.

_____. *Tibetan Yoga and Secret Doctrines*. sc, Oxford University Press 1967. If you want accurate data about Tibetan magic and religion, this is one author to start with.

Farrar, Janet & Stewart; *Eight Sabbats for Witches*. hc, Phoenix 1983.

_____. *The Life and Times of a Modern Witch*. sc, Phoenix 1988.

_____. *The Witches' Goddess*. sc, Phoenix, 1987.

_____. *The Witches' Way*. hc, Phoenix 1986.

The Farrar's are two of the most important writers on Neopagan Witchcraft in the 1980's. These recent books have been written with the cooperation of Doreen Valiente, and should be required reading for Neopagans of all persuasions.

Farrar, Stewart; *What Witches Do*. sc, Phoenix, 1983. An important classic of the Wiccan movement, revised for this edition.

Fell, Barry; *America B.C.* sc, Pocket Books 1976. Solid archeological evidence of multiple "discoveries" of North America prior to Columbus.

Feng, Gia-Fu & English, Jane (trans.); *Tao Te Ching*. sc, Random House 1972. My favorite translation.

Feng, Gia Fu & Kirk, Jerome; *Tai Chi — a Way of Centering — & I Ching*. sc, Random House 1971. First part is good instruction intro, second is my favorite translation for reading.

Findhorn Community; *The Findhorn Garden*. sc, Harper & Row 1976. Nature spirits, anyone?

Fiore, Edith; *You Have Been Here Before*. hc, Coward, McCann & Geoghegan 1978. A psychologist shares her hypnotic regression evidence for reincarnation. Very sensibly done.

Fodor, Nandor; *Between Two Worlds*. hc, Parker 1964.

_____. *Freud, Jung & Occultism*. University Books 1971.

_____. *Encylopaedia of Psychic Science*. sc, Citadel 1974.

Forbes, T.R.; *The Midwife and the Witch*. hc, Yale University Press 1966.

Fort, Charles; *Complete Books of Charles Fort*. Dover 1975. Includes *Book of the Damned*. (reprint of 1919 ed.), *New Lands*. (reprint of 1923), *Lo!* (reprint of 1931), *Wild Talents*. (reprint of 1932). Each is also available in sc, but get the hc edition as you may be using it a lot.

Fortune, Dion; *Practical Occultism in Daily Life*. sc, Samuel Weiser.

_____. *Psychic Self-Defense*. hc, Samuel Weiser 1967.

_____. *Sane Occultism*. sc, Samuel Weiser 1967.

The works of Fortune (especially the second one above) are highly recommended for the beginning magician with Christian tendencies. She gets a bit sugary-sweet now and then, and is a bit gullible about history, but is otherwise reliable.

Fox, Oliver; *Astral Projection — A Record of Out-of-the-Body Experiences*. sc, Citadel 1974. This is the classic work on astral projection, and still one of the best and most useful.

Frazer, Sir James; *The Golden Bough*. 15 volumes. hc, Macmillan 1900. This is NOT recommended for beginners.

Frazer, Sir James & Gaster, T; *The New Golden Bough*. sc, New American Library 1975. THIS is the edition for beginners to use. Among other things, Gaster has corrected several major errors of Frazer (most of which weren't Frazer's fault), and omitted a great deal of superfluous material.

French, Peter, *Philosophers in Wonderland*. sc, Llewellyn 1975. Philosophical implications of psi research.

Freud, Sigmund; *Studies in Parapsychology* (a collection of three essays). sc, MacMillan 1963.

Frost, Gavin & Yvonne; *The Witches Bible*. sc, Berkeley 1975. A modern eclectic system of magic, based on a Welsh Familial Tradition.

Fuller, John G.; *The Interrupted Journey*. sc, Berkeley 1974. Possibly the most detailed investigation of a UFO contact story available.

_____. *Incident at Exeter*. sc, Berkeley.

Furst, P.T. (ed); *Flesh of the Gods: The Ritual Use of Hallucinogens*. sc, Praeger 1972.

Gandee, Lee R.; *Strange Experience*. Unique and erotic memoirs of a Pennsylvania "Dutch" hexmeister. sc. Prentice Hall 1971.

Gardner, Gerald; *High Magic's Aid*. sc, Samuel Weiser 1975. OP.

_____. *Witchcraft Today*. sc, Citadel 1970.

_____. *The Meaning of Witchcraft*. sc, Samuel Weiser. OP.

The books that launched the Neopagan Witchcraft movement.

Gardner, Martin; *Fads & Fallacies in the Name of Science*. sc, Dover 1975. A classic job of scientistic debunking.

Garfield, Patricia; *Creative Dreaming*. sc, Ballantine 1974.

Garrett, Eileen J.; *The Sense and Nonsense of Prophecy*. sc, Berkeley 1968. A scathing denunciation (by a genuine psychic and parapsychologist) of fraud and quackery in the field.

Garrett, Randall; *Too Many Magicians*. hc, Doubleday 1967 (sc planned, Ace 1980).

_____. *Murder & Magic*. sc, Ace 1979.

The first is a classic novel and the second a collection of stories from Garret's "Lord Darcy" series of occult science fiction. Garrett presents the *best* depiction of magic of any fiction author.

Gauquelin, Michael; *The Scientific Basis of Astrology: Myth of Reality*. sc, Stein & Day 1970.

_____. *The Cosmic Clocks: From Astrology to a Modern Science*. sc, Contemporary Books 1974.

_____. *How Cosmic and Atmospheric Energies Influence your Health*. sc, Aurora Press, 1976. Research supporting parts of Astrology by a scientist who doesn't believe in Astrology.

Geller, Uri; *Uri Geller: My Story*. sc, Warner 1976. Autobiography. Compare with Puharich's book on him.

Ginzburg, Carlo; *Witchcraft & Agrarian Cults in the Sixteenth & Seventeenth Centuries*. sc, Penguin, 1985. An important text for those interested in theories of the witchcraft persecutions having been aimed at genius Pagan survivals.

Godwin, John; *Occult America*. hc, Doubleday 1972. A good antidote to overenthusiasm, has an excellent section on Scientology.

Goldberg, Herb; *Hazards of Being Male: Surviving the Myth of Masculine Privilege*. sc, New American Library 1977. The other side of the coin.

Goldberg, Steven; *the Inevitability of Patriarchy*. sc, Morrow 1974. Believers in matriarchal theories will have to deal with this well researched (though unclearly written) work.

Gonzalez-Wippler, Migene; *Santeria — African Magic in Latin America*. hc, Julian Press 1973.

Govinda, Lama Anagarika; *Foundations of Tibetan Mysticism*. sc, Samuel Weiser 1970.

_____. *Psychological Attitude of Early Buddhist Philosophy*. sc, Samuel Weiser 1970. OP.

Graves, Robert; *The White Goddess*. sc, Farrar 1970. Scholarship and logic are extremely shaky, but the poetic images are powerful.

Gray, William, G.; *Inner Traditions of Magic*. sc, Samuel Weiser 1978. Good training advice.

Gribbin, John & Plagemann, Stephen; *The Jupiter Effect: The Planets as Triggers of Devastating Earthquakes*. sc, Random House 1976. When is astrology not astrology? When you call it something else.

Grimm, Jacob; *Teutonic Mythology*. Four volumes. sc, Dover 1966.

Grof, Stanislav; *Realms of Human Unconscious*. sc, Dutton 1976.

Guillaumont, A.; *The Gospel According to Thomas*. Translated into English from Coptic. hc, Harper & Row 1959. A completely authentic "Lost" Gospel. Suppressed might be a better word.

Harner, Michael J. (ed.); *Hallucinogens & Shamanism*. sc, Oxford University Press 1973.

Harrington, Alan; *The Immortalist*. sc, Celestial Arts 1977. We don't really have to die, he says, we're just in the habit.

Henderson, Joseph & Oakes, Maud; *The Wisdom of the Serpent: The Myths of Death, Rebirth & Resurrection*. sc, Collier 1971.

Herskovits, M.J. & F.S.; *Dahomean Narrative*. hc, Northwestern University Press 1958. Useful background to Vodoun.

Hesse, Hermann; *The Journey to the East*. sc, Farrar, Straus & Giroux 1969.

_____. *Magister Ludi*. sc, Bantam 1972.

Holmes, Ronald; *Witchcraft in British History*. sc, Tandem 1976.

Holroyd, Stuart; *Psi and the Consciousness Explosion*. sc, Taplinger 1977.

Hope, A.D.; *A Midsummer Eve's Dreams: Variations on a Theme by William Dunbar*. hc, Australian Natural University Press 1970. Evidences of Scottish goddesses being worshipped in the 15th century.

Hughes, Pennethorne; *Witchcraft*. sc, Penguin 1965. Covers the Gothic Witchcraft period only.

Hurston, Zora Neale; *Mules and Men: Negro Folktales and Voodoo Practices in the South*. sc, Harper & Row 1970. A classic collection from the 1930's.

Huson, Paul; *Mastering Witchcraft: A Practical Guide for Witches, Warlocks and Covens*. sc, Berkley 1977. His folklore is still, but this is a surprisingly helpful book.

_____. *The Devil's Picture Book*. sc, Berkeley 1973. Good Tarot text.

Jackson, Kenneth H.; *A Celtic Miscellany*. sc, Penguin 1977. Good source of material for Celtic rituals.

James, William; *Pragmatism & Other Essays*. sc, Washington Square Press 1963.

_____. *Varieties of Religious Experience*. sc, Collier 1967.

Essays into the philosophy of perception and religion. Both are classics and both are recommended.

Jaynes, Julian; *The Origin of Consciousness in the Breakdown of the Bicameral Mind*. hc, Houghton-Mifflin 1977.

Jones, Marc Edmund; *Astrology: How and Why it Works*. sc, Penguin 1972. An interesting theory, and like his other books, clear and precise.

_____. *How to Learn Astrology*. sc, Random House 1977. A remarkably clear introduction to a difficult skill.

Jung, Carl Gustav; *Collected Works, Volume Nine, Part One: Archetypes and the Collective Unconscious*. hc, Bollingen 1969.

_____. *Collected Works, Volume IX, Part 2: Aion*. hc, Bollingen, Princeton University Press 1970.

_____. *Collected Works, Volume XI, Psychology and Religion, West and East*. hc, Bollingen, Princeton University Press 1969.

_____. *Psyche & Symbol*. sc, Doubleday 1958.

_____. *Synchronicity: An Actual Connecting Principle*. sc, Princeton University Press 1973.

Jung is probably one of the most important psychological theoreticians for magicians. All of his works are worth reading.

Jung, Carl Gustav & Kerenyi, C.; *Essays on a Science of Mythology ("The Divine Child" and "The Mysteries of Eleusis")*. sc, Princeton University Press 1969.

Jung, Carl Gustav & Pauli, W.; *Interpretation of Nature & Psyche*. hc, Bollingen 1955.

Kaplan, Stuart R.; *The Encylopedia of Tarot, Vol. 1.* hc 1978, and Vol. 2. 1985, U.S. Games. Possibly the definitive series on the history of Tarot cards. With superb bibliographies.

Katz, Michael, et al. (ed.); *Earth's Answer: Explorations of Planetary Culture at the Lindisfarne Conferences.* sc. Harper & Row 1977.

Kelly, Aidan; *The Rebirth of Witchcraft: Tradition and Creativity in the Gardnerian Reform.* Unpublished manuscript. The most scholarly examination of the origins of Neopagan Witchcraft ever done.

Kiev, Ari (ed.); *Magic, Faith and Healing.* sc, Free Press 1974. Papers on healing techniques.

_____. *Curanderismos: Mexican-American Folk Psychiatry.* sc, Free Press 1972.

Knight, Gareth; *Occult Exercises & Practices.* sc, Samuel Weiser 1976.

Koestler, Arthur; *The Roots of Coincidence.* sc, Random House 1973.

Kogan, I.M.; *The Information Theory Aspect of Telepathy.* A paper presented at a Symposium called "A New Look at ESP," held June 7–8, 1969 at the University of California Los Angeles. If you read Russian, look up Kogan in back issues (at least three) of "Radiotechnia." A mechanistic theory of telepathy as radio waves.

Kriss, Marika; *Witchcraft—Past & Present for the Millions.* hc, Tandem 1970. Despite the title, not bad.

Kubler-Ross, Elizabeth; *Images of Growth & Death.* sc, Prentice-Hall 1976.

_____. (ed.); *Death: The Final Stage of Growth.* sc, Prentice-Hall 1975.

Kusche, Lawrence David; *The Bermuda Triangle Mystery—Solved.* sc, Warner 1975. A very well researched deflating of the whole topic.

LaBarre, Weston; *Ghost Dance.* sc, Delta 1972.

_____. *The Peyote Cult.* sc, Schocken 1976.

_____. *They Shall Take up Serpents: Psychology of the Southern Snake-Handling Cult.* sc, Schocken 1974.

Lamb, F. Bruce; *Wizard of the Upper Amazon: The Story of Manuel Cordova-Rios.* sc, Houghton-Mifflin 1975. Shamanistic drug rituals leading to group psi experiences in Peru.

Langer, Susanne K.; *Philosophy in a New Key.* sc, Harvard University Press 1975. She goes the opposite direction from most authors, and considers magic to be 100% artistic in nature. But it's a very good book on symbolism in art, reason and ritual.

Larsen, Stephen; *The Shaman's Doorway.* sc, Harper & Row 1977. Traditional & changing functions of religions in daily life.

Layton, Eunice & Felix; *Theosophy: Key to Understanding.* sc, Theosophical Publishing House 1967. Theosophy from the viewpoint of modern theosophists, and much more readable than Blavatsky.

Leary, Timothy; *Exo-Psychology: A Manual on the Use of the Nervous System According to the Instruction of the Manufacturers.* sc, Peace Press 1977.

_____. *Neuropolitics: The Sociobiology of Human Metamorphosis*. sc, Peace Press 1979.

Strange but brilliant theories of psychology and evolution. Highly recommended for provoking arguments.

Leary, Timothy & Metzner, Ralph; *the Psychedelic Experience: A Manual Based on the Tibetan Book of the Dead*. sc, Citadel 1976.

Leek, Sybil; *Diary of a Witch*. sc, New American Library 1972.

_____. *Complete Art of Witchcraft*. sc, New American Library 1973.

_____. *My Life in Astrology*. sc, New American Library 1974.

Fascinating autobiographical materials from one of Britain's first Familial Witches to go public.

Leland, Charles; *Aradia — The Gospel of the Witches*. sc, Samuel Weiser.

_____. *Gypsy Sorcery and Fortune-Telling*. sc, Dover 1971.

LeShan, Lawrence; *Alternate Realities*. sc, Ballantine 1977.

_____. *The Medium, the Mystic & the Physicist*. hc, Ballantine 1975.

_____. *Toward a General Theory of the Paranormal*. sc, Parapsychology Foundation 1969.

Levi, Eliphas; *The History of Magic*. sc, Samuel Weiser 1969.

_____. *The Key of the Mysteries*. sc, Samuel Weiser 1970.

_____. *Transcendental Magic*. sc, Samuel Weiser 1970.

These three works are classics of W.M.O., but are not really very useful for practical work. You should read them at least once though.

Levi-Strauss, Claude; *Structural Anthropology*. sc, Doubleday 1967.

_____. *The Raw & the Cooked*. sc, Harper & Row 1970.

_____. *From Honey to Ashes*, sc, Harper & Row 1973.

Lilly, John; *Programming & Metaprogramming in the Human Biocomputer*. sc, Julian 1972.

_____. *The Center of the Cyclone*. sc, Bantam 1974.

_____. *Simulations of God — The Science of Belief*. sc, Bantam 1976.

_____. *Lilly on Dolphins: Humans of the Sea*. sc, Doubleday 1975.

One of the best interdisciplinary thinkers of our time.

Lilly, John & Antonietta; *The Dyadic Cyclone*. sc, Pocket Books 1977. A genteel introduction to sex magic for couples.

Long, Joseph (ed.); *Extrasensory Ecology; Parapsychology & Anthropology*. hc, Scarecrow 1978.

Long, Max Freedom; *The Secret Science Behind Miracles*. hc, DeVorss 1967.

_____. *The Secret Science at Work*. hc, DeVorss 1953.

Long has a tendency to go overboard with his historical theories, but these still remain the only major presentation of Hawaiian techniques of magic. The second book is a "work manual" to go with the first, and is good. *See* also Steiger, Brad.

Luzatto, Rabbi Moses C. Hayim; *General Principles of the Kabbalah*. hc, Research Center of Kabbalah 1970. A reliable if ponderous introduction to Kabbalah from the Jewish viewpoint, instead of the W.M.O. viewpoint.

Malinowski, Branislov; *Magic, Science & Religion*. sc, Doubleday 1954.

Maltz, Mazwell; *Psycho-Cybernetics*. sc, Pocket Books. A classic text of Orange Magic.

Manning, Al; *Helping Yourself with White Witchcraft*. sc, Prentice-Hall 1972.

————. *Helping Yourself with Psycho-Cosmic Power*. sc, Prentice-Hall 1976. More Orange Magic, for Blue Collars.

Manning, Matthew; *The Link*. sc, Ballantine 1976. Autobiography of a psychic.

Mao Tsi-Tung, et al.; *Chinese Guerilla Warfare Tactics*, sc, Paladin Press 1974. Interesting blend of Chinese philosophy with practical military science.

Maple, Eric; *Incantations and Words of Power*. sc, Samuel Weiser 1974. OP.

Marwick, M. (ed.); *Witchcraft & Sorcery: Selected Readings*. sc, Penguin 1970.

Maslow, Abraham H.; *Towards a Psychology of Being*. sc, Van Nostrand 1962.

————. *Religions, Values and Peak Experiences*. hc, Random House 1964. Maslow founded the Humanistic School of psychology, and deserves thoughtful reading.

Masters, Robert & Houston, Jean; *The Varieties of Psychedelic Experience*. sc, Dell 1967.

————. *Mind Games — The Guide to Inner Space*. sc, Dell 1973.

Mathers, S.L. "MacGregor"; The Kabbalah Unveiled. sc, Samuel Weiser, 1983. This is the book that organized Western Kabbalah into a clumsy but workable system, back in 1887. Try comparing it to Scholem or Luzzatto.

————. *Book of the Sacred Magic of Abra-Melin the Mage*. sc, Dover 1975. A complete system for a very expensive six month ritual to attain a link with one's "Higher Self." But Mather's translation is sloppy and you need to know enough Kabbalah to correct all the mistakes.

McCreery, Charles; *Psychic Phenomena and the Physical World*. sc, Ballantine 1973.

Mead, G.R.S.; *Fragments of a Faith Forgotten*. hc, University Books 1960.

————. *Pistis Sophia*. hc, Watkins 1963. These are only part of this great scholar's writings on Gnosticism and the origins of Christianity.

Metraux, Alfred; *Voodoo in Haiti*. sc, Schocken 1972.

Middleton, John (ed.); *Magic, Witchcraft and Curing*. sc, Natural History Press 1967.

Miller, David; *The New Polytheism*. hc, Harper & Row 1974. He argues for a return to Greek religion as being more relevant to our emerging worldview.

Mishlove, Jeffrey; *The Roots of Consciousness*. sc, Random House 1975. Good compendium of material.

Mitchell, Edgar & White, John (ed.); *Psychic Exploration; A Challenge for Science*. sc, Putnam 1976.

Monroe, Robert; *Journeys Out of the Body*. sc, Doubleday 1973. One of the more practical works on the topic.

Moss, Thelma; *The Probability of the Impossible*. sc, New American Library 1975. An excellent introduction to the field of parapsychology.

Muldoon, Sylvan & Carrington, Hereward; *The Phenomena of Astral Projection*. sc, Samuel Weiser 1969. A classic on astral projection, though not very practical.

Murphy, Gardner & Ballou, Robert; *William James on Psychical Research*. hc, Viking 1960. An analysis of the philosopher's views.

Murphy, Gardner & Dale, Laura A.; *The Challenge of Psychical Research: A Primer of Parapsychology*. sc, Harper & Row 1970. A modern classic of psi research.

Murray, Margaret A.; *The Witchcraft in Western Europe*. sc, Oxford University Press 1967.

_____. *The God of the Witches*. sc, Oxford University Press 1973.

_____. *The Divine King in England*. sc, Oxford University Press, 1974.
A respected Egyptologist whose theories about the medieval witchcraft persecutions are highly controversial.

Needleman, Jacob; *The New Religions*. sc, Dutton 1977.

_____. *A Sense of the Cosmos*, sc, Dutton 1977.

_____. (ed.) *The Sword of Gnosis: Metaphysics, Cosmology, Tradition, Symbolism*. sc, Penguin 1974.

Neumann, Erich; *Amor & the Psyche: The Psychic Development of the Feminine*. sc, Princeton University Press 1971.

_____. *The Great Mother: An Analysis of the Archetype*. sc, Princeton University Press 1972.

Niel, Fernand; *The Mysteries of Stonehenge*. sc, Avon 1975. One of the best single works on the topic.

Nybor & Bonewits, P.E.I.; *The Nybor Tarot*. Deck & Book. In preparation. An adult tarot deck focussed on the erotic aspects of the tarot archetypes.

Ophiel (pseud.); *The Art and Practice of Astral Projection*. sc, Samuel Weiser 1974.

_____. *The Art and Practice of Clairvoyance*. sc, Samuel Weiser. OP.

_____. *The Art and Practice of Getting Material Things Through Creative Visualization*. sc, Samuel Weiser 1975.

_____. *The Art and Practice of the Occult*. sc, Samuel Weiser, rev. ed. 1984.
His theories are slightly muddled, but his exercises are very good.

Ornstein, Robert; *On the Experience of Time*. sc, Penguin 1975.

Ostrander, Sheila & Schroeder, Lynn; *Psychic Discoveries Behind the Iron Curtain*. sc, Bantam 1971.

————. *The ESP Papers: Scientists Speak Out from Behind the Iron Curtain.* sc, Bantam 1976.

Two enlightening looks at how far behind we are.

Owen, Iris & Sparrow, Margaret; *Conjuring Up Philip: An Adventure in Psycho-kinesis.* sc, Pocket Books 1977. One of the most important books published in the field of psychical research. A major threat to survivalist theories.

Parrinder, Goeffrey; *Witchcraft: European & African.* sc, Barnes & Noble 1970.

Pauwels, Louis & Bergier, Jacques; *The Morning of the Magicians* (also published as *The Dawn of Magic*). sc, Stein & Day 1977.

————. *Impossible Possibilities.* sc, Avon 1973.

————. *The Eternal Man.* sc, Avon 1973.

Highly speculative materials, but well worth sifting through.

Peach, Ed (see "Ophiel")

Pearce, Joseph; *The Crack in the Cosmic Egg.* sc, Pocket Books 1977.

————. *Exploring the Crack in the Cosmic Egg.* sc, Pocket Books 1975.

Two fine works on expanding beyond our self-imposed limits of "reality."

Pensee Magazine, the Editors of; *Velikovsky Reconsidered.* sc, Warner 1977. A series of thoughtful articles from *Pensee*, the quarterly journal of the Student Academic Freedom Forum in Portland Oregon.

Perry, John Weir; *Lord of the Four Quarters: Myths of the Royal Father.* sc, Collier 1970. A Jungian traces the archetypes.

Piggott, Stuart; *Approach to Archeology.* sc, McGraw Hill 1965. Includes fascinating material.

————. *The Druids.* sc, Thames & Hudson, 1985. Undoubtedly the best single work ever written on the Druids, specifically designed to deflate a lot of romantic nonsense.

Pollack, Jack; *Croiset the Clairvoyant.* sc. Doubleday 1964. Biography.

Pollack, Rachel; *Seventy-Eight Degrees of Wisdom — Part 1: The Major Arcana.* sc, Aquarian Press 1980.

————. *Part 2: The Minor Arcana and Readings.* sc, Aquarian Press 1983.

I think this set is one of the best introductions to the meaning and use of the Tarot ever published.

Popenoe, Cris; *Books for Inner Development: The Yes! Guide.* sc, Random House 1976. A gigantic bibliography.

Prinn, Ludwig; *De Vermis Mysteriis.* hc, Starry Wisdom Press 1895. This book is not for people who move their lips when they read! OP.

Puharich, Andrija; *Beyond Telepathy.* sc, Doubleday 1973.

————. *The Sacred Mushroom,* sc, Doubleday 1974.

————. *Uri: A Journey of the Mystery of Uri Geller,* sc, Bantam 1975.

Randall, John; *Parapsychology & the Nature of Life,* sc, Harper & Row 1977.

Ransom, C.J.: *The Age of Velikovsky.* sc, Dell 1977. A rational discussion of Velikovsky's theories by supportive physicist.

Reed, Evelyn; *Woman's Evolution: from Matriarchal Clan to Patriarchal Family*. sc, Pathfinder 1975. Speculative and revisionist anthropology, marred by a dependence on political dogma.

Rees, Alwyn & Brinely; *Celtic Heritage*. sc, Thames & Hudson 1975. Folklore text, good antidote to a lot of rot about Druids & Fairies.

Regardie, Francis Israel; *The Golden Dawn*, in four volumes. hc in 2 volumes, Llewellyn 1970.

_____. *My Rosicrucian Adventure*. hc, Llewellyn 1971.

_____. *The Tree of Life*. sc, Samuel Weiser 1971.

_____. *How to Make and Use Talismans*. sc, Samuel Weiser 1972.

_____. *A Practical Guide to Geomantic Divination*. sc, Samuel Weiser 1972.

There are many other titles, all of which are highly recommended, though not all of them are easy. Regardie may well be the most articulate and scholarly spokesman for the Western Mainstream tradition alive.

Regush, Nicholas & June; *Frontiers of Healing; New Dimensions in Parapsychology*. sc, Avon 1976.

_____. *The Human Aura*. sc, Berkeley 1977.

Reich, Wilhelm; *The Function of the Orgasm*. sc, Pocket Books 1975.

_____. *The Murder of Christ: the Emotional Plague of Mankind*. sc, Pocket Books 1976.

Every occultist should be familiar with Reich's work. If he could die for his writings, the least we can do is to sludge through them.

Reifler, Sam; *I Ching: A New Interpretation for Modern Times*. sc, Bantam, 1985. For practical application to daily life, this is my favorite version.

Reik, Theodor; *Pagan Rites in Judaism*. hc, Gramercy 1964.

Rhine, J.B.; *Extra-Sensory Perception*. sc, Branden.

_____. *New World of the Mind*. sc, Morrow 1971.

_____. *The Reach of the Mind*. sc, Morrow.

_____. (ed.); *Progress in Parapsychology*. sc, Parapsychology Press 1971.

Rhine, Louisa E; *ESP in Life & Lab*. sc, Macmillan 1969.

_____. *Mind Over Matter*. sc, Macmillan 1972.

_____. *PSI:What Is It?* sc, Harper & Row 1976.

Rigand, Milo; *Secret of Voodoo*. sc, Pocket Books 1971. A good journalistic treatment, with some nice pictures.

Robbins, Rossell Hope; *Encyclopaedia of Witchcraft and Demonology*. hc, Crown 1959. Possibly the definitive work on Gothic Witchcraft, at least as far as data is concerned.

Rogo, D. Scott; *Exploring Psychic Phenomena*. sc, Theosophical Publishing House 1976.

_____. *Methods & Models for Education in Parapsychology* sc, Parapsychology Foundation 1973.

_____. *Mind Beyond Body: the Mystery of ESP Projection*. sc, Penguin 1978.

————. *Parapsychology*. sc, Dell 1976.

Rothenberg, Jerome; *Technicians of the Sacred: A Range of Poetries from Africa, America, Asia & Oceania*. sc, Doubleday 1969.

————. *Shaking the Pumpkin: Traditional Poetry of the Indian North Americas*. sc, Doubleday 1972.

Rush, Anne Kent; *Moon, Moon*. sc, Random House 1976. Feminist mythology of the Moon.

Russell, Jeffrey Burton; *History of Medieval Christianity*. sc, AHM Publishing 1968.

————. *Witchcraft in the Middle Ages*. sc, Citadel 1976.

————. *Witchcraft: Sorcerers, Heretics & Pagans*. hc, Thames & Hudson, 1979.

Sagrue, Thomas; *There is a River: The Story of Edgar Cayce*. sc, Dell 1977.

Sandford, Jeremy; *In Search of the Magic Mushroom*. hc, Crown 1973. Touristy but interesting adventures in Mexico.

Scholem, Gershom G.; *On the Kabbalah and its Symbolism*. sc, Schocken 1972.

————. *Major Trends in Jewish Mysticism*. sc, Schocken 1971.

————. *Kabbalah*. sc, New American Library 1978.

These are tough sledding but worth it. Authors who understand the context, contents and condense of the Kabbalah of Mysticism are rare.

Schonfield, Hugh J.; *A History of Biblical Literature*. sc, New American Library 1962.

————. *The Authentic New Testament*. New American Library.

————. *The Passover Plot*. sc, Bantam 1971.

————. *Those Incredible Christians*. sc, Bantam 1969.

Schonfield is the foremost nonchristian scholar of the New Testament alive. He exposes a lot of data that the orthodox theologians would prefer to remain buried.

Schuttes, Richard Evans; *Hallucinogenic Plants; a Golden Nature Guide*. sc, Golden Press 1976. For its size, the best book around.

Schwarz, Jack; *The Path of Action*. sc, Dutton 1977.

————. *Voluntary Controls*. sc, Dutton 1978.

Shah, Indries Sayed; *The Elephant in the Dark; The Diffusion of Sufi Ideas into the West*. sc, Dutton 1976.

————. *Oriental Magic*. sc, Dutton 1975.

————. *The Secret Lore of Alchemy*. sc, Citadel 1958.

————. *The Secret Lore of Magic*. sc, Citadel 1970.

————. *The Way of the Sufi*. sc, Dutton 1970.

The fourth book is especially useful for showing how useless medieval grimoires are in this century. All of Shah's works are highly recommended.

Shea, Robert & Wilson, Robert Anton; *Illuminatus!* Three volumes: *The Eye in the Pyramid, The Golden Apple, Leviathan*. sc, Dell 1975. Mind boggling, brilliant and satirical "fiction" every occultist, parapsychologist, political activist and conspiracy buff should read.

Shepard, Paul & McKinley, Daniel (ed.); *Subversive Science: Essays Toward an Ecology of Man.* sc, Houghton-Mifflin 1969.

Sherman, Harold; *How to Make ESP Work for You.* sc, Fawcett 1975.

_____. *Your Power to Heal.* sc, Fawcett 1975.

Sherman usually has very good exercises.

Siu, Ralph G.; *The Tao of Science.* sc, M.I.T. Press 1958.

_____. *The Portable Dragon: The Western Man's Guide to the I Ching.* sc, M.I.T. Press 1971.

Slater, ed. *A Book of Pagan Rituals.* Samuel Weiser 1978. These rituals were originally created for The Pagan Way, an "outer court" (screening group) for would-be Gardnerian Witches in the New York City area, back in the 1960's. The polytheology is Gardnerian/Valientian and you need no initiation to perform them.

Smyth, Frank; *Modern Witchcraft.* sc, Harper & Row 1973. Has some interesting and rare data on Gerald Gardner, as well as much silliness.

Spence, Lewis; *The History of Atlantis.* sc, Citadel 1973.

_____. *The Mysteries of Britain.* hc, Aquarian 1970.

_____. *The Magic Arts in Celtic Britain.* hc, Aquarian 1970.

Spence usually mixes a great deal of nonsense with some genuine scholarship. But then, I've been accused of that too!

Spraggett, Allen; *The World of the Unexplained.* sc, New American Library 1974.

_____. *New Worlds of the Unexplained.* sc, New American Library 1976.

_____. *The Case for Immortality.* sc, New American Library 1975.

_____. *Kathryn Kuhlman: the Woman Who Believes in Miracles.* New American Library 1971.

_____. *Arthur Ford: the Man Who Talked with the Dead.* New American Library 1974.

Starhawk: *Dreaming the Dark: Magic, Sex and Politics.* sc, Beacon Press 1982.

_____. *The Spiral Dance: A Rebirth of the Ancient Religion of the Great Goddess.* sc, Harper & Row 1979.

_____. *Truth or Dare.* hc, Harper & Row 1988.

Starhawk is the most significant writer and "non"-leader of the Feminist Witchcraft movement.

Steiger, Brad; *Secrets of Kahuna Magic.* sc, Universal 1971. A concise summation of the nearly unreadable writings of M.F. Long, OP.

_____. *In My Soul I Am Free.* sc, Zebra 1975. Biography of the founder of the Eckankar system.

_____. *Medicine Power.* sc, Doubleday 1974.

_____. *Medicine Talk.* sc, Doubleday 1976.

Steiger's work is often butchered by editors, so read carefully. The last two are on Native American magic and religion today.

Steiner, Claude; *Scripts People Live*. sc, Bantam 1975.

_____. (ed.); *Readings in Radical Psychiatry*. sc, Grove 1975.

All Steiner's work is highly recommended.

Stevens, John O.; *Awareness: exploring, experimenting, experiencing*. sc, Real People's Press 1971. Gestalt awareness exercises.

Stephensen, P.R. & Regardie, F.I.; *The Legend of Aleister Crowley*. sc, Llewellyn 1970. A compassionate and accurate biography.

Stone, Merlin; *When God Was a Woman*. sc, Harcourt-Brace Jovanovich 1978. Revisionist "herstory" based on the Universal Golden Age of Matriarchy theory.

Sullivan, J.W.N.; *The Limitations of Science*. sc, Random House 1969. This text on scientific methods is must reading.

Sundar; *Rainbow Bridge Sex Guide*. sc booklet, Rainbow Bridge Construction Co. 1976. One of the stranger little systems of sex magic around.

Swann, Ingo; *To Kiss Earth Good Bye*. sc, Dell 1977. Autobiography of a psychic Scientologist.

Szasz, Thomas; *Ceremonial Chemistry*. sc, Doubleday 1975.

Tart, Charles; *PSI: Scientific Studies of the Psychic Realm*. sc, Dutton 1977.

_____. *Learning to Use Extra-Sensory Perception*. sc, University of Chicago Press 1976.

_____. (ed.); *Altered States of Consciousness*. sc, Doubleday 1972.

_____. *States of Consciousness*. sc, Dutton 1975.

_____. *Transpersonal Psychologies*. sc, Harper & Row 1977.

Teish, Luisah; *Jambalaya: The Natural Woman's Book of Personal Charms and Practical Ritual*. hc, Harper & Row, 1985. An excellent blend of Feminist Witchcraft and Afro-American Mesopaganism.

Thomas, Keith; *Religion & the Decline of Magic*. sc, Scribner 1971. Interesting historical materials, marred by scientistic biases.

Thorsson, Edred; *Futhark: A Handbook of Rune Magic*. sc, Samuel Weiser 1984.

_____. *Runelore: A Handbook of Esoteric Runology*. sc, Samuel Weiser 1987.

_____. *At the Well of Wyrd*. sc, Samuel Weiser 1988. His work is the best now available on the divinitory and magical uses of runes.

Toben, Bob & Safatti, Jack; *Space-Time & Beyond: Toward an Explanation of the Unexplainable*. sc, Dutton 1975. Marvelous ideas to play with.

Tractenburg, Joshua; *The Devil and the Jews*. sc, Harper & Row 1966.

_____. *Jewish Magic and Superstition*. sc, Antheneum 1970.

Superb examinations of the Jews, magic, witchcraft accusations, the Church of Rome and antisemitism.

Tucci, Giuseppe; *The Theory and Practice of the Mandala*. sc, Samuel Weiser 1970.

Valiente, Doreen; *An ABC of Witchcraft Past and Present*. sc, Phoenix 1988.

————. *Natural Magic*. sc, Phoenix 1987.

————. *Where Witchcraft Lives*. sc, Phoenix 1988.

————. *Witchcraft for Tomorrow*. sc, Phoenix 1988.

More than anyone other than Gardner himself, Valiente is responsible for the revival/invention of Neopagan Witchcraft. Her work deserves serious attention.

Van Deusen, Edward: *Astrogenetics*. sc, Pocket Books 1977. Another nonastrological book about astrology.

Van Over, Raymond; *Psychology & Extrasensory Perception*. sc, New American Library.

Vasiliev, L.L.; *Experiments in Mental Suggestion*. hc, Institute for the Study of Mental Images 1963.

————. *Experiments in Distant Influence: Discoveries by the Father of Russian Parapsychology*. sc, Dutton 1976.

Von Daniken, Erich; *Chariots of the Gods*. sc, Berkeley 1977. The ideas are unoriginal, the research is dishonest and the logic is abysmal. He's set back the search for genuine evidence of extraterrestrial contacts several decades with his sloppy and lurid writings.

Von Juntz, Karl; *Unaussprechlichen Kulten*. hc, Starry Wisdom Press 1909. Recommended only for Sirius researchers and those with no ambiitons to die of old age. OP.

Von Reichenbach, Karl; *The Odic Force*. hc, University Books 1968. Yet another flavor of psychic energy is discovered.

Waite, Arthur Edward "Whiz Dumb While You"; *The Book of Ceremonial Magic*. sc, Citadel 1970.

————. *The Pictoral Key to the Tarot*. sc, Samuel Weiser 1973.

————. *The Brotherhood of the Rosy Cross*, hc, University Books 1961.

W.M.O. at its most mediocre. His grimoire is useless, the Tarot theory is full of deliberate confusion, and the "history" is absurd.

Waters, Frank; *Masked Gods: Navaho & Pueblo Ceremonialism*. sc, Ballantine 1975.

Watson, Lyall; *Supernature*. sc, Bantam 1974.

————. *The Romeo Error: A Meditation on Life & Death*. sc, Dell 1976.

Watts, Alan W.; *The Two Hands of God: The Myths of Polarity*. sc, Collier 1969.

————. *Beyond Theology: the Art of Godmanship*. sc, Random House 1973. A brilliant and subtle thinker. All his works are worth study.

Weinstein, Marion; *Earth Magic*. revised & expanded, sc, Phoenix 1986.

————. *Positive Magic: Occult Self-Help*. sc, Phoenix 1981.

Good beginner's works on theurgical magic as seen through rose colored glasses.

West, J.A. & Toonder, J.G.; *The Case for Astrology.* sc, Penguin 1973. Good summation of pro-astrology research evidence.

White, John & Krippner, Stanley (ed.); *Future Science: Life Energies and the Physics of Paranormal Phenomena.* sc, Doubleday 1977. Another book that belongs in every occultist's library!

Williams, Sheldon; *Voodoo and the Art of Haiti.* hc, Morland Lee Ltd. 1968. A nice picture book. And one picture is worth . . .?

Wilson, Robert Anton; *Sex and Drugs: A Journey Beyond Limits.* sc, Playboy 1975.

———. *Cosmic Trigger: The Final Secret of the Iluminati.* sc, And/Or Press 1977.

———. *Schrodinger's Cat.* sc, Pocket Books 1979.

———. *Masks of the Illuminati.* sc, Pocket Books 1979.

Wilson is probably the most Sirius writer on alternate realities and the occult now alive. He is certainly one of the best.

Wolman, Benjamin (ed.); *Handbook of Parapsychology.* hc, Van Nostrand Reinhold 1977. An outrageously expensive and *very* important text for professional researchers.

Wood, Ernest; *Yoga.* sc, Penguin 1968.

———. *Concentration: An Approach to Meditation.* sc, Theosophical Publishing House.

Woodroffe, John (writing as "Arthur Avalon"); *Hymn to Kali.* hc, Ganesh 1965.

———. *Principles of Tantra, Parts One & Two.* hc, Ganesh 1969 & 1970.

———. *Saki & Sakta.* hc, Ganesh 1969.

If you are at all interested in Tantra and/or E.M.O., this is one author you must read. Almost all his 60-odd books are direct translations of original Indian texts.

Woodroffe, John & Ellen (writing as "John & Ellen Avalon"); *Hymns to the Goddess.* hc, Ganesh 1964. Devotions of the Mother Goddess, useful for all interested in matriarchal cults.

Yram; *Practical Astral Projection.* sc, Samuel Weiser 1967. One of the better how-to-do-it books around.

Zimmer, Heinrich; *Philosophies of India.* sc, Princeton University Press 1969.

———. *Myths & Symbols in Indian Art & Civilization.* sc, Princeton University Press 1971.

———. *The King & the Corpse: Tales of the Soul's Conquest of Evil.* sc, Princeton University Press 1971.

Glossary

The following is a list of technical words and phrases used in this text, with the current definitions (1989) now favored by the author. A few words *not* mentioned previously, but which the readers are likely to come across from time to time, have been added for the sake of thoroughness. Those with an asterisk (*) were taken wholly or in part from *Webster's Third New International Dictionary*, which should not be held responsible for the uses to which I have put their definitions. Readers should remember that many of my definitions and coinages are my own, and that other authorities may violently disagree with me. But *all* definitions should be taken, regardless of the source, as tentative approaches to complex realities.

Absorption: An antipsi talent for absorbing the power out of psychic energy fields, including those around other beings. See *Tapping* and *Vampire, Psychic.*

Achromatics: The "colors" black, grey and white; used occasionally in this text to refer to moralistic schools of occultism.

Active Ritual: One in which those persons raising and focussing the psychic energies are *not* the main targets intended to be changed.

Active Talent: A psychic talent that involves the discharge of energy or data from the agent to the target.

Adept: One who is very skilled in magic or mysticism.

Agent: The person or animal exercising a psychic talent.

Air: One of the main "elements" in occultism; associated in the West with thought, knowledge, yellow, blue, swords, activity, daring, light, communication, heat, dampness, etc.

Akasa or *Akasha:* One of the "elements" in Indian and Tantric occultism, equivalent in most ways to the "ether" concept and/or that of "astral" matter.

Akasic Records: A concept in Indian metaphysics, of a gigantic repository of all the memories of every incarnation of every being; some gifted ones are said to be able to "read" these records (possibly through retrocognition or the clair senses) and to gain data about past events. See *Switchboard.*

Amplification: A psi or antipsi talent for boosting the power levels of psychic energy fields.

Anachronism: Something that appears to be from a time period other than the one in which it is perceived; as in medieval knights and ladies in modern America or astronomical computers in the Stone Age.

Angel: A personification of what we consider good or pleasant. In theoilogy, a being just below the main god(s) in power for good. In some magical systems, a sort of "psychic robot."

Angelology: Medieval science of studying angels. Question: how many angels can dance on the head of a photon? Answer: give the physicists who are working on quantizing consciousness another decade or two.

Animal-Psi or *Anpsi:* A little-used term for psychic phenomena involving the interactions of animals with humans, each other and the environment.

Animism: The belief that everything is alive. The Law of Personification taken as a statement of universal reality rather than as one of psychic convenience.

Anthropomancy: Divination from human entrails.

Anti-Psi or *Antipsi:* A categorical term for several genuine psychic talents that (for the most part) serve to frustrate, avoid, confuse, destroy or otherwise interfere with the operation of normal psi; they can affect the power and/or information content and/or vector of psi fields within range.

APK: See *Atomic Psychokinesis.*

Apopsi or *Avoidance:* An antipsi power that appears to generate an energy field into which no external psi field can penetrate; may work through transmutation, retuning or aportation; may interfere with internal psi fields as well.

Aportation: A PK talent involving the seemingly instantaneous movement of an object from one location in space-time to another, apparently without going through the normal space-time in between. See *Teleportation.*

Archetype: (1) Original astral form of a phenomenon; (2) *In the psychology of C.G. Jung, an inherited idea or mode of thought derived from the experiences of the species and present in the unconscious of the individual who picks it up from the collective unconscious of the species.

Asceticism: A method of altering the state of one's consciousness through the avoidance of comfort and pleasure; when extreme, may become masochism.

Aspect, Astrological: Angle formed between two items on an astrological chart.

Assimilation: A technique of psychic healing involving the picking up of a patient's pain and/or illness by the healer, who experiences it personally for a short time, after which it is supposed to vanish in both patient and healer; may also be done accidentally.

Association: Connection or correlation between two or more objects, ideas or beings; thus forming a pattern.

Association, Law of: "If any two or more patterns have elements in common, the patterns interact 'through' those common elements and control of one pattern facilitates control over the other(s), depending (among other factors) upon the number of common elements involved."

Astral Planes: Subjectively real "places" where some astral projectors perceive themselves as traveling; said to be multiple "levels" of (a) material density in the same space, and/or (b) awareness and concentration.

Astral Projection: An OOBE or Psi talent that may involve traveling GESP with the image of a body and/or the separation of a "less dense" body from the normal physical one.

Astrology: Divination through the correlation of earthly events with celestial patterns.

Athame: Ritual dagger used by Neopagan Witches, borrowed by Gerald Gardner from medieval grimoires.

Atomic Psychokinesis or *APK:* Psychokinesis done upon the molecular, atomic or subatomic levels; a subcategory of PK.

Augury: Divination by means of whatever is most handy at the time.

Aura: One or more energy fields supposedly generated by and surrounding all beings and many objects; those persons blessed with clairvoyance or other psychic talents can "read" the patterns of energy and determine information about the person or object. See *Kirlian Photography.*

Belle Indifference: Lack of interest or concern on the part of a "hysteric" or RSPKer towards unusual events occurring in or around him or her.

Beltane: Celtic fire festival beginning the summer half of the year; starts at sunset on May 4th and is also known as Bealtaine, Galan-Mai, Roodmas, Walpurgistag, St. Pierre's Day, Red Square Day, etc. Celebrated by most Neopagans and many Marxists as a major religious holiday.

Bibliomancy: Divination through the random selection of words or phrases taken out of books, especially the Bible.

Biocurrents: Electrochemical energy currents generated by living cells.

Biological Radio: One Russian term for telepathy.

Biophysics: The physics of biological phenomena.

*Bit: From "binary digit," a unit of data equal to the result of a choice between two equally probable alternatives, used in computer technology. Eight bits usually equals one "byte."

Black Magic: A racist, sexist, creedist and classist term used to refer to magic being done for "evil" purposes or by people of whom the user of the term disapproves.

Blessing: The use of magic to benefit an object or being.

Bon: The native Tibetan religion that later merged with Buddhism and Tantrism.

Bonding Control: A PK talent involving the creation and/or alteration of bonding patterns on the intermolecular, interatomic and subatomic levels; thus causing disintegration or cohesion. See *Geller Effect.*

Boomerang Curse: Spell designed to make an attacker suffer the effects of whatever hostile magic they may have launched at the user; a variation of the "mirror effect," probably operates through reddopsi.

Cabala: See *Kabbalah.*

Cartomancy: Divination through the use of cards, especially Tarot Cards.

Casting Runes: (1) Divination through the use of small objects which have been inscribed with runic letters. (2) A method of focusing or firing a spell through the carving or writing of runes.

Catapsi: An antipsi talent for the generation of strong fields of psychic static, frequently at such high intensity that all other psi fields within range are disrupted and/or drowned out, usually with the information content of those fields collapsing first.

Cause and Effect, Law of: "If exactly the same actions are done under exactly the same conditions, they will usually be associated with exactly the same 'results'."

Cellular Psychokinesis or *CPK:* A subcategory of PK, involving the use of what is probably several different APK talents in order to psychically affect the structure and behavior of living organisms, working primarily on the cellular level.

Centre or *Center, The:* Point of intersection of various planes or modes of existence, including space and time, and which can be used for (at least subjective) transportation between them.

Ceremonial Magic: Schools or methods of magic which place their emphasis upon long and complex rituals, especially of the Medieval and later European traditions; often degenerates into ritualism.

Chakras: Several psychic centers of power associated with different parts of the human body in Tantric systems of anatomy.

Chalice: Cup used in rituals and usually associated in western occultism with "element" of Water (though it often contains more potent fluids).

Circuit: A pattern or connection between whole or partial metapatterns within the Switchboard; often may be (or be associated with) an archetype, deity or other spirit.

Clairaudience: ESP input as if it were normal hearing, without the medium of another mind.

Clairempathy: A term I once tried to get people to use instead of "psychometry," but which I am no longer using myself.

Clairgustance: ESP input as if it were normal tasting, without the medium of another mind.

Clairolfaction: ESP input as if it were normal smelling, withut the medium of another mind or of a cosmetics company.

Clair Senses: General term for all the forms of ESP that start with the prefix "Clair-."

Clairtangency: ESP input as if it were normal touching, without the medium of another mind.

Clairvoyance: ESP input as if it were normal seeing, without the medium of another mind; often used as a term for clair senses, psychometry and/or precognition. See *Remote Viewing.*

Classification: Association of some phenomenon into a predetermined pattern or class of phenomena.

Cleric: A person who uses both passive and active talents and rites for both thaumaturgical and theurgical purposes, for personal and public benefit.

Cold Control: The use of temperature control to freeze or thaw objects or beings.

*Color: An interpretation of the ways in which photons hit your eyes; one way to see the difference between two objects of identical size, shape, distance and illumination.

Color Classifications: Sets of associations between various colors and particular concepts, interests or acts.

Computer: A network of electronic gates and memories that processes data; an unimaginative but very logical problem solving machine; a magnificient slave and miserable ruler; a great tool and toy for any technologically oriented occultist.

Cone of Power: Term for the focusing of a group's magical energies, visualized as a cone of psychic power based upon a ritual circle containing the participants (who are usually Neopagan or Feminist Witches). There is some confusion among various groups as to what exactly should be *done* with the energies at the moment of firing.

Contagion, Law of: "Objects or beings in physical or psychic contact with each other continue to interact after spacial or temporal separation."

CPK: See *Cellular Psychokinesis.*

Craft, The: (1) Old term used by Freemasons to refer to their activities and beliefs. (2) Current term used by Neopagan, Feminist and some other modern Witches to refer to their activities and beliefs.

Critique: A calm and unbiased evaluation of the structure and performance of a ritual, not usually done in American occult groups thanks to internal politics and delicate egos.

Crystallomancy: Divination through the use of (usually) spheres of quartz crystal, glass or plastic as focussing devices.

Cult: Any secretive religious, magical, philosophical or therapeutic group of which the user of this term does not approve.

Curse: The use of magic to harm an object or being.

*Cybernetics: Comparative study of the autonomic control system formed by the brains and nervous systems of humans and other animals, as well as electro-chemical-mechanical devices and communications systems.

Dactylogy: Finger signaling system of language (such as Ameslan) used by deaf and mute persons; can also be used as powerful mudras in rituals.

Dactylomancy: Divination by means of finger movements upon tripods, planchettes, pendulums, Oui-Ja Boards, etc., or through the use of finger rings.

Daemon: A "supernatural" spirit or being in ancient Greek religion and philosophy, far below the Gods in power for good, evil or neutral purposes; probably the actual sort of "demon" conjured by Goetic magicians.

Dagger: A ritual knife used for severing psychic bonds, exorcising, cursing and/or initiating.

Damping: A psi or antipsi talent for lowering the power levels of psychic energy fields.

Data: As used herein, information or concepts of any sort.

Definition: The meaning of a word; the classification pattern that it fits into during the time period and for the given population involved.

Deflection or *Bouncing:* An antipsi talent for altering the force vectors of incoming psi broadcasts, thus "bouncing" them away.

Deity: (1) The most powerful sort of "supernatural" being. (2) A powerful pattern in the Switchboard. (3) The memory of a dead hero(ine) or magician. (4) An ancient visitor from outer space. (5) An ancient visitor from inner space. (6) All of the above?

Demon: (1) A personification of what we consider to be evil or unpleasant (often repressed guilt feelings). (2) A nonphysical entity of a destructive and evil nature opposed to the will of the God(s), such as Maxwell's.

Demonology: Medieval science of studying demons.

Density Control: A PK talent for increasing or decreasing the density of an object or being.

Devil: A minor spirit perceived as a force for evil.

Devil, The: "Heir of Man," originally the Evil God of the Zoroastrians; later a creation of Christian and Islamic theologians (who called him Satan and Shaitan) consisting of old fertility gods, wisdom spirits and nature elementals combined with Ahriman into a figure of terror and malevolence fully equal to that of that Good God (Jehovah or Allah); the deity worshipped by Neogothic Witches.

Dharanis: One phrase creeds or statements of belief, often used as mantras, such as

"$E = mc^2$."

Dhyana: Tantric trance, possibly a form of hypnosis.

Difficult Passage: A common mythological motif involving a hard transition or journey from one state or location to another through impossibly dangerous or paradoxical territory.

*Discipline: Training or experience that corrects, molds, strengthens, or perfects (especially) the mental faculties or moral character; noted primarily by its absence in American occult groups.

Disk of Shadows: A grimoire or other magical text (especially one of witchcraft rituals) kept on a computer memory disk.

Divination: The art and science of finding out hidden information about the past, present or future through the use of psychic talents.

Diviner: Obviously, one who does divination.

Dowsing: See *Rhabdomancy.*

Druids, Ancient: From the root "dru-," meaning "oak tree, firm, strong;" the entire intelligentsia of the Celtic peoples, including doctors, judges, historians, musicians, poets, priests and magicians; 99.9% of what has been written about them is pure hogwash.

Druids, Masonic: Members of several Masonic and Rosicrucian fraternal orders founded in the 1700's (and since) in England, France and elsewhere; some claim to go back to the original Druids.

Druids, Reformed: Members of several branches of a movement founded in 1963 c.e. at Carleton College in Northfield, Minnesota; most are now Neopagans, though the original founders were not.

Dualism: A religious doctrine that states that all the spiritual forces of the universe(s) are split into Good Guys and Bad Guys (white and black, male and female, etc.) who are eternally at war.

Dualistic Polytheism: A style of religion in which the Good Guys and Bad Guys include several major and minor deities (though they may not always be called that by the official theologians); what most so-called "monotheisms" really are.

Duotheism: A style of religion in which there are two dieties accepted by the theoilogians, usually of opposite gender; all other deities worshipped are considered to be "faces" or aspects of the two main figures.

Dynamic Balance, Law of: "In order to survive, let alone to become a powerful magician, one must keep every aspect of one's universe(s) in a state of dynamic balance with every other one."

Earth: One of the main "elements" in occultism; associated in the West with matter, brown, black, pentacles, passivity, inertness, silence, food, fertility, wealth, practicality, cold, dryness, etc.

Earth-Mother: Female personification of the Life force, fertility of the Earth and its inhabitants. One of the most widespread deity concepts in the world (though far from universal); She is now worshipped in the West as Mother Nature.

Ego Trip: Modern slang for feeding one's ego or inflating one's pride.

Electric Control: An APK talent involving the control of electricity and other electron phenomena.

Electrochemical: Having to do with the interchanges between electrical and chemical energy, especially (in this text) those taking place in the body.

Electroencephalograph or *EEG:* A machine that records electromagnetic activity in the brain (the so-called "brain waves"), usually upon a moving roll of paper.

*Electromagnetic Spectrum: The entire range of frequencies or wave-lengths of electromagnetic radiation from the longest radio waves to the shortest gamma rays. Visible light is only a tiny part of this range.

Elementals: Personifications of the four or five "elements" of Western or Eastern occultism; in the West these are "Gnomes" for Earth, "Undines" for Water, "Sylphs" for Air, "Salamanders" for Fire, and "Sprites" for Spirit.

Elementals, Artificial: Term used by some Western occultists to refer to spiritual entities "created" by magicians, usually to perform specific tasks.

Elementals, Nature: Term used by some to refer to various minor spirits inhabiting or associated with various natural phenomena such as trees, streams, rocks, dust storms, etc.

Elements, The: A classification system based upon the division of all phenomena into four or five categories; in Western occultism these are Earth, Water, Air, Fire and sometimes Spirit or Ether (or in India, Akasha); in Chinese occultism these are Earth, Water, Metal, Fire and Wood.

Empath: One who can use the psi talent of empathy.

Empath, Controlled: As used in this text, someone who uses psychometry and/or empathy and/or absorption, occasionally to the point of draining others of their psychic energy.

Empath, Total: One who has trouble controlling their empathic and/or other passive psychic talents, and subsequently gets "overloaded" with data and power.

Empathy: As I now use it, a type of telepathic reception limited to the perception of emotions; obviously this talent would tie in nicely with absorption.

Energy Control: In Tantra, the control of biocurrents and their movements through the body; otherwise the control of energy in general.

*Energy Field: A continuously distributed something in space that accounts for actions at a distance; an area where energy does something. Don't blame me for the vagueness of this definition; it's a standard one used in modern physics.

Entity: A being, spirit, living creature or personification.

ESP: See *Extrasensory Perception.*

Ether: A hypothetical "substance" filling all space and conveying waves of energy. See *Space-Time Continuum.*

*Ethics: (1) That part of philosophy and theoilogy dealing with matters of "right and wrong," "good and evil," etc. (2) A set or system of moral values. (3) Principles of conduct governing an individual or profession.

Ethnography: Part of social and cultural anthropology emphasizing descriptions of individual cultures rather than cross-cultural comparisons; when engaged in by the untrained, often degenerates into scrapbooking.

Evocation, Law of: "It is possible to establish external communication with entities from either inside or outside of oneself, said entities seeming to be outside of oneself during the communication process."

Exorcism: The severing or disruption of all unwanted psychic circuits and circuit potentials within a specific object, person or place; hence the dismissal of ghosts and spirits.

Exorcist: (1) One who performs exorcisms. (2) A magician or psychic (often very religious) with strong talents for CPK, antipsi and the clair senses, who specializes in forcing or persuading unwanted psychic energies (including spirits) to depart from objects, persons or places.

Experiment: A test of an idea or guess.

Experimental Design: The way the test is put together, hopefully for maximum output of useful data.

Exponential Decay Function: A "decaying" or "falling apart" function in which an independent variable appears as one of the mathematical exponents.

Extrasensory Perception or *ESP:* The categorical term for several psi talents involving the reception of (usually) external data through other than the commonly recognized sensory means.

Faith Healing: CPK and/or other psi talents interpreted as religious phenomena in curing.

False: That which is improbable, unpleasant or inconvenient to believe.

Familiars: Animals supposedly used by Gothic Witches and others to help them with their magic; often believed to be incarnated spirits or the messengers of noncarnate ones.

Fam-Trad: Short term for "Familial Witchcraft Traditions." See *Witchcraft, Familial* and *Tradition.*

Feedback: Data returned as a reply or result, containing corrections and additions.

Filtering: An antipsi ability to use apopsi, reddopsi or deflection selectively, thus stopping part of a psi broadcast or field while letting the desired remainder (usually part of the information content) through.

Finite Senses, Law of: "Every sense mechanism of every entity is limited by both range and type of data perceived, and many real phenomena exist which may be outside the sensory scanning ability of any given entity." The Supreme Being(s) may be excepted from this law.

Fire: One of the main "elements" in occultism; associated in the West with flames, red, orange, wands or staves, activity, light, will, animals, energy, assertiveness, heat, dryness, etc.

Firing: The discharge of psychic energy in a ritual, the timing of which is frequently critical.

Folklore: The study of folktales and legends, a subject overlapping that of mythology.

Folktale: Story handed down among a people, such as "Cinderella," "Rumplestiltskin" or "Our Leader Knows Best."

Geller Effect: One or more psi talents (probably including bonding control) that enable the user to bend metal objects without touching them, named after this century's best known user, Uri Geller. The effect is real and has been done by Geller and others under impeccable laboratory controls, regardless of the tales told by Geller's supporters and detracters.

General Extrasensory Perception or *GESP:* A term used when two or more forms of ESP are operating at the same time.

Germ Theory: (1) In Tantra, the theory that every entity has a germinal or root sound, the repetition of which can create that entity. (2) In the West, a folk belief that all diseases are caused by miniature demons called "germs" or "viruses."

Ghost: Personification of data received as the result of a plug-in to an individual metapattern within the Switchboard, and/or the spirit of a dead person or animal, still existing in a nonphysical manner, and/or something(s) else entirely.

Goal: The general result one actually wishes to accomplish with a particular magical or psychic act. Compare with *Target.*

God or *Goddess, A:* See *Deity.*

God or *Goddess, The:* The particular masculine or feminine deity worshipped by a particular mono-, heno-, or duotheist.

"God or *Goddess, Thou Art:"* A statement of divine immanence common among Neopagans, originally from Robert Heinlein's book, *Stranger in a Strange Land.*

Godling: A young or minor deity.

Goetia: From words meaning "howling or crying," the medieval books of ceremonial magic, such as *The Greater & Lesser Keys of Solomon.*

Golem: An artificial person given life by the carving of a Sacred Name upon his or her forehead and usually used as a slave. Has deeper meanings in real Hebrew Mysticism, in which we are all golems in some sense.

Graphology: (1) An officially nonpsychic method of personality assessment based upon the study of handwriting samples. (2) A method of divination based upon the use of such samples as contagion links.

Gravity Control: A psychic talent for altering the gravitational fields in a particular location, such as in a room or around an object or being.

Gray Magic: Magic that is neither "black" nor "white," hence morally neutral, at least according to those who use these quaint terms.

Grimoires: So-called "Black Books" of (usually Goetic) magic, consisting of recipe collections, scrapbooks of magical customs, *Who's Who's* of the spirit worlds and phone directories for contacting various entities. Fairly useless unless you know enough Hebrew, Greek and Latin to correct all the mistakes.

Groupmind: A section of the Switchboard consisting of two or more metapatterns linked into an identity circuit. Term is used for those formed telepathically in rituals but can also be used to refer to mobs or other cases of crowd hysteria.

*Hallucination: (1) Perception of objects or beings with no reality or not present within normal sensory scanning range. (2) Experience of sensations with no exterior cause, usually as a result of nervous dysfunction. (3) Perceptions not in accord with consensus reality.

Hallucination, Veridical: One in which the content is essentially factual.

Hallucinogen: A chemical or biochemical substance capable of inducing hallucinations when introduced into the human metabolism.

Hauntings: Recurrent plug-ins to the Switchboard and/or perceptions of ghostly entities associated with a particular location or being.

Heathenism: The religion of those who live on the heath (where heather grows). See *Paganism.*

Hedonism: A method for altering the state of one's consciousness through the experience of intense pleasures; when extreme, may become tiring.

Henotheism: A polytheistic religion where one deity is the official Ruler and is supposed to be the prime focus of attention.

Hepatoscopy: Divination through the use of animal innards (see *Anthropomancy*), especially livers. When done with French hens, usually indicates cowardice.

Heat Control: The use of temperature control to start or stop fires and other heating phenomena, also called "psychopyresis."

Hixson's Law: "All possible universes that can be constructed out of all the possible interactions of all existing subatomic particles through all points in space-time, must exist."

Horoscope: A two-dimensional chart of the way "important" parts of the sky look at a particular time and location, especially at birth, used in astrology.

Hyperapotheosis: The promotion of one's tribal deity to the rank of Supreme Being, as in Judaism, Christianity or Islam.

Hypercognition: A categorical term for those psi talents consisting of superfast thinking, usually at a subconscious level, often using data received via ESP, which then reveals all or part of the "gestalt" (whole pattern) of a situation; this is then presented to the conscious mind as a sudden awareness of knowledge (or "a hunch"), *without* a pseudo-sensory experience. See *Retrocognition* and *Precognition.*

*Hyperesthesia: Excessive or pathological sensitivity of the skin or other senses; heightened perception or responsiveness to the environment; often mistaken for real ESP.

Hypnosis: (1) As used in this book, an altered state of consciousness within which the following can occur at will: increase in bodily and sensory control, in suggestibility, in ability to concentrate and eliminate distractions, and probably in psychic abilities as well. (2) A useful word and tool for those who cannot conceive of nor practice real mesmerism.

Hypothesis: Scientific term for wild guess, hunch, tentative explanation or possiblity to be tested.

Iatromancy: The divination of medical problems and solutions.

I Ching: Chinese "Book of Changes;" key to sortilege system.

Identification, Law of: "It is possible through maximum association of the elements of one's own metapattern and those of another being's to actually become that being, at least to the point of sharing its knowledge and wielding its power."

Imaging or *To Image:* Term for strong visualization of a concept being used for focusing.

Imbolg or *Imelc:* Celtic fire festival beginning the second quarter of the year (or spring); starts at sunset on February 3rd and is also known as Candlemas, St. Bridget's Day, Bride's Day, Lady Day, etc. Celebrated by most Neopagans as a major religious holiday.

Impossible: Unlikely, difficult, implausible, uncomfortable, new.

Incantation: Words used in a ritual or spell; should always be chanted or sung.

Infinite Data, Law of: "The number of phenomena to be known is infinite and one will never run out of things to learn."

Infinite Universes, Law of: "The total number of universes into which all possible combinations of existing phenomena could be organized is infinite." See *Hixson's Law* and *Personal Universes, Law of.*

Information Theory: Study of communication.

Information Transfer: Communication.

Initiation: An intense personal experience, often of a death and rebirth sort, resulting in a higher state of personal development and/or admission to a magical or religious organization.

Input: The way incoming data is interpreted or classified.

Instrumental Act: One which is useful, even if for no other purpose than to relieve stress.

Interdisciplinary Approach: The use of data and techniques from more than one art or science in order to analyze phenomena.

Invocation, Law of: "It is possible to establish internal communications with entities from either inside or outside of oneself, said entities seeming to be inside of oneself during the communication process."

Jargon: Any technical terminology or characteristic idiom of specialists or workers in a particular activity or area of knowlege; often pretentious or unnecessarily obscure.

Kabbalah: (1) A Hebrew word for "collected teachings," referring to several different lists of books and manuscripts on various occult and mundane topics. Sloppy translations of a handful of texts in the Kabbalah of Mysticism, with Christian names and concepts forcibly inserted, are responsible for much of what is now called "Cabala" by western metaphysicians. If you can't think fluently in Hebrew, you have no business trying to do Kabbalistic magic. (2) A general term for collections of magical and mystical texts from various cultures, thus "Greek Kabbalah," "Arabic Cabala," etc.

Kachina: A (usually benevolent) supernatural being in Hopi religion; may be a personification of an aspect of nature, an ancestor, or something revealed in a dream.

Kāma-kali: Ritual sexual intercourse in Tantra.

Karma: In many eastern religions, the load of guilt or innocence carried from one incarnation to the next, determining one's lot in the next life; often used by American occultists as a general term for moral responsibility, as in "You can do that if you want to, but it's your karma."

Karma Dumping Run: American occult slang for a ritual process of visiting someone's "just deserts" upon them, by "concentrating the karma" they may have earned in their life (or recent past) and delivering it back to them in one brief period of time; usually done when someone is suspected of evil doing but proof is lacking, since it is considered a morally neutral way of stopping them.

*Kinesis: Physical movement including quantitative, qualitative, and positional change; sometimes movement caused by stimulation but not directional or aimed.

Kinetic Energy: Energy associated with motion.

Kirlian Photography: A lenseless electrical photographic technique invented by Russian parapsychologists S.D. and V. Kirlian in 1939 and which can be used to record energy fields around living or once living objects and beings. Although the "Kirlian auras" vary with emotional excitement and intent, there is as yet no proof that they are the same as the "psychic auras" traditionally seen by clairvoyants. Time will tell.

Klutzokinesis: Term invented by Arlynde d'Loughlan to describe the use of CPK to make people more clumsy (or agile) through interference with neuron or muscle activities.

Knowledge, Law of: "Understanding brings control; the more that is known about a phenomenon, the easier it is to exercise control over it."

Koran: The sacred books of Islam.

Ksana: The "favorable moment;" a temporal Centre.

Law: A statement of the ways phenomena seem to work.

Law of Magic: A statement of the ways magical phenomena seem to work.

Laws, Law of: "The more evidence one looks for to support a given law, the more one finds."

Law, Sturgeon's: From science fiction writer Theodore Sturgeon: "90% of everything is crap."

Left-Hand Path: (1) The people we don't like who are doing magic. (2) Occultists who spend their time being destructive, manipulative and "evil."

Levitation: A psi talent involving the combination of PK proper with Gravity Control and/or Mass Control in order to produce floating effects.

Light Control: An APK talent for the control of photons.

Linguistics: The study of human speech, including the units, nature, structure and development of language(s).

Litany: Long prayer or incantation with constantly repeating refrain.

Lodges: Groups of magical and mystical workers similar to (1) the old European guild systems, with apprentices, journeypeople and masters, or (2) church organizations with rank based upon goodness or evilness. In America at least, these are usually tiny, incompetent and riddled with internal and external warfare and politics.

Lughnasadh: Celtic fire festival beginning the third quarter of the year (or fall); starts at sunset on August 6th or 7th and is also known as Lammas, Apple Day, etc. Celebrated by most Neopagans as a major religious holiday.

Mage: A general term for anyone doing magic, especially of the active kinds; often used as synonym for "magus."

Magi: Zoroastrian priests. Later used for powerful magicians of any sort.

Magic: (1) A general term for arts, sciences, philosophies and technologies concerned with (a) understanding and using various altered states of consciousness within which it is possible to have access to and control over one's psychic talents, and (b) the uses and abuses of those psychic talents to change interior and/or exterior realities. (2) A science and an art comprising a system of concepts and methods for the build-up of human emotions, altering the electrochemical balance of the metabolism, using associational techniques and devices to concentrate and focus this emotional energy, thus modulating the energies broadcast by the human body, usually to affect other energy patterns whether animate or inanimate, but occasionally to affect the personal energy pattern. (3) A collection of rule-of-thumb techniques designed to get one's psychic talents to do more or less what one wants, more often than not, one hopes. It should be obvious that these are thaumaturgical definitions.

Magic Circle: A mandala-mudra-mantra combination used around an area where all or part of a ritual is to take place, so that an individual or group can more easily control the energies generated.

Magician: (1) As a general term, anyone who does any sort of magic at all. (2) More specifically, someone who uses mostly active talents and rites for mostly thaumaturgical purposes.

Magician, Goetic: A magician and psychic who frequently "summons up" various nonhuman entities (good, bad or ugly) in order to gain both occult and mundane knowledge, which is then used for thaumaturgical, theurgical and nonmagical purposes.

Magister: Master, teacher or magician.

Magnetic Control: An APK talent involving the control of magnetic, diamagnetic and paramagnetic lines of force and other magnetic phenomena.

Magos: Greek word for "magi."

Magus: Originally, the singular form of "magi." Later, a powerful magician.

Mana: Polynesian word for psychic energy.

Mandala: Sights (especially drawings, paintings and carvings) used primarily as associational and/or trance inducing devices.

Mantic Arts: The various methods of divination.

Mantis: A diviner or seer.

Mantra: Sounds used primarily as associational and/or trance inducing devices.

Mass: The property of a body that is a measure of its inertia, that causes it to have weight (in a gravitational field), and that is a measure of the amount of material it contains.

Mass Control: An APK talent for increasing or decreasing the mass of an object or being.

Maya: (1) Sanscrit for "illusion." (2) A tribe of Cental American Indians.

Mayin: One who controls the worlds of illusion, a magician or mystic.

Mechanistic: A word used (usually as an insult) to refer to those who prefer to analyze even supposedly nonphysical phenomena in terms of physical or mechanical patterns of behavior.

Medicine Person: A tribal official who combines the modes of magician, psychic and cleric, using her or his talents for personal and tribal benefit; especially in such matters as healing, hunting, fertility, weather and war magic.

Medium: A psychic (and frequently cleric as well) who specializes in being possessed by, or otherwise communicating with, various spirits especially those of dead humans; someone who knows how to plug-in to the metapatterns of the recently dead, or can arrange such plug-ins for others. See *Necromancer.*

Mental Projection: An OOBE or psi talent that may involve traveling GESP without the image of an "astral body" being brought along.

Mesmerism: From Franz Mesmer, a form of telepathic sending in which the data sent consists of suggestions backed by the insistent power of the sender.

Mesopaganism: A general term coined by Robin Goodfellow for a variety of movements both organized and nonorganized, which have attempted to revive or recreate various forms of Paleopaganism, but which suffer(ed) from being locked into a Judeo-Christian worldview. Examples would include many Renaissance artists and philosophers, the Masonic Druids, Aleister Crowley's Thelemic religion, Gleb Botkin's "Long Island Church of Aphrodite," etc. See *Neopaganism* and *Paleopaganism.*

Metabolism: The sum or gestalt of the processes going on inside your body.

Metamorphosis: Change, especially of the outward appearance. See *Werewolf,* or your local politicians.

Metapattern: As used in this text, the sum and gestalt of all the interlocking patterns that make up an individual, including the body (or bodies), the various levels of mind or awareness, the psychic and artistic abilities, memory and intellectual capacities, and perhaps whatever it is that is usually called "the soul."

Metaphysics: Philosophy of the relations between "underlying reality" and its manifestations.

Miracle: A paranormal act or occurrence done by or for someone who belongs to a religion that you approve of, usually credited to divine intervention.

Miracle, Counterfeit: A paranormal act or occurrence done by or for someone who belongs to a religion that you do *not* approve of; usually credited to demonic intervention.

Monotheism: A style of religion in which the theologians (or thealogians) claim that there is only one deity (theirs of course) and that all other spirits claiming (or claimed) to be deities are "actually" demons in disguise. If other deities have cults that can be made to support the One Deity, they are kept on as "angels" or "saints." See *Hyperapotheosis.*

Moon Sign: In astrology, the zodiacal sign that the moon appeared to be in at the time and location for which the chart is cast.

Motif: A common pattern running through stories, folktales or myths.

Motion: The act or process of a body passing from one place or position to another. Completely relative.

Mudra: Physical gestures, positions or postures (including dance movements) used primarily as associational and/or trance inducing devices.

Mundane: Worldly, ordinary, common, simple; pertaining to "the earth plane."

Mysteries: Secret rituals usually involving the display of sacred mandalas and other objects to, and the performance of various mudras with and in front of, and the chanting of mantras and dharanis in the hearing of, properly initiated worshippers, for theurgical purposes in this life and the next.

Mystery Cult: A group of people who get together regularly to perform sacred mysteries and to study their meanings.

Mystery School: In theory, a group of magicians and/or mystics who have gathered together to share their wisdom and secrets with each other and with new seekers. In practice, usually a group of would-be "enlightened masters" who are primarily interested in impressing each other and in fleecing the gullible. After all, "there's a seeker born every minute!"

Mystic: (1) One who practices mysticism. (2) A person who uses mostly passive talents and rites for mostly theurgical purposes.

*Mysticism: (1) The doctrine or belief that direct knowledge of the God(s), of spiritual truth, of ultimate reality, or of comparable matters is attainable through immediate intuition, insight or illumination and in a way differing from ordinary sense perception or conscious thought. (2) The concepts and theories behind the theurgical approach to occultism.

Myth: Technically, a traditional story with its emphasis upon the actions of deities; commonly, a false or simplistic belief.

Mythology: The study of myths, and thus a field overlapping folklore; sometimes used to refer to a specific body of myths pertaining to a given culture or motif. The study of someone else's religious stories.

Mythos: A system of myths within a society or culture.

Names, Law of: "Knowing the complete and true name of an object, being or process gives one complete control over it."

Necromancer: (1) A magician and psychic who specializes in "summoning" the spirits of dead persons, usually without possession, in order to gain both occult and mundane knowledge, which is then used for thaumaturgical, theurgical and nonmagical purposes. (2) Generally, anyone who does any form of divination involving the dead. See *Medium.*

Negapsi or *Reversing:* An antipsi ability to reverse all or part of the information content of a psi broadcast or field.

Neopaganism: A general term for a variety of "Aquarian Age" movements both organized and (usually) nonorganized, which have attempted to revive or recreate various forms of Paleopaganism in terms of modern humanistic ideas of personal growth needs. As "Neo-Paganism," term was popularized in the late 60's and early 70's by Tim Zell, who has a different and much longer definition. Examples would include the Gardnerian Witches, the Church of All Worlds, Feriferia, the New Reformed Druids, the Church of the Eternal Source, etc. See *Mesopaganism* and *Paleopaganism.*

Neotarot Cards: A collection of divination cards designed to be used in the same general ways as regular Tarot Cards, but which have different (non-Tarot) archetypal images as their main contents. Examples would include "Morgan's Tarot," "The Illuminated Tarot," etc.

*Nervous System: The bodily system made up of nerves, senses, and brain, including all connectors such as the spinal cord.

Numerology: Divination by means of numbers and numerical "values" of letters.

Objective: "Reality" as it supposedly is "in itself," instead of as it may be perceived.

Observation: A part of the scientific method that involves a careful cataloging of perceptions involving any particular phenomenon.

*Obsession: Being besieged or impelled by an outside force (often perceived as demonic) to entertain thoughts or perform actions of an unpleasant, malign, pathological or unprofitable nature; thus causing anxiety and fear to be experienced by the person involved and/or observers. See *Possession.*

Occam's Razor: A philosophical axiom credited to William of Ockham: "Entities should not be multiplied without reason." Or as I put it, "Don't complicate theories unnecessarily, but beware of being simplistic."

Occult: That which is hidden or known only to a few.

Occultism: The study and/or practice of that which is occult, especially (in this century) in reference to the powers of the mind.

Oneiromancy: Divination by means of dream interpretations.

OOBE: See *Out of the Body Experience.*

Oui-Ja Board: A flat board with letters, numbers and/or words upon it, used with a planchette or pendulum for divination.

Out of the Body Experience: A perception of one's consciousness as being outside of one's physical body and usually as movable. See *Astral Projection* and *Mental Projection.*

Pagan: From the Latin *paganus,* meaning "civilian" or "country dweller;" used in ancient Rome to refer to those who were not part of the army, or who were "hicks" and "bumpkins;" later used by the Christians to refer to those who were not part of the "armies of the Lord." Now used as a general term for polytheistic religions and their members, it should always be capitalized just as other religious noun/adjective combinations are, such as "Buddhist," "Hindu," "Christian," etc.

Paleopaganism: A general term for all of the ancient and current polytheistic religions, practiced by intact (usually tribal) cultures. Most often refers to beliefs and practices of the ancient Romans, Greeks, Slavs, Celts, Babylonians, Egyptians, etc., but can also be used for the original inhabitants and their current tribal descendants in Africa, Australia, Oceania, Asia, and the Americas.

Palmistry: Divination by means of the folds and other features of the hands.

Pantheon: The organization of deities and lesser spirits in any given religion.

Para-anthropology: The study of paranormal phenomena in tribal, traditional and/or nonliterate cultures.

Paranoia: Slang term taken from psychology, used to refer to general terror or anxiety, usually with associated feelings of persecution.

Paranormal: Unusual or "supernatural."

Paraphysics: (1) The physics of paranormal phenomena. (2) The study of PK.

Parapsychology: (1) The general and interdisciplinary study of paranormal phenomena. (2) The study of that which is "beyond" the field of "normal" psychology. (3) The scientific branch of occultism.

Passive Ritual: One in which those persons raising and focusing the psychic energies *are* the main targets intended to be changed.

Passive Talent: A psychic talent that involves the reception of energy or data by the agent from the target.

Path: A method, system or approach to magical or mystical knowledge.

Path, The: The One-True-Right-And-Only-Way followed by the user of the term.

Pendulum: Any small object on a string or chain, the movements of which can be used for divination. See *Rhabdomancy.*

Pentalpha: A five pointed star made by interweaving five letter A's.

Pentacle: Originally a talisman of a five pointed star, now used as a general term for talismans in general. When made of clay, glass, metal or wood, often used in western occultism as a symbol of the "element" of Earth.

Pentagram: Another word for a five pointed star, used as a symbol for the occult in general and Neopagan & Feminist Witchcraft in particular.

Perception: The process of classifying sensations.

Personal Universes, Law of: "Every sentient being lives in and quite possibly creates a unique universe which can never be 100% identical to that lived in by another." See *Hixson's Law* and *Infinite Universes, Law of.*

Personification, Law of: "Any phenomenon may be considered to be alive and to have a personality, and may be effectively dealt with as such."

Perversity, Law of: "If anything can go wrong, it will—and in the most annoying manner possible." Also known as "Murphy's Law."

Perversion: A variation in a process that effectively negates or contradicts what the user of this term considers to be the original purpose of the process.

Phrenology: Divination by means of the features of the head (exterior).

Physiology: The study of the living body.

PK: See *Psychokinesis.*

Placebo Effect: Term used to refer to the process by which the belief of a target may cause results (physical or psychic) to occur with no known effort being made by the supposed agent.

Placebo Spell: Obviously, a spell that works by the placebo effect.

Planchette: A triangular object with short legs used as a divination tool, usually by moving it over a Oui-Ja Board.

Plant-Psi or *Planpsi:* A little-used term for psychic phenomena involving the interactions of plants with humans, each other and the environment.

Plug-in: To "close a circuit" or otherwise make a connection with a part of the Switchboard or a smaller groupmind.

Poet: (1) One who fashions words artistically. (2) One who can control the power of words and is thus a magician. (3) To the ancient Greeks, one who is a specialist in retrocognition.

Polarity, Law of: "Any pattern of data can be split into (at least) two patterns with 'opposing' characteristics, and each will contain the essence of the other within itself."

Poltergeist: From the German, meaning "noisy spirit;" an old term for RSPK, resulting from a personification of the phenomena.

Polytheism: A style of religion in which the theoilogians claim that there are many deities, of varying power, and many lesser spirits as well, all of whom are considered to be "real" and to be worthy of respect and/or worship.

Possession: The process or experience of having another being (divine, demonic or other) inside of one's own body, usually as the result of a conscious or unconscious invocation. See *Obsession.*

Pragmatism, Law of: "If a pattern of belief or behavior enables a being to survive and to accomplish chosen goals, than that belief or behavior is 'true,' 'realistic,' and/or 'sensible'."

Precognition: Hypercognition done about future phenomena.

Priest or *Priestess:* A cleric who is an official representative of a given religion, sect or cult, and who is responsible for leading other people in rituals.

Prophet: (1) A person (usually a cleric) who "speaks out for" a deity or other powerful spirit, usually about future events. (2) A diviner of the future.

Props: Tools, physical emblems and other objects used primarily as associational and/or trance inducing devices.

Psi: Short for "psychic."

Psi Corps: Organizations set up by governments in order to use psychic talents for the benefit of the governments involved, especially in matters of espionage, sabotage and assassination.

Psionics: A scientistic way to get around using the dirty word "magic;" probably coined by John Campbell, the word is usually used to refer to technologically oriented parapsychology.

Pseudo: Fake, deceptive, erroneous or otherwise "unreal."

Psychic: As used in this text, a word referring to rare or seldom-used powers of the (usually) human mind, which are capable of causing effects that appear to contradict the mainstream worldview of western science and philosophy.

Psychic, A: Anyone who uses mostly passive talents and rites for mostly thaumaturgical purposes.

Psychoenergetics: A fashionable term for parapsychology in Russia.

Psychokinesis or *PK:* A categorical term for those psi talents that involve the movement of matter and energy through space-time.

Psychokinesis Proper: A specific term for the psychically induced movement of objects (including the physical bodies of beings) through normal space-time.

Psychology: Divination by means of the features of the head (interior).

Psycholuminescence: See *Light Control.*

Psychometry: (1) The science of statistical measurements in the field of psychology. (2) An undefeatable term for a psychic talent involving the reception of data "from" objects or surroundings about events and/or persons connected to those objects or surroundings; quite possibly the ability to use objects or places as contagion links for telepathic reception, the clair senses, and/or retrocognition.

Psychopyresis: See *Heat Control.*

Psychotronics: Another new way to avoid saying "magic;" the popular term in Eastern Europe.

Radiation Control: An APK talent for speeding up and slowing down the decay rates of radioactive materials.

•Radio Waves: Waves on the electromagnetic spectrum between infrared radiation (less than 1 cm from crest to crest) and those called "Very Low Frequency" (over 10,000 km); only a tiny portion of this wavespread is used for common radio and television broadcasting.

Reality: (1) The result of consensus opinion. (2) That which is most comfortable and convenient to believe. (3) My universe.

Reality, Levels of: The concept (resulting from the Law of True Falsehoods) that a given idea may be "true" in some situations and "false" in others, depending upon the aspects, sections, areas or other subsets of the personal or consensus universes involved; such subsets may be considered "levels" of reality.

Recurrent Spontaneous Psychokinesis or *RSPK:* New term coined by William Roll. Refers to the unconscious use of PK and APK talents (usually by adolescents) as a release for frustration and means of obtaining attention.

Reddopsi or *Returning:* An antipsi talent for reversing the force vectors of incoming psi broadcasts, thus returning them to their senders. Probably a variation of deflection.

Reincarnation: A belief concerning the supposed process by which souls reinhabit body after body, life after life. The mathematics are implausible and most of the evidence has other possible explanations.

•Religion: (1) The body of institutionalized expressions of sacred beliefs, observances and practices found within a given cultural context. (2) A magical system combined with a philosophical and ethical system, usually oriented towards "supernatural" beings. (3) A psychic structure composed of the shared beliefs, experiences and related habits of all members (*not* just the theologians) of any group calling itself "a religion."

Remote Viewing: The currently fashionable term being used by parapsychologists in the U.S.A. to refer to clairvoyance, presumably because it sounds "more scientific." So far, no one has said anything about "remote hearing," "remote smelling," etc.

Repeatability: The ability of a phenomenon to be repeated at will, especially as the result of a scientific experiment; one of the major dogmas of scientism is that an unrepeatable experiment is not a valid one.

Retrocognition: Hypercognition done about past phenomena.

Rhabdomancy: Divination by means of wands, sticks, rods and pendulums, usually when searching for water, minerals or other valuable items. Sometimes called "dowsing" or "water witching."

Right Hand Path: (1) The people we like who are doing magic. (2) Occultists who spend their time being constructive, manipulative and "good."

Rising Sign: In Astrology, the zodiacal sign that was coming over the eastern horizon at the time and location for which the chart is cast.

Ritual: As used in this text, any ordered sequence of events, actions and/or directed thoughts, especially one that is repeated in the "same" manner each time, that is designed to produce a predictable altered state of consciousness within which certain magical or religious (or artistic or scientific?) results may be obtained.

Ritual Cannibalism: The eating of all or part of the physical or symbolic body of a given person or personified entity in hopes of gaining one or more of their desirable attributes.

Ritualism: Devotion to the use of rituals and ceremonies above and beyond the call of sanity; often, an uncritical acceptance of rituals constructed in the past.

Role Playing: A flavor of "modern" psychology, discovered by Aeschylus and Shakespeare, saying that we all wear masks and play various roles as conditions seem to require, even when alone.

Runes: Letters in the old Celtic, Teutonic and Scandinavian alphabets; the word is based on roots meaning "secret" or "occult." If you try to practice any form of magic within these cultural contexts, especially for deceptive purposes, then your career will lie in runes.

Samhain: Celtic fire festival beginning the winter half of the year and being the Day Between Years; starts at sunset on November 7th and is also known as La Samhna, Nos Galen-gaeof, All Hallow's Eve and Halloween. Celebrated by most Neopagans as a major religious holiday.

Satan: See *Devil, The.*

Satya-vacana: In Tantra, the solemn uttering of a Great Truth, used as a mantra for magical or religious effects such as exorcisms.

Schemhampheres: One of several spellings of a word from Christian Cabala, meaning "the expository" or "the 72 Names of God and His Angels;" originally the title of a collection of magical names, now used as a magical word itself.

*Science: Accumulated and accepted knowledge that has been systematized and formulated with reference to the discovery of general truths or the operation of general laws; knowledge classified and made available in work, life or the search for truth; comprehensive, profound or philosophical knowledge, especially knowledge obtained and tested through the use of the scientific method.

*Scientific Method: The principles and procedures used in the systematic pursuit of intersubjectively (consensus reality) accessible knowledge and involving as necessary conditions the recognition and formulation of a problem, the collection of data through observation and if possible experiment, the formulation of hypotheses, and the testing and confirmation of the hypotheses formulated.

Seer: One who can see the hidden, a diviner.

Self-Knowledge, Law of: "The most important kind of knowledge is about oneself; a magician must be familiar with her or his own strengths and weaknesses."

Sensation: The noticing of a change in the internal or external environment; the activity of a sense before classification.

Sense: A mechanism that notices or causes sensation.

Shaman: A medicine person and medium who frequently uses astral and/or mental projection to fly into "the spirit world," in order to represent his or her tribe to the spirits there and who is often possessed by them as well.

Shield: An area around a being or object within which one or more forms of (usually) antipsi energies are operating in order to defend the being or object from unwanted psychic intrusions; the process of setting up and maintaining such an antipsi field.

Sign: A pattern of sensory stimuli which is intended to communicate data.

Signs of the Zodiac: In astrology, twelve approximately equal segments of the Ecliptic (the belt of sky through which the planets appear to move "around the Earth"); in many systems of astrology, these no longer occupy the same space as the constellations, after which they were originally named.

Silver Cord: Supposed umbilical cord connecting an astral projector to her or his body.

Silver Dagger: A traditional weapon for destroying various monsters.

Similarity, Law of: "Effects are liable to have one or more outward physical or inward mental appearances similar to one or more of said appearances of their causes."

Sorcerer or *Sorceress:* Indiscriminate terms for those who use (or are suspected of using) magic, especially when acting as independent agents and/or using their magic for "evil" purposes.

Sortilege: Divination by means of sticks, coins, bones, dice, lots, beans, yarrow stalks, stones or any other small objects.

*Space: A three-dimensional something that extends without bounds in all directions (this week) and is the field of physical objects and events and their order and relationships.

*Space-Time or *Space-Time Continuum:* The four-dimensional system consisting of three coordinate axes for spacial location and one axis for temporal location, upon which any physical event may be determined by citing its four coordinates; also, the four dimensional space formed by these four axes.

Spell: (1) A magical act designed with an emphasis upon the use of mantras and the literal spelling of words. (2) Any magical ritual.

Spiritualism: A religion based upon the belief in life after death and the experiences of various mediums over the last hundred years; organized primarily to provide legal protection for the mediums and their followers.

Splodging or *Yelling:* An antipsi talent for the generation of specific psi broadcasts (usually of emotions) so strong that all other psi signals in range are drowned out or disrupted, with the information content of those signals collapsing first; may be a form of reversed empathy or of single-content telepathic sending.

Sprites: Disembodied spirits, elves, fairies or daemons; often the term used for the Air elemental known as "sylphs," or as the name of the elementals of Spirit.

Statistics, Three Magical Laws of: "Once is dumb luck, twice is coincidence and three times is Somebody trying to tell you Something."

Stimuli: Those things that arouse sensations; energy fluctuations.

Subject: In science, someone or something being observed and/or experimented upon.

Subjective: "Reality" as it is perceived, instead of as it may be "in itself."

Sun Sign: In astrology, the zodiacal sign that the sun appeared to be in at the time and location for which the chart is cast. In isolation, the sun sign reveals very little data.

Supernatural: Rare, unusual, beyond the common, extraordinary, unexplainable at the time, paranormal; usually input as "religious" phenomena.

*Superstitions: (1) Fixed irrational notions held stubbornly in the face of evidence to the contrary; beliefs, practices, concepts or acts resulting from ignorance, fear of the unknown, morbid scrupulosity, erroneous concepts of causality, etc., as in the words and actions of many critics of parapsychology and the occult. (2) "A belief not founded in any coherent worldview" (J.B. Russell). (3) Someone else's religious or philosophical beliefs.

Supplication: The normal form of prayer, that is to say, begging; occasionally, asking an entity to give you her or his attention for a moment.

Survival Phenomena: Paranormal phenomena that appear to bear relevance to the questions of survival after physical death; at one time the main area of study in parapsychology when it was still being called "psychic research."

Suspension of Disbelief: Temporary curtailment of critical faculties for a specific time and specific purpose, it is absolutely necessary during the performance of a ritual. Before and after the ritual, however, the participants can and should criticize all that they can.

Sutra: Book or traditional collection of sayings.

Switchboard, The: A theory of the author's concerning a postulated network of interlocking metapatterns of everyone who has ever lived or who is living now, expressed as constantly changing and infinitely subtle modifications of current telepathic transmissions and receptions. Many phenomena interpreted as "spirits" may actually be "circuits" within this Switchboard, as may be many other "archetypes" of the "collective unconscious." See *Akasic Records, Archetype, Circuit,* and *Unconscious, Collective.*

Sword: An archaic weapon used in western occultism as a symbol of the "element" of Air, as well as for fighting psychic battles, concentrating and directing energies, and for severing psychic links or bonds.

Symbol: A sign plus an associated concept.

Synchroncity, Law of: "Two or more events happening at the 'same' time are likely to have more associations in common than the merely temporal."

Synthesis, Law of: "The synthesis of two or more 'opposing' patterns of data will produce a new pattern that will be 'truer' than either of the first ones were."

Table Tipping: The use of tables for dactylomancy.

Talent: As used in this text, an ability to use psychic energies in one or more forms, including ESP, Hypercognition, PK and the Antipsi powers. Talents may be active, passive or both.

Talisman: A psychically charged mandala carried about (or placed in a special spot), expected to work via contagion.

Talmud, Babylonian and Palestinian: Records of the processes by which Hebrew scholars debated and developed their laws and rulings.

Tantra: Indian systems of theurgical concepts and magical training methods, easily adaptable for thaumaturgic purposes.

Tantrism: The religious window dressing added to Tantra.

Tapping: The absorption of psychic energy from the ether or from groups or individuals who are willing (such as congregations of worshippers or various deities). See *Absorption* and *Vampire, Psychic.*

Target: The person, object or process one wishes to effect in order to accomplish one's goal.

Tarot Cards: Ancestors of modern playing cards, originally designed for divination use and now used for meditational and magical focussing as well.

*Technology: The study of applying scientific, artistic, psychic or other knowledge to practical ends; the use of methods, skills, crafts, arts, sciences, knowledge and beliefs to provide the material needs of a people.

Telekinesis: Synonym for "psychokinesis."

Telepathy: A type of ESP involving the communication of data from one mind to another without the use of the normal sensory channels. Note that telepathic sending and reception may be two different talents.

Teleportation: A PK talent involving the seemingly instantaneous movement of a person or other being from one location in space-time to another, apparently without going through the normal space-time in between. See *Aportation.*

Temperature or *Thermal Control:* An APK talent for altering the speed of atoms and molecules, so as to change the temperature of an object or being; see its two main subsets: *Heat Control* and *Cold Control.*

Thaumaturgy: The use of magic for nonreligious purposes; the art and science of "wonder working;" using magic to actually change things on the Earth Plane.

Thaumaturgical Design: Experimental design for magic.

Thealogy: Intellectual speculations concerning the nature of the Goddess and Her relations to the world in general and humans in particular; rational explanations of religious doctrines, practices and beliefs, which may or may not bear any connection to any religion as actually conceived and practiced by the majority of its members.

Theoilogy: Intellectual speculations concerning the natures of the Gods and Their relations to the world in general and humans in particular; etc., etc., etc.: see *Thealogy.*

Theology: Intellectual speculations concerning the nature of the God and His relations to the world in general and humans in particular; etc., etc., etc.: see *Thealogy.*

*Theory: (1) A belief, policy or procedure proposed or followed as the basis of action. (2) An ideal or hypothetical set of facts, principles or circumstances. (3) The body of generalizations and principles developed in association with practice in a field of activity. (4) A judgement, conception, proposition or formula formed by speculation or deduction, or by abstraction and generalization from facts. (5) A working hypothesis given probability by experimental evidence or by factual or conceptual analysis but not conclusively established or accepted as a law.

Theurgy: The use of magic for religious and/or psychotherapeutic purposes, in order to attain "salvation" or "personal evolution."

Three M's: Mantra, mandala and mudra; the prime associational and trance inducing devices.

Time: A function of the ways in which humans perceive their universes, as being composed of phenomena that occur "before," "during" or "after" each other. There is no adequate definition.

Torah, The: The first five books of the Bible.

Tradition or *Trad:* A term used by Neopagan and other Witches to refer to the exact distinctions between each body of organized sectarian beliefs and practices, thus some groups refer to themselves as Manx Traditional Witchcraft, Scottish Trad, English Traditional, Continental, German, etc. The assumption or claim is usually that each "tradition" represents several centuries' worth of an organized system of witchcraft, though in point of fact the overwhelming majority of trads can be easily proven to be less than twenty years old. The term, however, seems to be evolving to mean just a sect or flavor of witchcraft, with no implied claims of antiquity.

Trance: An altered state of consciousness (at least for most people) which is characterized by disassociation and withdrawal from the mundane environment.

Transmutation: An APK talent for changing the atomic structure of matter, so as to alter its elemental or molecular nature.

*Treatise: A writing that treats a subject; specifically, one that provides in a systematic

manner and for an expository or argumentative purpose a methodical discussion of the facts and principles involved and conclusions reached.

Tribal Magical Systems: All systems of magic and mysticism practiced by peoples living in tribal cultures at any time in the past or present, anywhere in the world.

True: That which is probable, pleasant or convenient to believe.

True Falsehoods, Law of: "It is possible for a concept or act to violate the truth patterns of a given personal universe (including a single person's part of a consensus reality) and yet to still be 'true,' *provided* that it 'works' in a specific situation." See *Pragmatism, Law of* and *Reality, Levels of.*

Unconscious, Collective: A theoretical construct of C. G. Jung, who believed that all human beings have access to the collected mental experience of all their ancestors and that, in essence, these memories (usually in highly symbolic forms) are carried genetically from one generation to the next; sometimes called "racial" unconscious, though whether the species as a whole or specific gene pools are referred to is unclear.

Unity, Law of: "Every phenomenon in existence at any point in space or time is linked, directly or indirectly, to every other one."

Universals, Cultural: Patterns of belief or behavior that show up in all or a majority of human cultures, that are related to specific topics.

Universe: The total gestalt of all data patterns one may have about that which seems to be oneself and that which seems to be not-oneself; depending upon whether or not one believes in an objective reality, the universe can be considered to be a part of one's metapattern or vice versa.

Vampire: A person who has supposedly risen from the dead and who survives through a process of inducing willing or unwilling blood donations.

Vampire, Psychic: A person or institution practicing the absorption of psychic energy to the point of actually damaging the people they attack. See *Absorption* and *Tapping.*

Variable: A factor, as in an equation or experiment, that changes from situation to situation and thus affects the outcome.

Varna: In Tantra, the principle that sound is eternal and that every letter of the alphabet is a deity.

Vodun or *Voudoun:* (1) A West African word meaning "deity" or "power." (2) General term for a variety of eclectic religions and associated magical systems practiced throughout the Americas, consisting of mixtures of various African tribal beliefs with various Native American tribal beliefs, Roman Catholicism and Protestantism, Spiritualism, Theosophy and other systems (including Hinduism, Islam, Neopagan Witchcraft and anything else that seems useful). Different names include Candomble, Macumba, Santeria, Hoodoo, Voodoo and many others. (3) In the United States and Canada, systems of thaumaturgic magic and religion practiced by people who are usually poor, uneducated and nonwhite. Therefore, see *Black Magic.*

Vortex Field: An energy field causing rapid circular movement around an axis.

Wand: A short stick of wood or metal, used ritually in western occultism as a symbol (usually) of the "element" of Fire, as well as for concentrating and directing energies.

Warlock: (1) One who bends (or bends with) words, a magician and/or liar. (2) Used by some to refer to male witches.

Water: One of the main "elements" in occultism; associated in the West with emotions, intuition, blue, green, silver, cups, bowls, wisdom, passivity, cleansing, passive psychic arts, cold, dampness, etc.

Water Witching: Rhabdomancy when done for finding water.

Web, The: The total pattern formed by all the interactions of all matter and all energy.

Weight: The effect of gravity upon mass.

Weight Control: Mass control and/or gravity control when done in a gravity well (on the surface of a planet, for example).

Werewolf: Someone who can supposedly change their body into that of a wolf's, as a result of deliberate intent or unfortunate curse.

White Magic: A racist, sexist, creedist and classist term used to refer to magic being done for "good" purposes or by people of whom the user of the term approves.

Wic-: An Old English root meaning (1) to bend, turn or twist, and (2) to practice magic. No connection to "wisdom."

Wicca and *Wicce:* The male and female terms in Old English that eventually became "witch" in Modern English.

Wiccan: (1) The original plural form for "wicca/wicce" or "witch." (2) An adjective used to describe their religion by the followers of Neopagan Witchcraft.

Wiccian or *Wigle:* The Old English words for the activities of a "wicca/wicce."

Window Dressing: The scenery and passive props used to provoke and reinforce specific moods and associations.

Witch: Anyone who calls themself a "witch" or is called such by others; an utterly useless term without a qualifying adjective in front of it. The only thing the definitions of "witch" have in common is the idea of magic or other techniques of change being practiced.

Witchcraft: From "wiccecraeft," the craft of being a witch.

Witchcraft, Alexandrian: A variety of Gardnerian Witchcraft founded by British magician Alex Sanders.

Witchcraft, Anthropologic: Anything called "witchcraft" by an anthropologist, usually referring to (a) the practices of independent magicians (real or supposed) who are outside of their society's accepted cultural patterns of behavior and/or (b) a state of being (often involuntarily) a monster who can curse people with the "evil eye."

Witchraft, Classic: The probable practices of the persons originally called "witches" in Europe, to wit: midwifery; healing with magic, herbs and other folk remedies; providing abortions, love potions and poisons; divination; casting curses and blessings, etc.

Witchcraft, Dianic: (1) A postulated medieval cult of Diana and/or Dianus worshippers. (2) Term used by some henotheistic Neopagan Witches to refer to their concentration on the Goddess. (3) Term used by some Feminist Witches to describe their practices and beliefs.

Witchcraft, Ethnic: The practices of various non-English-speaking people in the United States who use magic, religion and alternative healing methods in their own communities, and who are called "witches" by English speakers.

Witchcraft, Familial or *Fam-Trad:* The practices and beliefs of those who claim to belong to families that supposedly have been underground occultists for several centuries in Europe and the Americas, using their wealth and power to stay alive and secret, and mixing fragments of Paleopagan customs with every new occult wave that hit the West.

Witchcraft, Feminist: Several new monotheistic religions started since the early 1970's by women in the feminist community who belonged to the women's spirituality movement and/or who had contact with Neopagan Witches, the religions involve worshipping only the Goddess and using Her as a source of inspiration, magical power and psychological growth.

Witchcraft, Gardnerian: The origin of what has now become Neopagan Witchcraft, founded by Gerald Gardner in the 1940's and (with help from Doreen Valiente and others) the 1950's, based upon his alleged contacts with British Fam-Trads. After he finished inventing, expanding and/or reconstructing the rites, laws and other materials, copies of them were "borrowed" by numerous others who then claimed Fam-Trad status and started new religions of their own.

Witchcraft, Genetic: see *Witchraft, Familial & Grandmotherly.*

Witchcraft, Gothic: A postulated cult of devil worshippers believed in by the medieval Church and used as the excuse for raping, torturing and killing hundreds of thousands (if not millions) of women, children and men. The origins of the modern Disney stereotype. Russell calls this "Diabolic Witchcraft."

Witchcraft, Grandmotherly: Refers to the common habit among modern witches of claiming to have been initiated at an early age by a grandmother who belonged to a Fam-Trad but who is conveniently dead or otherwise unavailable for questioning.

Witchraft, Hereditary: see *Witchraft, Familial & Grandmotherly.*

Witchcraft, Immigrant or *Imm-Trad:* Refers to the customs and beliefs of partially-Pagan peasants and supposed Fam-Trad members who immigrated to the Americas and mingled their magical and religious customs with each other, the Native Americans and enslaved Blacks, and the previous immigrants.

Witchcraft, Neoclassic: The current practices of those who are consciously or unconsciously duplicating the activities of the Classic Witches and who call themselves (or are called by others) "witches."

Witchcraft, Neogothic: The beliefs and practices of modern Satanists, most of whom work very hard to be everything that the medieval Church and current Fundamentalists say they should be.

Witchcraft, Neopagan: Several new duotheistic religions founded since the 1960's, many of which are variations of Gardnerian Witchcraft but some of which are independent inventions and/or reconstructions based on real or supposed Fam-Trads. Worship centers around a Moon/Sea/Earth Goddess and a Horned Sun/Hunting/Vegetation God.

Witchcraft, Neoshamanic: The practices of those modern persons who are attempting to rediscover, duplicate and/or expand upon the practices of the original (postulated) Shamanic Witches.

Witchcraft, Shamanic: The beliefs and practices of postulated independent belladonna/ Moon Goddess cults throughout premedieval Europe, remnants of which might have survived into the Middle Ages.

Witchcraft, Traditional: See *Tradition* and *Witchcraft, Familial.*

Witchcult of Western Europe: A European-wide cult of underground Pagans postulated by Margaret Murray as having been the actual cause or spark of the medieval persecutions, but which is not believed in by most of the historians, linguists, folklorists or anthropologists who have examined her arguments.

Witchdoctor: A medicine person or shaman who hunts down and fights "evil" Anthropologic Witches.

Witchfinder: A cleric or other person who seeks out and tortures alledged Gothic

Witches.

Witchmark: Blemish supposedly placed upon a Gothic Witch by The Devil as a sort of membership card or identification device.

Wizard: From the Old English "wys-ard," meaning "wise one." Originally may have referred to anyone whose wisdom was respected; later came to mean a male witch; now used to mean a powerful and wise magician.

Words of Power, Law of: "There exist certain words that are able to alter the internal and external realities of those uttering them, and their power may rest in the very sounds of the words as much as in their meanings."

Xenophobia: A morbid fear of that which is new, different or strange; common among professional debunkers of minority belief systems.

Yantra: A Tantric diagram or chart.

Yin-Yang: Chinese symbol for the Laws of Polarity and Synthesis.

Yoga: Literally means "yoke" or discipline. With no qualifying adjective, usually refers to Hatha Yoga (discipline of the body).

Yule: The feast of the Winter Solstice, Birth of the Sun, etc.

Zener Cards: Cards used in most of the early ESP experiments, developed in the Parapsychology Laboratory at Duke University.

Zombie: (1) Someone supposedly raised from the dead by a Vodun magician, possibly never really dead at all but rather drugged, who is used as a slave. (2) Someone who has joined a repressive "cult" movement, lost their own personality and other intellectual faculties, and is used as a slave. Easily identified by the characteristic "glazed eye" look and inability to continue their conversation if interrupted several times in mid-partyline.

Note:

Depending upon the currently fashionable trends in physics, biology, history, anthropology, psychology and cybernetics at the time of observation, a few of the Laws of Magic, some of the various modes of practicing magic, and many of the psi and antipsi powers may be easily considered to be identical to each other, and/or to include each other, and/or to be culturally and politically threatening to the insecure (and therefore as phenomena the existence of which is to be denied and eradicated as quickly as possible). Research is progressing (and academic fashions are shifting) at an incredible pace, so if you don't like the latest explanations — wait a minute.

Index:

The following Index is by Randall Millen and P.E.I. Bonewits, and does not include Glossary or Bibliography listings. Page numbers printed in *italics* indicate where in the text a definition or explanation of the concept or entity shown by the keyword will be found. Most keywords are in singular form only.

I see by your sickle that you are a Druid...

Do you want to know what the Author's been up to lately? Are you curious about what the Old Religions *really* were like? Do you have a concern for the environment and an attraction towards Earth-centered spirituality — but you don't want to throw away your computer just yet? Want to have the best of Paleo-, Meso-, and Neopaganism in a European-American path?

Ár nDraíocht Féin: A Druid Fellowship, is North America's largest tradition of Neopagan Druidism, planted by Isaac Bonewits. With hundreds of members and groves and protogroves across the U.S. and Canada, A.D.F. is leading the Neopagan community into the mainstream with serious scholarship, beautiful arts, powerful ceremonies, college-level training and organic organizational patterns based on common sense and Neopagan ideals.

A.D.F. is: non-sexist, non-racist, polytheistic, pluralistic, creative, open, inclusionary, accessible, accountable, rowdy, dedicated, tax-exempt, hard working, hard playing, exoteric, esoteric, and controversial.

If it sounds like A.D.F might be just your cup of mistletoe tea, write to: A.D.F., Box 15259, Ann Arbor, MI 48106-5259, or visit them on the web at www.adf.org. The author's website is at www.neopagan.net.